The
Custom
HARLEY

The *Custom* HARLEY

JOHN CARROLL

Photographs by
GARRY STUART

Foreword by **ARLEN NESS**

SMITHMARK

A Salamander Book

This edition published in 1995 by SMITHMARK Publishers Inc.
16 East 32nd Street, New York, NY 10016

1 3 5 7 9 8 6 4 2

SMITHMARK books are available for bulk purchase for sales
promotion and premium use. For details write or call the manager
of special sales, SMITHMARK Publishers Inc. 16 East 32nd Street,
New York, NY 10016; (212) 532-6600

Photographs © Garry Stuart, 1995
Text © Salamander Books Ltd, 1995

ISBN 0 8317 5512 1

All correspondence concerning the content of this
book should be addressed to
Salamander Books Ltd,
129–137 York Way, London N7 9LG, England

Credits
Editor: Richard Collins
Designer: John Heritage
Photographer: Garry Stuart
Filmset by Flair plan Photo-typesetting Ltd
Color reproduction P & W Graphics, Singapore
Printed in Italy

Additional captions
1 Hamsters MC detail on a Harley speedo.
2 A trio of riders on customized Evos.
4 Clive Maye's custom rigid Panhead.
6 The Evolution engine in Nigel Saxon's custom bike.
8 An Evo with a custom, urban grafitti paint scheme.
10 The Xzotic Eye, a bike built by Lawayne Matthies.
Endpapers A Softail chopper built by Arlen Ness.

CONTENTS

FOREWORD BY ARLEN NESS

I GOT MY FIRST HARLEY in 1966. I had no idea then that that bike would change my life so completely. I never set out to be any kind of celebrity. All I wanted was to have one of the coolest bikes in town.

That word 'cool' has sure had a lot of definitions over the years. Long forks, sportster tanks and raked frames have come and gone. Custom paint has gone from murals, to graphics, to monochrome jobs. Bikes have gotten tall, gotten low, gotten stretched, gotten bobbed. The only thing that remains constant is the fact that we just can't seem to leave them alone. Why not? In my case, I would have to say that I like things to be a little more personalized than they come from the factory. I like to change things. Many times, a stock bike just doesn't look right. Maybe the wheel doesn't sit over the fender right, or the handlebars are ugly, or it sits too high off the ground, or … you get the picture.

It's a question of vision. A successful custom bike builder can **see** how a bike will look finished before he ever begins. He can conceive how the lines of the bike will flow and create a unified image, and also reflect the current (or upcoming) trends in custom bikes. This conceptual process is really the hardest part of the whole thing. You have to know what you're building, or how will you know when you're done? I have been lucky enough to be blessed with this sort of vision, and to be able to associate with many talented people to help me achieve these visions.

These last few years have seen such a dramatic increase in interest in custom motorcycles, it's hard to believe we used to do this just for fun. I have watched my company go from a three-man operation ten years ago to employing over thirty people. We have had to keep moving to bigger and bigger locations as we've grown, to the point where, as I write, we are now preparing to build a brand new facility to house our operation.

Where is the custom bike scene going? I've noticed an increasing sophistication in the custom bike owner. When I started doing this, you couldn't buy **anything** to customize a bike. You had to adapt things off of other bikes, or make them from scratch. For better or worse, the custom builder today has things much easier. Parts availability for the custom builder has never been as great as it is now, and companies like mine are constantly expanding the possibilities. Custom bikes are getting very high tech, and we anticipate that the demand for our style of parts will only grow.

The American motorcycle aftermarket has grown to such an extent that it is possible now to build an American V-Twin custom bike completely from aftermarket parts, without using **any** parts from Milwaukee, and, since the quality of the aftermarket manufacturers generally has improved a great deal, that bike is as roadworthy as one from the factory. In our case, I feel our smaller production runs allow us to be far more innovative in our designs, and at the same time keep a tighter reign on quality.

The future of the custom bike has never looked brighter. The many new bike owners, for the most part, have more money to devote to their machines than in the old days. It may sound slightly mercenary, but it sure does make it easier to produce expensive parts if there is someone out there to buy them. Also, many very talented people are being attracted to custom bike building because of the money that has become available. An infusion of talent like that cannot help but improve the field.

I feel we are entering a new golden age of American motorcycles. With as many talented people involved in custom bike building as there are today, what lies in the future is far more exciting than anything that has happened yet! As you will see in the pages to come, the sky is the limit for the custom bike. I hope you enjoy it.

Arlen Ness

Arlen Ness
San Leandro, California

INTRODUCTION

TEN THOUSAND or more black biker T-shirts proclaim their wearers' allegiance to Harley–Davidson with the slogan, 'If I had to explain you wouldn't understand'. Like so many clichés there is a ring of truth to it. This might appear to negate the need for an introduction to a book on the very subject but its purpose is to set the scene rather than explain.

As with so many aspects of life in the second half of the twentieth century, motorcycling on both sides of the Atlantic was affected by World War Two and this theme crops up throughout this book. In America the returning GIs flooded into motorcycling using Uncle Sam's dollars to buy a Harley or an Indian. Some guys came home and wanted things to get back to 'normal' but for others it wasn't so easy and they were looking for more action. It was to be found in the saddle of a big motorcycle. Many rural American towns saw their first tourists arrive in the shape of city boys on motorcycles who were more interested in the tavern and the local girls. The prevailing social conditions of the time and the problems of the returning servicemen have been well documented by the likes of James Jones and Bill Mauldin. Those early days seemed to reach a pinnacle in terms of notoriety in July 1947 at the AMA races at Hollister in northern California. At the event things got somewhat out of control: a few riders were hospitalized, a few were jailed and most of them rode home after the weekend. The American Motorcyclist Association made the statement that only 1 per cent of riders behaved in such a fashion. The label stuck and outlaw clubs still sport a One Percenter patch today.

It is possible that nothing would ever have come of custom biking beyond being a niche within the whole thriving motorcycle scene as it was then, with a small percentage of riders aboard flat track-style Bobbers, except for the fact that Stanley Kramer read the reports of the incident in **Life** magazine. He made a film with a fictionalized screenplay of the incident that starred Lee Marvin and Marlon Brando. It hit the cinemas in 1954 and inspired young, white, working class kids from the cities to emulate the 'heroes'

from **The Wild One** – especially the style of bearded Lee Marvin in a sleeveless jacket on a chopped Hog. Irrevocably the link between modified motorcycles and trouble had been made and, as is so often the case, the media as a form of communication fanned the flames. This may seem somewhat removed from the core subject of a book dedicated to custom Harleys but there is however a direct connection. Several decades after that particular film was made motorcycles and motorcycling apparel is being sold using words like 'individual', 'freedom', 'rugged' and even 'rebellious'. Riders are said to be 'living life their way', they are claimed to be the 'last frontiersmen' and the last in a line that stretches back through cowboys and pirates to Vikings and Celts. The reality is that the image, and the trade, is based on a sanitized version of the wild and lawless image, the seeds of which were sown on that 4 July in Hollister, and harvested on celluloid. Harley–Davidson themselves have used a clip from the film in their official video that has been released worldwide.

The sixties saw the chopper inexorably linked with the outlaw motorcycle clubs, especially in the eyes of the newspapers and film makers. Newspapers seemed to delight in lurid reporting of the salacious goings-on involving motorcyclists. For once it was the same in Europe – Britain at least, where motorcycle borne 'rockers' clashed with scooter-mounted 'mods' at English holiday resorts. A series of films that continued to portray chopper riders as hoodlums were made, including Roger Corman's **Wild Angels** of 1966. Three years later though, another film arrived that placed chopper riders firmly beyond the pale of normal society: **Easyrider**. Released in 1969 it redefined the chopper rider as dope smoking hippy, coming as it did during the uncertainties of the Vietnam War and highlighting the conflict between the redneck culture and that of the emerging 'longhairs'. The custom bike scene on both sides of the Atlantic would for a while, at least, co-exist alongside the hippy culture. Ultimately though the bike culture would be the only one that would survive without metamorphosizing into something else.

Unlike **The Wild One** (which was banned in Britain until 1968) **Easyrider** was screened worldwide and had an immediate effect. In the same way as **The Wild One** it tried to show the shocking truth about a minority within motorcycling and succeeded in spawning thousands of imitators. It is hard to overestimate just how powerful the influence of each of these films was. There were others such as the dramatic **Electra-Glide in Blue** and the nostalgic and nihilistic **The Loveless** of the early seventies and eighties respectively, but neither had the impact of the earlier movies. Films such as **Any Which Way But Loose** simply portrayed bikers on custom bikes in the role of circus clowns and beyond that the motorcycle was on the whole relegated to a supporting role, with

the possible exceptions of **Mask**, which starred Cher, and **Stone**, which was made in Australia. Alongside the movie business there was an industry that generated pulp fiction stories that dwelt on the real and imagined doings of certain motorcycle clubs.

Maybe it is true that there ain't no such thing as bad publicity because, despite such adverse reporting, custom bike building flourished; as chapters in this book show, many of the famous names in American custom bike building worked right through this period. The actual motorcycles themselves have been ever changing and ever evolving. There are several reasons for this; for example, custom bike builders have been quick to take advantage of new technology as it becomes available. In the fifty years since World War Two the materials used in motorcycle construction have undergone nothing short of revolutionary change so it is inevitable that styles will have progressed. Similarly metalworking techniques have also progressed; the advent of Mig and Tig welding means that certain jobs can be carried out to a higher standard while

Below: The chopper gives the rider an upright, disdainful view of the world from behind apehanger handlebars (left). Flathead Phil's bike (below) is an early chopper based around Harley's venerable 45cu. in. flathead. Phil has styled himself on Willem Dafoe's role in **The Loveless**.

other jobs become possible, such as heavily modifying gas tanks with a welder. Thirdly, custom motorcycle building is a competitive business; new customs are unveiled at big shows and the best take home the trophies. However, the winner cannot rest on his laurels because the losers will be working on a new creation. Certain shows such as The Oakland Roadster Show and The Rat's Hole Custom Show at Daytona and more recently at Sturgis have become institutions, while other shows around the world have followed. In England, for example, the Kent Chapter of the Hells Angels MC organize the annual Kent Custom Bike Show. One of the rules is that all entered bikes have to be ridden to be eligible for any of the trophies. The longstanding annual event attracts bikes and bikers from all over Europe. One aspect of the factory sponsored Harley Owners' Group events is that at events there will be a ride-in custom show. In fact the importance of riding Harleys and entering custom shows has partially eclipsed the competitive origins of events at Daytona, Sturgis and Laconia which were started around races, hillclimbs and gypsy tours.

Because of the ever changing nature of custom biking there is no constant reference beyond the annual aftermarket catalogues and the monthly magazines, of which **Easyriders** is undoubtedly the most famous. There have been a number of others and there is a range of newcomers about at present. Old issues of **Easyriders** are custom biking's equivalent of the Dead Sea Scrolls. The magazine is decades old and charts the changing styles of choppers, whether it was the trend toward shorter front ends after the excesses of the seventies, or toward gold plating, the decline of the cissy bar and Maltese cross mirrors. It also chronicled in its own inimitable way the introduction of the Evolution engine, the return of apehangers, the formation of the Harley Owners' Group and every other shift within the custom bike world.

To bring the whole scenario up to date, recent years have seen a shift toward respectability because professional people also want a piece of the action. They have flooded into Harley riding in unprecedented numbers, bringing a flood of dollars to both dealers and custom builders doors. The Harley–Davidson factory is steadily increasing production to meet a still growing demand; in the twelve months to December 1994 Harley shipped 95,811 motorcycles, a growth of 17 percent over the previous year. Of this figure 20 percent, a total of 29,313 Harley–Davidsons, were exported from the USA; such is the worldwide demand. Export markets include Europe, Australasia and Japan. To some the newcomers are seen as unwelcome intruders and are derisorily referred to as RUBs – Rich Urban Bikers – but they don't seem to care. They are too busy enjoying themselves riding their bikes – just like the original hardcore riders did – which is, when all is said and done, what it is all about.

Left: Wide handlebars and a big Harley on a country backroad. The forward mounted footpegs and the low seat height allow the rider to sit relaxed and upright – just easyriding. This differentiates the chopper rider from the sportsbike rider who adopts a forward leaning position.

The formation of the Harley Owners' Group (HOG) was seen by some as an attempt by Harley–Davidson to reclaim motorcycling's family traditions from the one percenters. The traditions they sought to reclaim were those of the forties and fifties when Harley (and Indian) ownership revolved around dealer-sponsored events and competitions such as Hare and Hounds, Gypsy Tours and picnics. This was in some ways something of a contradiction because the styles of officially licenced leather jackets – and indeed of factory choppers – were based on the styles that had been made famous by the 'rebels'. Others saw the whole thing through more cynical eyes and considered it to be little more than a massive marketing exercise. Either way, the contradiction exists – Harley want their bikes to be ridden by 'nice' people but rely on their rebellious image to sell the bikes to those people. Nowhere is this dichotomy more pronounced than in the fact that both The Law and the outlaw ride Harleys. Now, maybe there's a bit of the cowboy in both sides; after all, the James Gang rode horses as did the various law enforcement

Above: It's hard to overestimate the impact of the film **Easyrider**. This chopper was built twenty-five years after the film was made but is based around the same frame and has similar lines overall, albeit with some modern touches. Roll 'em boys …

officials who pursued them. The difference is in the way they did it, and so it is with both motorcycle cops and those on choppers. The motorcycle cop wears a uniform that includes a leather jacket, motorcycle boots and shades; so does the outlaw. The motorcycle cop rides a Harley that is customized in a specific way; so does the outlaw. The difference is simply that one group are seen as the guardians of law and order while the others are seen to be in defiance of it. Harley are no doubt aware of this and see a potential problem if such attitudes are perpetuated. One of the things they have done in an attempt to alleviate the situation is to market official Harley–Davidson T-shirts that read, 'Good Guys wear Black'. And so they do.

ORIGINS AND INFLUENCES

CUSTOM BIKE BUILDING has been continually evolving for more than fifty years. It started in the last years before World War II but really took off immediately after the war as thousands of former GIs flooded into motorcycling. Back then customizing, or 'bobbing' as it was known, meant modifying your Harley or Indian yourself. The tools used were the rider's own or those of a buddy and the parts were from other motorcycles or home-made. 'Bobbers' had all the surplus parts chopped off and so the term 'chopper' was born. The debut of the K-model Sportster in 1953 meant that smaller, lighter parts, such as the now ubiquitous Sportster tank and solo seat, could be substituted for the cumbersome saddle and big tanks of a big twin Harley. Other alternative gas tanks came from Mustang mopeds and, later, from dirt bikes. The latter were fitted with tiny tanks that became known as 'Peanut' tanks. Eventually small, specialist companies started manufacturing these items and the foundations for the huge custom parts industry of today were laid.

The fad for long forks started in an attempt to increase the ground clearance of a bobbed Harley. It was easily possible to lean a big twin over enough to ground out the primary case. One solution was to fit longer forks and there were two popular ways of doing this. The first was to find the cast springer forks off a Harley VL model. They were an inch longer and fitting these changed the bike's appearance and helped out with ground clearance. The second possibility was to find a set of war surplus experimental Harley XA springers; these too were slightly longer. Later riders started extending their own tubular springers after someone discovered that Ford car axle radius rods were in the same section as Harley–Davidson springer forks. With accurate measuring and welding it was possible to extend forks to almost any length. Customizing Harleys incorporated new parts from the factory's bikes as they became available; telescopic forks appeared on the Hydra-Glide and these soon appeared as customized bikes. The 1955–57 'straight-leg' frame rapidly became a favorite around which to build a chopper because of its clean lines. It was described as a straight-leg to differentiate it from the 1948–55 'wishbone' frame. The descriptive terms refer to the shape of the front downtubes – the straightleg is regarded by many as the first custom frame. Certainly its lines are still being emulated by frame makers more than thirty-five

Harry, of Chopper Club Wales, aboard his custom FLH (far left), while the almost spindly lines of a chopped seventies Shovelhead (left), with its long forks and modified frame, contrast with a solid looking Pro-street drag-style nineties custom (right).

years after the last one was made by Harley themselves. The Duo-Glide, a Harley with rear suspension, arrived in 1958 and custom bikes from then on were often based around swingarm frames. This was despite some feeling that a chopper should have a rigid frame. The irony is that something that appears so alternative and radical is, in fact, steeped in tradition. Frames were lengthened, raked, stretched and modified as choppers became more extreme through the sixties and seventies. In these decades modifications were frequently, but not always, to change a Harley's appearance rather than improve its handling or performance. Hunter S. Thompson provided a snapshot of a mid-sixties chopper in his seminal book, **The Hell's Angels**. He points out that outlaw bikes of that era carried only the extras required by law, such as lights and a rear view mirror (even this latter item was sometimes reduced to a minimum through the use of a dentist's mirror – apparently there was no mention of a minimum size in California highway laws). The Angels' (and other clubs) bikes used small gas tanks, no front fenders, bobbed rear fenders, skinny front wheels, upswept exhausts, tiny headlights and tall sissy bars as well as all sorts of chrome and flame painted trim. In awed tones, Thompson wrote of the chopper of the time, 'it is a beautiful, graceful machine and so nearly perfect mechanically . . .'. And so it was.
The seventies saw the Shovelhead engine in a swingarm frame become the raw material for the next generation of custom Harleys. This happened alongside trends to increasing sophistication and ostentation in the diverging styles of custom motorcycle and subsequent growth in custom parts industry, as well as a brief dalliance with Japanese bikes on the part of many builders. The current Evolution engine, introduced during the eighties, would bring builders and riders back to the Milwaukee fold in droves as well as new styles of custom Harley. These styles have been boosted further as longstanding hot rod builders and designers such as Pete Chapouris, Boyd Coddington and Thom Taylor have turned their attention to Harleys.

Above and right: Tall, skinny front wheel, no front fender or brake, springer forks, apehanger bars, jockey shift, solo seat, pillion pad, rigid frame and flames. This '42 Knucklehead is a perfect reincarnation of an early chopper. It belongs to Mark Finstad from Watertown, South Dakota, who built it over the past three years. Craig's Custom in Watertown rebuilt the engine and Randy Lauen sprayed the base coat and the flames.

Larry Pitts is a resident of New Jersey. He is seen here (far left) riding the early style chopper he built using only the correct period parts from the fifties. These include upswept fishtail pipes and a tiny, Sparto, tail-light (left). Vintage style horns and jockey shifts (above) were also popular then. One of the reasons for jockey shifts was that they did away with the cumbersome linkages to a tank-mounted gearlever. This meant that it was possible to change gear more quickly while racing from the stoplight. Their removal also cleaned up the lines of the bike. Jockey shiftlevers have been adorned with everything from door knobs through dice and poolballs to pistons.

Left and right: A Panhead chopper based around the Duo-Glide style of bike – it has suspension both front and rear. The frame has been modified to accommodate the 8in. over length telescopic forks. It has belonged to Jeff Lorimer from Omaha, Nebraska, for four years. The bike features a foot clutch and hand gearchange lever, which is located behind the rider's left leg. This system is referred to as a 'jockey shift', or sometimes as a 'suicide shift', because the rider cannot put his left foot on the ground at junctions. On this bike the shifter (right) is a chromed .38 pistol.

Below: Choppers such as this Shovelhead have several inches extension built into the downtubes of the Harley FX frame; this raises the headstock sufficiently to fit extended forks but still keeps the engine and bottom frame rails level in relation to the ground. The wheels are Invader custom parts and the rear shock absorbers Smith Strutters.

Left: An FL Harley '74 chop built in the nineties. It uses the late sixties swingarm frame and engine as well as a variety of other Harley parts. The solid looking bike is a timeless combination of 21in. front wheel and 16in. rear, cut down rear fender, slightly overstock length forks, apehangers and flames. Disc brakes are a concession to modernity.

Below left and right: In the seventies, Ness and others pioneered the Bay Area Lowrider style of custom. The bikes, which were not always Harley powered, were long and low. Ness built this bike in 1975 using a '65 Sportster engine, a custom frame and springer forks of his own manufacture. It features a 15in. rear wheel and a 21in. front and a prism tank. The whole bike was adorned with wild graphics. By chance, the bike was stored in a garage in its original form for seventeen years until Bill Haar bought it and wheeled it into the sunshine again.

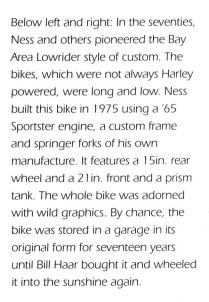

Left and below: Dark Star, a custom painter from Texas, built this Evo chop along traditional lines but with modern components. He used a Denver's Choppers rigid frame which is based on the old Harley straightleg design and fitted an FXR engine, an '89 transmission and a '91 FXR front end. Dark Star has been riding rigid choppers for thirty years. The seat is an old custom part re-upholstered and the taillight and sissy bar are new custom parts.

Right: In the legendary movie **Easyrider**, both the heroes ride Panheads. Peter Fonda, as Captain America, rode a chopper with a stars and stripes paint scheme. That movie, more than any other before or since, focused attention on the chopper as a symbol of freedom and has inspired many to base their bikes (as right) on Fonda's.

Above left: Although this is a contemporary custom Harley–Davidson, its influences are clearly drawn from Indian's post-war range. The Indian Chief motorcycles featured such hugely valanced fenders and enjoyed an opulent standard of fittings.

Above: Modern versions of the Bay Area Lowrider such as this neatly assembled custom are probably what the nineties will be remembered for. Billet aluminum, high tech brake parts, painted graphics and a long low look are all fashions that have come to the fore recently.

Left: Performance-styled machines such as this, which formerly belonged to Cory Ness, have always existed but, despite the fitting of a turbo and massive carburetors, its function is more for show than serious racing action.

Right: Paint schemes such as this are not exclusively reserved for custom Harleys or even motorcycles in general but can be found on jet skis and sail boards. This, from Paragon Custom Cycles, was the first Harley a nineteen-year-old painter had done.

This bike was built in the nineties to replicate a fifties-style custom Harley and uses only parts that would have been available then; the pipes, taillight and apehangers are typical. The Panhead engine was available from 1948 to 1965.

SPECIFICATION

Name
Tavern to Tavern
Owner
Larry Pitts
Builder
Owner
Location
New Jersey, USA

Engine model
H–D Panhead
Capacity
74cu. in.
Year
1964
Modifications
Fishtail exhausts

Frame model
H–D rigid
Type
Straightleg
Modifications
None
Forks
H–D Springer

Front wheel
21in. spoked
Front brake
H–D drum
Front fender
None
Rear wheel
16in. spoked
Rear brake
H–D drum
Rear fender
H–D bobbed

Handlebars
Apehangers
Gas tank
H–D Fatbob
Seat
Solo saddle

Paint
Owner
Plating
Stock

THE PROCESS OF CUSTOM BUILDING

AS CUSTOM BIKES have evolved so have the processes involved in building a custom Harley. Where once all it took was a hammer, a hacksaw, a welder and a little imagination, now it is considerably more complex but still requires imagination. In many ways the processes involved have diverged enormously; at one end of the scale is the huge and well-equipped commercial custom bike shop where the only limit to what can be built is the amount of money in a customer's pocket. At the other end of the scale altogether is the person who is modifying his or her only bike through a combination of ingenuity, catalogue and homemade parts. Often as not this person is working in a domestic garage with limited numbers of tools. Having said that, the small operator still benefits from the commercial operations as the recent growth in aftermarket parts suppliers and their ranges means that it is usually possible to buy a custom part knowing it will both fit and look good. The aftermarket industry has done the research and development for the customer. While it could be that the big custom shops don't need help with the techniques involved with building custom Harleys, the individual rider often does. Over the years magazines – such as **Easyriders** – have pointed riders and builders the right way and often led the fashions for custom bikes by featuring particularly spectacular and avant garde machines. Other publications have helped out too. In the late seventies, **Street Chopper** magazine published a series of small guides to chopper building that covered aspects such as electrics, frame and tank modifications, custom front ends and a styling guide. A truly excellent publication aimed squarely at home builders is Mike Geokan's **Custom Chopper Cookbook**: it is something of a combination of Zen and the art of motorcycle maintenance and a Clymer workshop manual! Whichever end of the scale you're looking at custom building from, it is still a combination of aluminum and steel, paint and chrome, rubber and leather and hours at the work bench, for these are the things that make a custom bike. Whether it is built in an air-conditioned factory or on the floor of a garage the same basic process must be followed. First the builder has to decide what sort of custom Harley is to be built: chopper, lowrider or drag-inspired performance bike? Mild custom or radical? Nostalgic or up to the minute? Once these questions have been answered then work can begin. The key to the whole bike is the type of frame used; a lowrider, for example,

The beginnings of a custom project (far left) – English B&I Engineering replica frames. Hours at the work bench are what ensures that bikes built by their owners, such as Denny Lueders' Shovel (left) end up looking exactly right. Nostalgic-style choppers often require traditional techniques such wheel building.

must have a long, low frame that sits close to the road while a chopper may need an early type rigid frame. Is the frame to be modified? The lowrider might want the frame stretching, as lengthening is described, to enhance its long low lines while the chopper frame might require the downtubes modifying to enable the headstock to be raised to accommodate longer than stock length forks. It could be that a frame will be purchased from a specialist frame shop. Further components for the custom have to be picked to suit similar criteria. The type of forks, tank, seat, wheels and brakes are all affected by the style of bike being constructed. Many of the current wave of high tech customs incorporate high quality aircraft-style engineering and use materials from this industry such as anodized aluminum and stainless steel. The advent of the CNC milling machine has fueled an industry dedicated to manufacturing parts, everything from wheels to handlebar grips, from billet aluminum. A more traditional Harley custom may require older parts and lead the builder to shops that stock genuine old Harley parts or pattern copies. In many ways building a traditional chopper is more like restoring a vintage ride than pure innovation.

The hours in the workshop are taken in assembling the bike to make sure that the parts both fit physically and look right. After all, the aesthetics of the finished bike are what it will be judged on and no matter how much money is spent, if it doesn't look exactly right it will always be an also ran. Those who still perceive bikers as an unwashed horde of surly misanthropes would probably be surprised at just how state of the art the technology that is used in the fabrication of custom bikes is. Both machining and welding, for example, are carried out to the highest standards as a poorly constructed custom bike soon deteriorates once it is ridden. The vibration from a V-twin engine will crack welds and bondo, as will the loads imposed by braking and cornering. All these aspects of a custom bike have to be finished before the parts go to the chromers or the paint shop.

Left: Back Off is a completely custom built Harley. It uses an Arlen Ness 2in. stretched frame, a Ness swingarm and wideglide telescopic forks. Performance Machine brakes, wire spoke wheels and numerous billet parts complete the ensemble.

Above: This performance style Harley was built by La Fores of Lakewood, CO. It is based around a Shovelhead engine and a rigid frame. The frame was stretched 2in. and lowered. Modifications were also made to fit the wide rear wheel and tire.

Below: Harley's Softail frame has rear suspension but looks like a rigid, or hardtail. Use of such a frame requires rear fender struts. In Ron Simms' Bay Area Custom Cycles workshop (see also pages 94–5) a billet strut is being tried for fit.

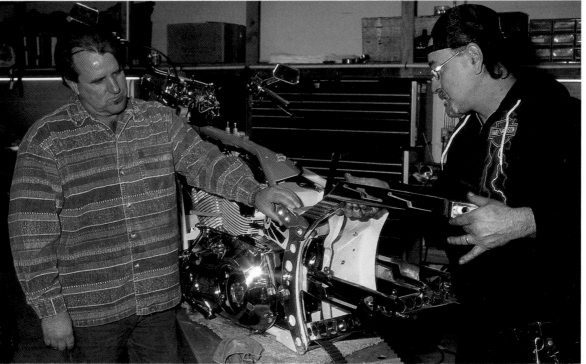

Left: The headstock of a frame must be precisely engineered to the correct angle to suit the forks. This extreme Sportster chopper has very long forks that necessitate a high headstock, evidenced by the space above the engine. The headstock must be braced to prevent vibration cracking it. The engine is also steadied by a bracket on the frame.

Above and below: The headstock of this Ness chopper (above) is braced by a combination of horizontal tube and steel gusset while the Knuckle-head chop from Texas (below) relies solely on a gusset. This style of frame is extended forwards and described as a 'gooseneck'. Like the prism tank it was popular in the seventies but turns heads in the nineties.

Above and right: Rear suspension is not uncommon on custom Harleys. The swingarm (above) mounts the rear wheel and the bottom shock absorber as standard but is a tubular item designed by Arlen Ness. Plunger rear suspension – a spring mounted axle – (right) is an antiquated design of motorcycle rear suspension. Custom builders have kept it in use, notably Amen of California with the 'Savior' frame in the seventies. This is a nineties Cobra Engineering plunger frame.

Left: Springer forks, so-called for obvious reasons, were the type of forks fitted to Harleys by the factory in the thirties and forties and so appear on many early custom bikes. These are standard length, another early feature before later extended forks became popular.

Below: In 1949 the Harley factory started using telescopic forks in a model called the Hydra-glide. This also used a Panhead engine and a rigid frame. It was a look that became popular for choppers. This bike, on Daytona Beach, is a variation on that theme. It uses extended forks and a custom frame.

Above: This chopped Sportster uses what are commonly known as girder forks. These were common on pre-war British bikes but offered advantages to the custom builder in that they could be made to any length and their slender, minimal components looked attractive, especially when chromed. Long girder forks became popular in the seventies but have largely been superseded.

Left: The high tech braking and suspension components used by the Japanese manufacturers have started a trend toward more high tech Harleys, particularly in Europe. This British owned Harley uses a complete Suzuki front end including 'upside down' forks. These are named because the lower part of the fork leg slides inside the upper. Traditionally, telescopic forks are the other way about.

Left: In the late seventies and early eighties Arlen Ness used to manufacture custom Springer forks that were more delicate than Harley's own. As recently as 1994 he used some new old stock ones on his Knucklehead powered chopper. The bike also uses a rigid frame, a taildragger rear fender and apehanger bars and certainly echoes earlier times.

Above right: Pat Kennedy from Tombstone, Arizona, is building choppers with long forks. Although some would say this is an outdated concept, Kennedy's bikes are bang up to date and perfectly engineered – with careful calculation of rake and trail angles – to ensure that they are easy to ride. The forks on this Alien machine are 30in. over stock length.

Below right: Another current custom Harley that echoes earlier times is Danny Franssen's Bobber. Franssen is from Genk in Belgium and based his bike around genuine stock length Harley Springer forks and Hydra-Glide rigid frame to give an immediate post-war appearance but used a new Harley Evolution engine and four-speed transmission.

All that these wheels have in common is that they are round and fitted with disc brakes; widths, diameters and methods of construction vary. Traditionally, Harleys have wire spoked wheels that have forty spokes. Custom builders have found a way to increase the number of spokes used (above) and can lace them up in different configurations. A minimal number of spokes are used in this American chromed steel wheel (above right) and this English made stainless steel wheel (below). Current cast alloy wheels (below right) need even less. This is a three-spoked wheel sourced from a Japanese bike. The style of wheel is chosen to suit the style of bike.

A contemporary style of wheel is that machined from a single piece of billet aluminum such as the solid wheel (above) partially hidden by a huge fender of the more visible spoked design fitted to this custom Springer (above right). Alloy combines both strength and lightness of weight, making it ideal for performance applications.

Right: The wheels for this custom Sportster were made by Performance Machine Inc. from California. They are machined out of billet aluminum and are one of the range of wheels supplied by this company who also manufacture braking components. The bike was built by Battistinis in Bournemouth, England.

Top left and above: Rear wheels and brakes are equally important; the origins of solid wheels (top left) are in drag racing. A very strong wheel was required to withstand the power of a competition engine. Three-spoke cast alloy wheels such as this (above) give a sporting appearance, even in a rigid frame, and can easily be matched to a different sized front wheel.

Left: Brake calipers such as this have become very popular in recent years. They offer excellent braking capability. Billet-6 calipers are made in England, although similar products are made in both America and Europe. The number 6 indicates that there are three pairs of hydraulic pistons and brake pads inside the caliper.

Right: The idea of modifying the existing bike rather than simply replacing everything is still current. This rigid framed (ie without rear suspension) chopper uses a stock Harley wheel, brake disc and caliper. These parts have been fitted to a custom frame with a neat variation on the flames theme.

Below: The choice of wheels and brakes is determined by the style of custom that the builder is trying to achieve. On this recent custom the current style of wheels and brakes is reflected in the choice of billet handlebar fittings, foot controls and boards and engine and gearbox parts. It is finished with a suitably modern paint job.

Left: Many custom Harleys retain the stock fatbob gas tank: it is attractive, strong and designed to fit a big twin Harley frame as well as holding several gallons of gas. The dash-mounted speedo and ignition switch enable the builder to keep the handlebars clean looking.

Below left: Another advantage of the big fatbob tank is that there is room for special paint. Flames are traditional custom paint on both choppers and street rods. There are, however, endless variations on the theme. Shapes and sizes vary quite considerably, as do colors.

Right: The airbrush paint work on this tank shows Miraculous Mutha, a lewd character who starred in **Easyriders** magazine for many years. The bike's owner, Ken Schultz from Nebraska, admitted that the guy at the window is a caricature of himself – the Moonlight Bandit.

Above: This custom tank is described as a 'Mustang tank' because it is the type originally fitted to a Mustang moped. Demand for such tanks exceeded supply so they are now manufactured especially for Harleys and available through custom parts suppliers. Both single and twin cap versions are made.

Left: Sportster tanks are a popular choice with custom builders. In the early days of chopper building they had to be obtained from the K model Sportster but replicas are now manufactured. Mounting it on the frame's top rail, as this bike, is described as 'Frisco style'.

Above: One off custom tanks are another way to go. Pat Kennedy used this faceted steel tank on his Alien machine to continue the unnatural theme throughout the bike. Its angles are reflected in most of this chopper's components, including the handlebars and air filter.

Right: Tanks, of course, do much more than just hold gas. They provide another area of the Harley that can be extensively modified. This Sportster tank, on another Pat Kennedy bike, has been fitted with a sight glass fuel gauge, ensuring it is one of a kind.

It is hard to believe that this completely rebuilt and beautifully finished custom cruise, photographed on Daytona's famous beach was once a worn out Sheriff's Patrol bike sitting in an auction yard.

SPECIFICATION

Name
FXRP Custom
Owner
Mike Tockey
Builder
Owner
Location
Fort Myers, Florida

Engine model
FXRP
Capacity
84cu. in.
Year
1987
Modifications
+.020in. Wiseco pistons
Milled heads
Andrews cam

Frame model
FXRP
Type
Swingarm
Modifications
Rake increased 4°
Swingarm stretched 3.5in.
Forks
Showa telescopic
Front wheel
18in. billet aluminum
Front brake
H–D discs and calipers
Front fender
Ness
Rear wheel
18in. billet aluminum
Rear brake
H–D disc and caliper
Rear fender
Ness

Handlebars
Ness
Gas tank
H–D FXR
Seat
Corbin Gunfighter

Paint
Jim Perno/Pat Clelland
Plating
The Chrome Factory

ENGINES

BECAUSE SO MANY of the roots of custom biking are in competition Harleys which emulate the style of early competition bikes, it is perhaps not surprising that much of the aftermarket parts industry produces parts that make Harleys go faster. Particularly in these high tech days such parts seem to be used as often on street ridden bikes as on race bikes. Many of the early tuners have left a legacy in that their hard won and homespun experience laid the foundations for the performance Harleys of today. Most people have heard of S&S Cycle Inc. and their performance parts. The company was founded by George J. Smith from Chicago in 1958. He founded it with his wife Marge as partner using the experience he gained drag racing a big twin called Tramp. And Tom Sifton, a Californian Harley dealer before World War Two, made his name tuning Harleys in order to win races around California. More than fifty years later aftermarket camshafts still bear his name and the company he founded, Sifton Motorcycle Products, still thrives. Tom Sifton passed away in 1990.

The popularization of the V-twin by both the Harley–Davidson and Indian motorcycle factories is what ensured that custom biking of today would be almost totally reliant on V-twin engines. Both factories made 45cu. in. V-twin engined bikes that were the mainstay of each company's racing efforts. The races saw crowds of partisan fans cheering on their riders which of course boosted the image of each factory's products. This brand loyalty extended across the range of bikes produced, including the larger capacity flatheads also made in both Springfield and Milwaukee. Harley–Davidson introduced their first overhead valve engine in 1936. Known as the EL model, it ensured that things would never be the same again. The EL soon became known as the Knucklehead because of the shape of the rocker cover castings. It was so revolutionary that many of the features pioneered on it are still aspects of Harley–Davidson styling today, notably the wraparound oil tank and the fatbob gas tanks. Production of the Knucklehead was interrupted by World War Two but resumed briefly after the war until the Panhead was introduced in 1948. The Panhead is so described because its rocker covers look like upturned cooking pans. The Panhead engine appeared in a rigid frame with springer forks for one year and was then upgraded to a rigid framed bike with telescopic forks and called the Hydraglide. Rear suspension and electric

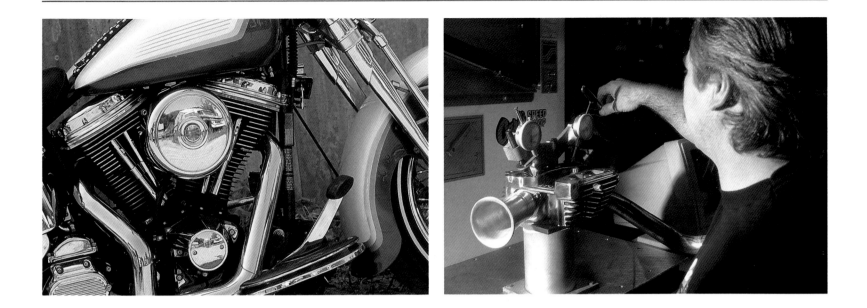

While the bike (far left) is fitted with a genuine Panhead engine, the one above is an Evolution made to look like one through the use of parts made by Xzotic Cycle Products. An altogether different approach is employed at Carl's Speed Shop (right) where they make Harley engines to go a lot faster.

starters came later, in 1958 and 1965 respectively, but it was the early Panheads that reinforced the trends established by the Knucklehead. Bikes with panniers, screens and other unnecessary accessories were referred to as 'garbage wagons' and were seen by many as merely detracting from the power of the Panhead motor because of the weight. In the mid-sixties the Shovelhead engine made its appearance and once again its nickname arose from the shape of its rocker covers which are considered to look like upturned shovels. The Shovelhead engine would stay in production throughout the seventies and early eighties, including the entire period of AMF ownership. Eventually it was superseded by the Evolution, so-named because it could trace its design roots right back to the EL model of 1936. It is the Evolution engine – which has acquired two nicknames, Blockhead and Evo – which has been responsible for the upsurge in popularity of Harley–Davidsons. It sometimes attracts disparaging remarks from the older and possibly more traditional bikers. A not uncommon T-shirt slogan reads 'See no Evo, Hear no Evo, Speak no Evo, Ride no Evo'.

There are, of course, thousands and thousands of riders who wouldn't agree with this, having experienced the advantages of greater reliability, longevity and performance of the newer engines. Having said that, it should be remembered that the nostalgic look is enormously popular to the extent that Harley–Davidson themselves have offered current bikes with fifties and earlier styling features such as two-tone paint schemes, studded saddlebags and springer forks. There are any number of aftermarket custom parts designed to make an Evolution engined bike look old including parts to disguise the engine and make it look like a Panhead or a Knucklehead. The finished appearance of engines so equipped is undoubtedly assisted by the fact that Harley–Davidson have stuck to manufacturing V-twin engined motorcycles for more than fifty years. And there is nothing quite like the spine-tingling rumble of a big V-twin.

Left: In 1936 Harley–Davidson introduced their first overhead valve V-twin engine. It was officially known as the 61E model because it displaced 61cu. in. It soon became known as the Knucklehead because of the shape of its rocker covers. In 1937, riding a machine powered by one of these engines, Joe Petrali took a motorcycle speed record off Indian on the beach at Daytona, averaging over 136mph. The legend was born.

Above: The Panhead, so named because its rocker covers looked like upturned cooking pots, superseded the Knucklehead in 1948 and remained in production until 1965. Knucklehead and Panhead engines powered the majority of early custom Harleys, notably Bobbers and Choppers. This engine may appear to be in a standard motorcycle but no Harley came from the factory sporting so much chrome.

Above: The Panhead is many people's favorite engine and is still used in freshly built custom Harleys. Fatal Attraction, built in 1992, features a monster Panhead motor that displaces 101cu. in., has dual Morris Magnetos, a dual throat carb and most of its internal components from both S&S and STD. These two companies are renowned for their performance parts. The engine was rebuilt by Williams Motors.

Above: The Shovelhead is so named because the rocker covers look like the backs of upturned shovels. They first appeared on Harleys from the factory in 1965. This particular Shovel is unusual in that it is assembled completely from parts available from the giant aftermarket parts company, Custom Chrome Inc. from Morgan Hill, California.

Right: This Shovelhead is from the factory; it was made in 1974 and fitted to an FX model. It now powers the chopper ridden by Ken and Jo Schultz from Mead, Nebraska. The original FX frame has been considerably modified while the engine has been equipped with an SU carb and Drag Specialties coil.

Left: The Evolution engine was introduced in the early eighties and it soon appeared in custom bikes. Custom Chrome Inc. had this orange FXR built around an Evo engine but used parts from their extensive catalogue, including the RevTech cylinder heads and carb as well as a custom exhaust and a points cover.

Below left: A less modified Evo engine, but it does have the popular S&S Teardrop airfilter cover fitted which means that one of the S&S range of performance carburetors has been installed. George Smith, one of the founders of S&S, started out drag racing and was introduced into the Motorcycle Hall of Fame in 1994.

Below right: Another popular aftermarket carburetor upgrade is the fitting of a Dellorto and manifold. Such a carb is fitted to La Bonne Vie, a Ness-inspired, British-built custom Harley. Also fitted are a Ness points cover and a custom exhaust system. Engine oil is circulated in braided steel hoses.

Left and above: Customizing is about being different and one way to achieve that is to build a performance engine with race styling for street use. This Harley (left) belonging to Trik Cycles from Florida has been fitted with a turbocharger in front of the engine. Twin Dellorto carbs on chromed manifolds supply the fuel. The Paragon Custom Pro-street style bike (above) clearly borrows its styling from the drag strip and features a 96cu. in engine with Nitrous Oxide.

Right: Technoplus, a custom shop from Aiguillon in southern France, have fitted this Harley with Mega-Four four-valve heads. There is a French connection with these parts as they are manufactured in Longueuil, Quebec, Canada, by Mega-Performance.

Left: The Harley–Davidson Sportster is also regularly used as the basis for a custom bike. Many of these are based on performance-style machines which perhaps reflects the success that the Sportster has had over the years in competitive motorcycling, especially such sports as flat track and dirt track racing. This Ironhead Sportster features exactly that style of modification, including wide flat bars and a single disc brake as well as a performance carburetor and exhaust system.

Above: Another performance enhanced Sportster is this later Evolution model that features a trick twin carburetor set-up. The carbs are fitted with race-style air filters and have been partially painted yellow, as has the timing cover, to coordinate them with the oil and gas tanks.

Above: John Williamson of the RMD Performance and Custom Shop in Reading, England, built this big twin as a street bike although it is used to contest the UK Supertwins series of drag racing. The engine displaces 106cu. in. and is fitted to an all-aluminum monoshock frame. The bike produces 110 bhp at 5800 rpm. It is being ridden here by Dave Bartz.

Above and left: Mike Corbin devised the Warbird bodykit for Harley's FXR but this particular street bike is raced by Doug Morrow, son of Carl Morrow, who is the proprietor of Carl's Speed Shop. The 88cu. in. engine has been completely rebuilt for vastly improved performance and features a number of parts manufactured by Carl's Speed Shop. These include the magneto, camshaft, exhaust, cylinder heads and carburetor (left). Axtell pistons are also used. The transmission is five-speed although a prototype heavy duty clutch made by Barnett is installed. The frame and forks are modified FXR parts and the wheels were made by Performance Machine. The completed bike was painted in Persimmon-Tangelo pearl with flames.

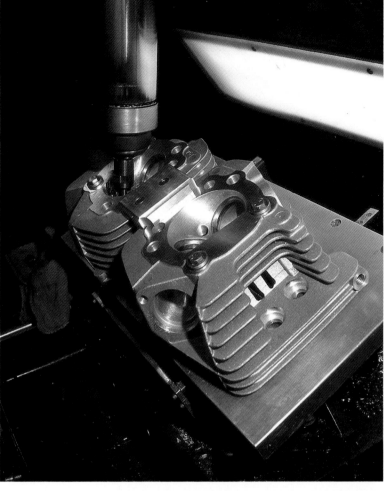

Above and right: Carl's Speed Shop is located in Santa Fe Springs, California. Carl Morrow has been in the business of making Harleys go faster since 1969 and over the years has acquired enormous expertise in engine building. He started – working from home – building engines for his own race bikes and a number of customers. His son now does the racing and the number of customers has grown immensely. The father and son team hold a number of drag racing records. His workshop now uses computers (right) in the quest for speed but still modifies engine parts, such as these cylinder heads (above) to make the engine run faster.

This Harley is typical of 1990's performance custom bikes. It features an engine with vastly increased power but the brakes and handling have been enhanced to match.

SPECIFICATION

Name
Home Brew
Owner
Steve Kenny
Builder
Owner
Location
Oxfordshire, England

Engine model
FXRS
Capacity
96cu. in.
Year
1992
Modifications
Rebuilt with increased displacement for performance by RMD Performance and Custom

Frame model
H–D FXRS
Type
Swingarm
Modifications
JMC Swingarm 3° extra rake
Forks
White Power

Front wheel
19in. Revtech
Front brake
Discs with ISR calipers
Front fender
Custom part
Rear wheel
16in. Revtech
Rear brake
Disc with ISR calipers
Rear mudguard
Owner made

Handlebars
Custom Part
Gas tank
Stock modified
Seat
Paul Nahoulakian

Paint
Owner
Plating
Bourne End Polishers

Paint and Finish

THE PAINT AND VARIOUS other finishes applied to a custom motorcycle have to fulfill two functions: they have to be hardwearing to protect the motorcycle from corrosion and they have to be attractive in appearance. Paint technology has evolved considerably since the beginnings of custom biking as has the technology of other metal coat techniques such as plating. Custom painting started with brush-applied pinstripes and has evolved into an intricate art through the use of the airbrush. Like everything else the types of paintwork chosen follow fashions. In the seventies murals often showing mythical scenes of dragons were enormously popular and were sprayed on the cycle parts of motorcycles. This followed the trend of the times to adorn most motor vehicles, including cars and vans, with murals. The popularity of such paintwork has waned while beautifully detailed graphics have become the style of the nineties. There are exceptions, however, and although the style of execution has evolved the themes have remained constant. Examples are paintwork involving skulls and flames. Flames are completely timeless, traditional and they show movement as they flow around the curves of a tank or fender. Skulls are slightly more sinister, being associated with death, and seemingly reflect the flirting with danger that can be involved in riding a motorcycle with a certain bravado. The skull and crossbones symbol was long ago flown by sea-going pirates and over the years there has been an imagined affiliation with those buccaneers. A current airbrush design is achieved by spraying different colored details onto the base coat and gradually building up the finished artwork which is then coated with lacquer to give a smooth and shiny finish.

Another early influence on the development of custom painting is generally accepted to have been the nose-art painted on aeroplanes during World War Two. American pilots of both bombers and fighters often adorned the noses of their aircraft with artwork copied from or inspired by airbrush artists like George Petty and Alberto Vargas whose work appeared in magazines such as **Esquire**. The copies were done with paintbrushes and incorporated humorous names, names of girlfriends or songs. Examples are 'Jamaica' [Did ya make her?], 'Enola Gay' and 'Shoo Shoo Shoo Baby'. Many crews took this one step further and painted the backs of their jackets with the designs and the name of their ship. Many of the flyers who survived were those who

The FLH (far left) received a modern splatter paint design while this gas tank (above left) features a modern combination of two of custom biking's perennially favorite designs: skulls and flames. Gold plating such as on this wild Ness bike (above right) with twin Sportster engines was popular in the seventies.

came home from the war and bought motorcycles and so it was inevitable that nose art would appear on motorcycles and that club colors would never be quite the same again.

Steel motorcycle parts have been plated with a variety of other metals over the years: brass, nickel, cadmium, chromium, even gold. Chrome both protects steel from corrosion and is decorative. Many custom builders have considerably more of their motorcycle chrome plated than that executed at the factory. There are those who consider chrome an unnecessary extravagance – it's not uncommon to see stickers that read 'Chrome don't get ya home'. Such an attitude was possibly spawned during the late seventies when many custom bikes were so ostentatious that they bordered on the garish. It was at this time that gold plated parts were popular – if expensive. More recently, as billet aluminum parts have become popular, other types of metal coatings are seen, such as anodising. This prevents aluminum parts such as brake calipers from corroding and can be done in colors to suit a custom bike. Polishing is another way of getting a shiny finish on motorcycle parts and metals such as stainless steel and aluminum buff up to a high gloss finish. Often this is achieved by polishing the parts up with a buffing mop and, once it is refitted to the motorcycle, keeping it polished with a proprietary brand of metal polish.

Other non-metallic areas of a custom bike, such as a seat, often receive special treatment too; leather seats, for example, are often trimmed with studs and conchos, particularly on nostalgia style bikes. On more radical customs it is possible to find seats which feature colored flames that contrast with the main color of the seat.

As with so many aspects of custom bike building, the limitations on the standard of paint and finish on a particular motorcycle tend to be determined by the individual builder's imagination and ability, the technology available or the amount of money which can be spent.

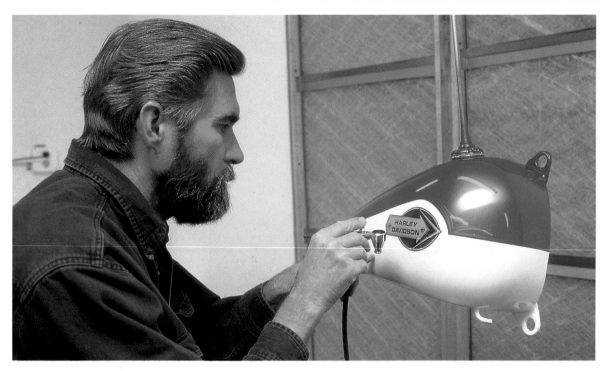

Left: Jeff McCann from Stockton, California, has been painting custom bikes for around twenty years. Here he is seen airbrushing the finishing touches of a traditional two-tone paint scheme on a gas tank. The screen behind the tank is a huge extractor fan to remove paint fumes and dust from the atmosphere.

Below: While the airbrush is one of a custom painter's most important tools because of its versatility, other older techniques are still important. McCann is painstakingly pinstriping the edges of a flame paint job on a Mustang tank in gold with a brush.

Right: The Corsa is a European built custom Sportster although it incorporates work from various American specialists, including Carl Morrow, Arlen Ness and painter Jeff McCann. It was intended to combine the elegance of Europe with the get-up-and-go of California. Jeff painted the bike in candy red and yellow. To detail the bike further he applied the goldleaf by hand to the tank, fenders and headlamp shell.

Left: Flames are traditional but on this Shovelhead chop, Arlen Ness has taken the flamed theme a step further with both flames and ghost flames. He has also incorporated flames into the points cover, air cleaner and handlebar grips. Flames are just visible stitched into the seat.

Right: Ron Simms has taken a different approach with his Evo. Not only has he used a matching selection of ball-milled billet parts, triple trees, handlebar clamp, dash panel, gas caps and aircleaner, but he has continued the flames of the tank on the speedo face.

Left: Yet another interpretation of flames on a custom Harley is seen on this street racer. The flames are painted gradually, changing color from white to purple. The tips of the flames are intertwined and on top of this are licking the orange outline of ghost flames.

Above right: The flames on Ron Rupp's custom Springer Softail (right) are still another variation on the theme. They were painted by Californian Jeff McCann before Ron rode his bike the 1500 miles to Sturgis. Rupp is a member of the Hamsters MC, a club dedicated to riding fine custom bikes.

Below right: Not the colors of flames you would perhaps expect – purple and magenta pearl. They were sprayed over the yellow paint by Damon's Motorcycle Creations on the stunning Panhead, Fatal Attraction. The flames and colors are continued on the fenders, frame and engine.

Left: Custom paintwork follows trends: flames may be a perennial favorite but murals covering whole bikes, for example, have declined in popularity since the seventies while paintwork such as this has become very popular in recent years.

Right and below: The idea behind a custom paint scheme is often a personal thing. It could be that the idea behind this character (right) is known only to the owner and the painter. The modern graphics (below) lend a contemporary touch to a classic Panhead.

Above: Photographed at Mule Creek in Wyoming on the road to Sturgis was the Harley with this she-devil on the tank. The owner said it was his ex-wife in a way that meant he definitely wasn't joking . . .

Left: Splash paintwork such as this is another recent trend. Like flames, it shows movement and is often painted so that it appears to be flowing the length of the Harley from front to back covering the fenders, gas tank, parts of the frame and other components such as the fender struts.

Right: Skulls, and to a lesser extent, skeletons, are another favorite subject for airbrush artists to paint onto custom Harleys. This probably originates from the piratical 'Jolly Roger' flag flown by sea-going pirates of earlier times. One of the earliest and biggest outlaw motorcycle clubs – The Outlaws MC – uses a skull and crossed pistons on its colors.

Like flames though, there are endless variations on the theme. A humorous interpretation is found on the rear fender of this bike from Ron Simms' Bay Area Custom Cycles. It was painted by Horst and the 'skulls and skeletons' theme covers several other parts of the Harley, too.

Left: Starr is from Dallas, Georgia, where she runs Starr Custom Paint. She painted her Panhead yellow and then spent a further two weeks masking it up before spraying the asymmetrical black graphics. Once finished the bike won first place at the Atlanta World of Wheels Show.

Above right: Scott Entrekin left his bike with Starr to be painted. He asked for purple and left the rest to Starr. She painted the custom Harley FLH, which is unusual in that it still carries its panniers, purple but with a few neat touches of her own.

Below right: Scott's brother, James Entrekin from Dallas, Georgia, rebuilt this FLH from a basket case. He wanted it painted black in time to ride it at Daytona. Starr painted it an eyecatching blue with a modern splatter design. James liked it and agreed it turns more heads this way.

The Corsa was built in England, in a
style which was intended to evoke
1950's Italian race bikes, by
Battistinis, an English custom bike
builder, who follow Arlen Ness's lead.
Battistinis have shown that it is
possible to base a stunning bike
around a Sportster.

SPECIFICATION

Name
Corsa
Owner
Jeff Duval
Builder
Battistinis Custom Cycles
Location
Bournemouth, England

Engine model
H–D Sportster
Capacity
89cu. in.
Year
1992
Modifications
Rebuilt as a performance engine by Carl's
Speed Shop

Frame model
Cobra Custom
Type
Plunger
Modifications
Custom built to order
Forks
Battistini Telescopic

Front wheel
21in. spoked
Front brake
Performance Machine
Front fender
Special Fabrication
Rear wheel
18in. spoked
Rear brake
Performance Machine
Rear mudguard
Special Fabrication

Handlebars
Arlen Ness
Gas tank
Battistinis
Seat
Battistinis

Paint
Jeff McCann
Plating
Battistinis

AMERICAN BUILDERS

WHILE NO BOOK COULD ever adequately cover all the custom builders in America let alone the world, such is the scale of the custom industry of the nineties, there are certain people whose names come up again and again. One such is the first of the American builders, the acknowledged King of the Custom Bike, Arlen Ness. He is a quiet, unassuming man whose wild bikes having been winning shows, turning heads and pushing the boundaries of motorcycle customizing ever wider for more than two decades.

Arlen Ness came to California as youngster from the Mid-west with his parents in the post-war years. He graduated from high school in the fifties, married at twenty and moved furniture for a living. He bought his first motorcycle, a '47 Knucklehead, in 1967 with money won at the local bowling alley. While he had already been modifying and painting cars, this was the first two-wheeler that he customized. It was taken apart and given a custom paint job. The result was that it drew a lot of comment and admiration and caused other riders to ask if Arlen would paint their bikes. The work carried out by Ness, who was still working a day job too, quickly progressed to more elaborate paint. He also started stretching tanks, modifying fenders and making up handlebars. It was a particular design of bars, ones he tagged Ramhorns, that were his first commercial success. Arlen Ness opened his first shop on a part-time basis; it was open in the evenings when he got home from his day job. He was pleased to see that somedays when he got home people were already waiting outside the shop. After customizing the Knucklehead for the second time he entered it in the Annual Oakland Roadster show. It won the ultimate accolade, the Best in Show, and made people take notice of its builder, a then unknown motorcycle customizer. He was soon able to quit his day job and turn his attention to full-time custom bike building. He still owns that first Knucklehead and, although it has been rebuilt many times over the years, it remains among his favorite bikes. Currently it is in the museum above his original shop in San Leandro in the form in which it was finished fifteen years ago. It uses unexpected components such as a Sportster transmission separated from its unit construction engine, a pair of Weber carburetors and a Magnusson Supercharger.

A particular style that Ness introduced and which soon caught on, so that

Another creation close to completion on the bench in the Ness workshop (far left)
contrasts with the early style chopper (above left) built far more recently than the
rigid frame, apehangers, Ness springers and Knucklehead engine might imply.
Housed above the workshop is this 1980 Shovelhead (above right).

numerous shops emulated and developed the style, was that of the Bay Area
Lowrider. It happened in the early seventies and his bikes had long, low
frames, kicked out front ends but with swept back handlebars and shortened
front ends. The bikes were lean and mean, narrow and almost spidery. The
lowrider style is still being developed.

Over the years he has been in business, Ness has built in excess of one
hundred show-stopping bikes using turbochargers, superchargers, a twin
engine configuration, Knucklehead, Panhead, Shovelhead, Evolution and
Sportster engines. He has also worked on other bikes – such as one a couple
of years ago in conjunction with Drag Specialties to promote their range –
and supplied parts for countless numbers through the ever expanding parts
side of the business. The newest color catalogue runs to more than 200
pages and features both Ness custom motorcycle products and clothing but
showcases many of the parts through inclusion of bikes built in the San
Leandro shop and beyond. These include bikes such as Flamin' Ape and
collaborative projects such as Drag-Ness, a machine built with Drag
Specialties and a number of bikes built in other countries by companies using
his parts. All this of course wouldn't be possible without assistance and, as
well as his employees, Arlen Ness can rely on three particular members of his
family – Bev, Sherri and Cory. Bev, Ness's wife of over thirty years, works in the
office as does daughter Sherri, while son Cory now runs a lot of the business
and builds a neat line in bikes too. He built his first custom around a 1974
Sportster while he was still at school and it made a magazine feature in
January 1981. There is a certain irony in the fact that Bev is so involved in the
motorcycle business because she is one of the reasons Arlen didn't buy his
first motorcycle until he was twenty-eight. Neither Ness's father nor Bev would
allow him to ride a motorcycle. When Arlen turned up at home with that first
Knucklehead, Bev is reported to have told him that either it went or she did.
History shows that they did resolve their differences.

Left: Arlen Ness builds himself a new bike each year for the ride up to Sturgis. For 1994 he built the luxury liner that he describes as a custom bagger. It is the bike in the background of this photograph and is so-called because it carries custom panniers. Ness is standing with another bike that he built at the same time. He describes this as a hot rod because it is powered by an 89cu. in. Sputhe motor built by Jeff Border and uses a lightweight chrome molybdenum frame.

Left: This sleek motorcycle is a current version of the Bay Area Lowrider style that has existed since the seventies. The style has always verged toward long and low. Ness has long been a proponent of such motorcycles. He built this one recently using many handcrafted parts and incorporated neat touches such as the almost completely enclosed rear tire. For this reason it might be described as 'where Bay Area lowrider meets luxury liner'.

Above: The fact that Arlen Ness has, in recent years, built a selection of old style choppers has helped popularize such Harleys again. The two seen here were built by him in California and shipped to Europe to showcase his custom parts through European distributors. The yellow one – a Softail Evo – is a progression from the other – a hardtail Shovel.

Pat Kennedy

THE OWNER OF THE eponymous Pat Kennedy's Custom Motorcycles in Tombstone, Arizona, Pat Kennedy recently relocated his business there from California. Pat and partner Brook Bryant had been considering a move but were finally spurred into action when California's helmet law came into force. Pat Kennedy is a longstanding custom bike builder; he never really wanted a stock bike and built his first custom – a BSA chop – at the age of twelve. The way he saw it back then was that choppers were cool so that is what he wanted to ride. From that first BSA he has never looked back, believing that despite all the refinements in factory produced bikes there is still a place for the innovative custom builder. Pat Kennedy started building bikes at home for himself and for others who appreciated his work. One thing led to another and in 1979 he opened his first shop in Oceanside, California. He built bikes with long forks in tune with the trend and fashions of the time but, perhaps because of his early influences, stuck to building long-forked bikes although the detailing, components and craftsmanship evolved with the times. After a trip to Sweden he was impressed with the long-forked style of chops that the Swedes seemed to have made their own. Somewhat ironically, he found himself reimporting the concept of the long forked chopper to America.

The bikes that roll out of his Tombstone shop are truly bespoke. Pat, Brook and a carefully selected team concentrate on building extremely high quality custom motorcycles by limiting the shop's output to as few as six motorcycles per year. Before a bike is commissioned Pat Kennedy and the prospective owner discuss the details, such as what sort of bike the customer wants and how he wants to ride. Assuming it is all to go ahead Pat will take a number of measurements including height, weight and arm reach. From there graphic artist Jeff Cahill draws up seven scale drawings of how the finished bike might look including varying paint schemes. Jeff has been working with Kennedy for more than six years. Once the customer has seen the drawings and chosen one then work on the actual bike itself will start.

One bike built in this manner was for Bandit from **Easyriders** magazine who reportedly weighs 225lb and stands over six feet. He came to Kennedy's shop with an idea for his bike: a hardtail Evo chop with springer front end and any number of neat touches. Pat Kennedy liked the notion. The engine was rebuilt by Lee Clemens of Departure Bike Works in Richmond, Virginia, and

Pat Kennedy (far left) with two of the bikes he has built. He built this bike (above left) for his business partner and fiancée Brook Bryant. It features 20in. over stock forks and 120-spoke wheels. His own bike (above right) has a completely alien theme reflected in the angular appearance and fiendish paint.

Pat Kennedy built a frame to suit Bandit's size and to match Cahill's concept of the finished bike. The bike utilized a Sportster tank that was both narrowed and lengthened and a completely handmade rear fender. Brook Bryant laced up a pair of 80-spoke wheels an 18in. rear and 21in. front. Darrell Pinney, who paints all the bikes that Kennedy builds, sprayed the bike which was completed for Sturgis in 1992. Similarly painstaking work has been carried out on the bikes that Pat Kennedy and Brook Bryant themselves ride. Pat had an idea for a futuristic chopper with an alien theme and with his assistant Ray Neff created it around one of Kennedy's own chrome molybdenum frames and a pair of 32in. over stock forks. To give the bike an alien feel, almost everything on the machine was angled and faceted including the handlebars, frame tubes, air cleaner, gas tank and rear fender. To take that theme a step further Brook laced up 80-spoke wheels with diamond cut spokes. The final touch was the paint, applied by Darrell Pinney, which features any number of skulls and extra-terrestrial characters.

Brook Bryant's bike is dark red and silver with 20in. over forks. The curved shapes of the tank and other components are slightly more traditional but based around a similar chrome molybdenum rigid frame with a 10in. stretch and 45° rake. It is proof that with correct engineering in terms of rake, trail and seat height the rider does not have to be over six feet tall to ride a really long forked chopper. The ruby bike features glassfiber fenders and gas tank of Kennedy's manufacture. The oil tank is made from aluminum as are the forward controls and handlebars. The latter items are anodised to match the bike. Brook laced up her own 120 spoke wheels: 19in. in diameter for the front and 15in. in diameter for the rear. The brakes are made by ISR. The bike features any number of neat touches such as a one-off aircleaner. Darrell Pinney, who Brook also considers to be the best, then applied the paint in a complex scheme of skulls and graphics. The result is, as one would imagine it to be, quite outstanding.

Ron Simms

RON SIMMS BUILT HIS first bike – a custom Panhead – over a few months of 1969 and rode it around California's Bay Area. This particular Panhead was fat bobbed, lowered, fitted with a Wideglide front end and painted gloss black. The bike was different – and hot – enough to get noticed around the Bay Area. Two years later he discovered that a Harley dealer on Mission Boulevard, Hayward Harley, was moving premises so he called the realtor and signed the lease the following day. He drove down to Los Angeles for some stock and opened the place as Bay Area Custom Cycles. He didn't intend just to stock other people's parts for long though, and was intent on building bikes. Ron Simms started by building Sportster choppers – they were lowered and featured springer front ends and straight bars. Building such bikes when the fashion was for very long front ends soon ensured Ron earned a reputation for doing things differently. Ron acknowledges one of his early influences as a guy called Ron Granato who built bikes in the late sixties. As late as 1972 most custom bikes were black but Ron started using lots of color and the foundations for his reputation were laid. He is still in the same shop on Mission Boulevard today and over the course of more than two decades has seen a lot of custom-bike fashions come and go. He believes that much of the custom scene started around the Bay Area as in the sixties the styles were in the main NorCal or Frisco-style choppers; but then guys around the bay started using rigid frames with wideglide front ends, short rear fenders and Sportster tanks, high bars and foot pegs up high and of course jockey shifts. To be different, though, Simms started building bikes with understock length front ends and a correspondingly decreased rake – bikes that appeared short and fat when they were complete. Around the turn of the decade adverts for Bay Area Custom Cycles in magazines such as **Street Chopper** read 'Fat's where it's at but lean is mean' and offered frame kits and springers for Fat-Bob and Lowrider motorcycles. A particular bike built at this time by the shop was known as Gold Rush. Built for Paul Brill, it was based around a 1962 Sportster engine and used a BACC frame and springers. Also used was one of Bay Area Custom Cycles' own custom glassfiber rear fenders. Mechanically the Sportster was upgraded by the fitting of a Rajay turbo. The whole lowrider was painted white with goldleaf and approximately six ounces of gold were used to plate parts such as the

Far left and above: Ron Simms on one of his custom Harleys outside his Hayward, California, shop. The low and wide classic FL custom shown in the pair of Softails seen above, has been a trademark of Simms' for many years. Lowered frames, full fenders and wide handlebars enhance the fat look.

wheels, forks and turbo. Years ago, Simms, who has degrees in Mechanical Engineering and Architecture, saw some billet aluminum parts on a racing motorcycle. Keen to innovate, he fabricated some aluminum triple trees for his shop built bikes. It was several years later before such components became popular and more widely used.

While fabricating custom parts has always been a part of Bay Area Custom Cycles' business, as evidenced by the custom rear fenders supplied years ago, it is, alongside the custom building, an increasing part of the business now. The Bay Area Custom Cycles' catalogue lists 800 billet parts that are available off the shelf to dress up a Harley. The shop also stocks a range of quality parts from other manufacturers. A recent development is the custom frame which is the result of a joint project between Ron Simms and Ron Paugh of Paughco. It is a Softail frame but engineered so that a builder can use up to a 6in. wide rear wheelrim and a 180 rear tire but retain the factory belt drive system. Bay Area Custom Cycles has eight employees who build approximately forty-five original custom bikes per year with around twenty being worked on at any one time. Some of these are speculative builds and put on the showroom floor for sale after completion while others are built to order. They'll build whatever the customer wants. The shop does all its own work with the exception of upholstery and plating. Bay Area Custom Cycles offers service, repairs and restoration service. One thing that Ron Simms is proud of is that all his custom bikes are built for riding.

He describes his main goal as always having been to build motorcycles that not only look great but are also fully functional; otherwise he feels that it's not worth it. As proof of this, Simms' catalogue contains a number of shots of bikes he built both for himself and from customers being ridden to and from shows. Also included are old pictures of his and Carl Simms' choppers back in the early seventies. Ron rode a Panhead with apes and Carl a colorful rigid Shovel.

Bob Dron/Donnie Smith

STARTING OUT IN the custom bike world at the end of the sixties, **Bob Dron** entered a bike in the San Francisco International Motorcycle Show in 1969 and won. He started out in business in 1970 in Concord, California, and has been a central figure in the Bay Area Custom scene ever since. His first business was an outfit called American Chopper Enterprises which he ran until 1981 when he bought a Harley–Davidson dealership in Oakland. His first bike was a Triumph Thunderbird which he customized himself in the maintenance shop of his father's trucking business. Bob admits that he was influenced by guys such as George Barris who were building lead sled cars and indeed he worked on some cars himself. A lot of the bikes built by Bob Dron ended up as magazine features, such as one featured by **Street Chopper** in April 1976. The list of parts and contributing workers reads like a who's who of customizers from the seventies. It featured a Shovelhead engine in a Jammer frame with 12in. over Ness springer front end; gas and oil tanks were from Paughco. The chopper was painted by Arlen Ness and featured artwork by Horst. A particularly unusual machine he built was The Indycycle which was a Harley and sidecar with a body like an Indycar. The finished machine was track tested at Sears Point by Bob Bondurant. Another radical three-wheeler from Dron's shop was the Cycletron which had a wild design of bodywork and paint by Art Himsl. Bob fondly recalls the seventies as a decade of paisley patterns and psychedelic paint jobs.

The official Harley–Davidson dealership he runs – Oakland HD – is the largest in the world but it wasn't an altogether easy transition. He took on the franchise in 1981 and stuck with the company through the uneasy early days of their return to private management. It was, of course, worth it and trade picked up and continued to grow, so in the nineties Dron moved into new 21,000 square feet premises. In this shop there are displays of bikes and a hot rod or two as well as the expected parts department and a Motorclothes department. The latter segment of the business is run by Dron's wife, Tracey. The service department boasts an area specifically reserved for building custom bikes such as the awesome Heritage Royale.

Donnie Smith was born in Minnesota and started out as part of a team campaigning a Willys Gasser at the drag strip. One thing led to another and before long Donnie Smith was one of the brothers behind the Smith Brothers

Recently Bob Dron has been noted for building full fendered custom bikes such as the red Heritage Royale (far left) that won a major trophy at the '92 Oakland Roadster show and the purple Heritage II (above left). Donnie Smith rode his (above right) striking custom Evo to the 53rd Sturgis Rally.

and Fetrow shop in Minneapolis. The other guys were Happy Smith and Bob Fetrow. This was in the late sixties and SB&F was a respected chopper shop. It stocked many of the custom brands available then and manufactured lines of its own. In the early eighties the shop moved into larger premises and as well as stocking custom parts the shop was busy building bikes. Engine building was farmed out to Jim Ulasich who was famous for racing a Knucklehead while paint went to guys like Kevin Winter and David Bell. Fetrow and Happy Smith ran the workshop while Donnie handled the retail side of the business. In the mid-eighties the three partners moved with the times and in, view of the changing nature of the custom bike business, closed their shop. Donnie intended to take some time off then get another job at another chop shop but in the event started building bikes in a small shop attached to his home. Part way through building a customer's bike he got bitten by the bug to finish a project that he had started in the old Smith Brothers and Fetrow shop. It was a radical machine involving lots of hand-made parts but, despite this, Donnie felt that it needed some updating. One area he felt needed attention was the engine; the project had been started around a Shovelhead but in the intervening years the Evolution engine had become widely accepted. Jim Ulasich converted the Shovelhead bottom end to accept Evolution cylinder components which he drilled and tapped for a second set of spark plugs. Kevin Winter painted the bike which was widely acclaimed and ensured more customers would be seeking his skills. Among them were Drag Specialties who contacted Donnie Smith with a view to having a bike built to showcase their products. Smith built a headturning, hot pink Fat Boy which appeared on the cover of the company's 1992 catalogue. The custom styling enhanced the low fat lines of the stock Fat Boy by almost exaggerating them. The finished custom sat lower than stock and featured fuller fenders and a chainguard that followed the lines of the fender. The pink paint was detailed with scallops of a different shade.

Rick Doss/Mike and Felix La Fore

BASED IN DANVILLE, Virginia, **Rick Doss** started with customized Harley–Davidsons in 1976 when he purchased his first Harley, a 1976 Super Glide. Like so many of the talented and prolific American custom Harley builders he produces a large number of custom bikes. Custom builders may produce catalogues showing examples of their work and of their finished project bikes but, unlike motorcycle factories, they don't produce an annual catalogue of new models mainly because each new bike is one of a kind. As a result it would be hard to keep a track on the progress of the top notch builders but for the monthly output of custom Harley magazines. There is a huge variety of them worldwide now, their numbers increasing in direct proportion to the growing Harley and custom market around the globe, but undoubtedly the most famous is **Easyriders**. It is claimed to be the world's largest selling motorcycle magazine and for more than two decades has entertained, shocked and informed in its own unique style. The magazine contains a mixture of news, events coverage, pretty girls wearing nothing but a smile and of course customized Harley–Davidsons. While it has moved with the times it still relies on this successful formula. It is noticeable that certain builders appear on a not-infrequent basis: Arlen Ness, Al Reichenbach, Dave Perewitz and Bill Gardner to name but four. Yet another is Rick Doss, who once traded under the name of Rick's Custom Harlees but is now known as Rick Doss Inc. The change of name is not particularly important when it is possible to find examples of fine bikes built or worked on by Rick Doss in copies of **Easyriders** magazine that are more than ten years apart. In 1984, for example, he helped out on a custom '63 FLH; in 1986 there was the Knucklehead he built for his wife Dixie and in 1987 it was a hardtail shovel. In May 1988 a Shovelhead he had built that had won the café class at The Rat's Hole Show in Daytona made the magazine. In August of the same year another Shovelhead, this time a '76 model, appeared. In 1989 a trick Evo Softail custom appeared and so it goes on. In August 1994 a similarly trick Shovelhead complete with some of Rick's own design of parts was shown. Given the competition to get bikes featured in the magazine that is a very impressive list and it no doubt enhanced Rick Doss's reputation as a first-rate custom builder.

The giant aftermarket manufacturer Custom Chrome Inc. obviously liked what

Rick Doss (far left) built this Softail Evo custom (above left); it is one of a long line of custom Harleys built by Doss since 1976 when he first started out. The Evo Softail (above right) was built by Mike and Felix La Fore in their Lakewood shop for Hawaiian tattooist Thomas Dias.

they saw and had Rick build some of their custom project bikes using lines from their catalogue. Some people would claim that bikes built from bolt-on parts aren't true custom bikes; Rick Doss proved otherwise. Through careful selection of parts he created a stunning FXR-type custom based around a CCI five speed, rubbermount frame and a number of RevTech engine parts. A second bike he built for the company was based on a stock Harley Softail frame and featured a variety of Custom Chrome, GMA brakes and a number of Rick's own parts. It is no surprise then to find many Rick Doss Inc. parts alongside those of Ron Simms and Arlen Ness among the range distributed worldwide by Custom Chrome Inc.

While the custom bike building shop run by **Mike and Felix La Fore** is perhaps smaller and definitely younger than the others described here, it is up and coming. The brothers are based in Lakewood, Colorado, and build varying styles of bike from rigid Shovelheads that they describe as café sport (because of their low lines and bikini fairings) to Harleys that feature trick engineering. One such is a bike built for a customer, Thomas Dias, that features an incredibly trick primary cover in which the billet Derby and Inspection covers rotate when the engine is running. The Derby cover has been machined with 'directional' slots. The rest of the particular Softail is similarly trick; molded within the handmade rear fender are both the turn signals and taillight. The gas tank features an aircraft-style flush fitting alloy filler cap. The engine has been rebuilt to displace 93cu. in. and features twin-plugged heads and an S&S Super carb. High tech brake master cylinders from Performance Machine and Bill Gardner's Omaha-made GMA brake calipers are installed. Each component on the bike has been chosen either for its function or its form and then polished or painted to suit. The painted parts are finished in a lustrous black that contrasts perfectly with the alloy and chrome and the whole Harley has an air of impeccable finish and phenomenal attention to detail.

Lawayne Matthies

BORN AND RAISED in Sioux Falls, South Dakota, Lawayne Matthies saw the annual Black Hills Motor Classic take place each August in nearby Sturgis from an early age. He hasn't missed a rally in Sturgis in twenty-five years despite having relocated to Grand Prairie, Texas, in 1980. He's been building and buying, swapping and modifying bikes since he can remember. After moving to Texas he started making plans for his own aftermarket business actually to market some of the parts he had ideas about, the pivit of all those hours spent working on Harleys. The business he established is called Xzotic Cycle Products and he has taken a different route to many other custom builders. While they set out to change most of the cycle parts of the Harleys they work on but retain a stock-looking Harley engine even it is fitted with aftermarket parts, Lawayne set out to change the appearance of the engine. It would still look like a Harley engine but one considerably older than it actually was. His timing fitted in with the trend toward nostalgia and retro bikes so parts that suited this style would be popular. The Evo engine was introduced in 1984 but Lawayne didn't buy one until 1986 when he purchased an accident damaged bike from Corpus Christi. He refurbished the damaged big twin and began manufacturing retro parts to make current FL models look like much older FLs. The major parts he designed and subsequently had manufactured were a set of parts to make the heads of an Evolution look like those of a Panhead. These comprise a Panhead-type rocker cover and gasket, an adapter ring and gasket that bolts to the cylinder heads. To allow the kit to be used with later model frames the Panhead covers are available slightly shallower than Harley's originals. To increase the similarities with a Panhead he made an early style ribbed generator cam cover that retains the modern electronic ignition. He also supplies a kit that simulates the generator and distributor for further subterfuge. The parts were a success and Lawayne followed them with vintage style exhaust pipes, coil covers, battery boxes and footboards. He also turned his attention to the front end of Harleys. Following the vintage theme he design a shrouded headlamp nacelle conversion for the forks of a late model Softail.
Following a much more up to date theme in the opposite direction, Lawayne developed an electronic speedo for the tank mounted Harley dash that fits into the existing dash and features an LED display. He also designed

Lawayne Matthies runs Xzotic Cycle Products which specializes in making current model Evos look like fifties Panheads (far left). He is seen here (above left) astride the Xzotic Eye on Daytona Beach. The bike has a theme of ellipses running through it, even in Dark Star's paint on the tank (above right).

innovative headlamps that he has called the Xzotic Eye. These are typical Harley headlamps, both Bates-style and nacelle mounted, except that they are elliptical in shape rather than circular and lend a decidedly custom appearance to a Harley. Then, in time to be unveiled for Sturgis, one year he followed the success of his Panhead covers with components made to make the Evolution engine look even older. He devised a kit that recreated a Knucklehead top end on an Evolution motor. Each head is refitted with a number of castings and fittings to give the classic appearance of the Knuckleheads. When they are used in conjunction with a circular air cleaner it takes more than a second glance to verify whether or not it is a real thirties engine.

To display all his products Matthies has built bikes that incorporate them. A retro FL first came with Panhead covers and all the associated early engine parts, including the timing cover and generator/distributor assembly. The cycle parts also benefitted from the Xzotic battery box, coil cover and headlamp nacelle used in conjunction with a Corbin seat and wide handlebars. He built the Xzotic Eye, a motorcycle which not only used an elliptical headlamp but carried the theme of ellipses throughout. Elliptical taillight, footboards, turnsignals, mirrors and dash are all to be found as well as high tech parts such as R.C. Components drag race wheels. Both these bikes were painted by Dark Star, as was his third machine built to showcase the Knuckleheads. It played on Harley's advertising for the Road King which read, 'Grandpa was a Knucklehead'. Matthies built one of his custom machines that looked similar to a Road King right down to the paint scheme but actually had a 'Knucklehead' engine.

Recently Lawayne Matthies has moved his business to larger premises to allow the business to grow. Some of his parts have been used on bikes built by the likes of Pat Kennedy and are now distributed by one of the biggest American distributors as well as a major European one.

Corporate Custom

TOWARD THE END OF the sixties it became apparent that there was a market for custom parts for motorcycles and, while lots of shops made a few parts and carried out modifications, some guys were intent on bigger things. Among the first was Mil Blair who founded Jammer Cycle Products with Joe Teresi. The company produced a series of publications, **Jammer's Handbooks**, which featured technical information and a catalogue of Jammer parts and helped bikers get custom motorcycles on the road. Other companies were started back then too: Drag Specialties based in Minneapolis started out making Maltese Cross taillights and mirrors. Tom Rudd founded the company in a small retail shop and saw the operation grow massively during the seventies. In 1971 Custom Chrome Inc. also started in a small store; there were others, too, including Paughco and Gary Bang. The market continued to grow and other companies joined the line up, including Chrome Specialties Inc. from Texas and Zodiac International BV from Holland, both of which were founded in 1984. Chrome Specialties was founded by two brothers, John and Greg Kuelbs, after they sold their official Harley–Davidson dealership in Texas. They moved to Arlington, and established their aftermarket business. Recently they acquired the famous Jammer brand and launched a new line of parts under the Motor Factory name. Zodiac International BV, as the European arm of an American company, started in a small Amsterdam warehouse with only three staff and 2000 square feet of warehouse. In 1990 the company moved into a 50,000 square feet facility in Mijdrecht, Holland.

What all these companies do is produce a selection of parts for Harley–Davidsons. The parts range from being service items such as filters and brake pads to replacement standard parts for repairs and restoration and, of course, a huge selection of custom parts. The major companies produce huge catalogues – often in excess of six hundred pages – that show their range, list part numbers and often cross refer them with Harley's own part numbers. The beauty of this is that it is possible for a customer to choose the components he or she requires, find the part number for the item to fit his or her own bike and order it through the local dealer who stocks that brand. The aftermarket parts companies have highly organized distribution networks and many local bike shops carry one or more of the brands. Another aspect

This FXR (far left) was built by Rick Doss for Custom Chrome Inc. using parts from their catalogue. John Reed is an expatriate Englishman who works for CCI. He built this Evo (above left) for the Fiftieth Anniversary of Sturgis. This custom Shovelhead (above right) was built by the company from products out of their catalogue.

of these big companies is that they distribute specialist products from smaller or more specialist manufacturers.

The major companies produce such a comprehensive range of parts for Harley–Davidsons that it is possible to build a complete and rideable motorcycle from the products in the catalogue. What each company does is build project bikes to showcase its own components; these take various forms. In some cases the company has teamed up with a particular custom builder to produce an extra special custom bike. Arlen Ness collaborated with Drag Specialties on at least one bike, while Rick Doss worked with Custom Chrome Inc. on several projects, for example. Another type of corporate custom are bikes such as the Custom Chrome Inc. and Chrome Specialties machines which are built solely from that company's products. Recently Chrome Specialties have even prepared a 'shopping list' of the parts required, to help a prospective builder order sufficient compatible parts to build a custom bike – there are 266 part numbers on it. While these companies and others such as Nempco and V-Twin Manufacturing are the largest concerns in the corporate custom business there is a new wave of manufacturers growing with the market. Arlen Ness and Ron Simms are long-established custom builders but are increasingly producing product ranges for sale through other motorcycle shops and both produce color catalogues of their ranges. Ness produces a huge range of billet aluminum parts and items such as frames and swingarms. Ron Simms produces his own range of billet parts and has collaborated with Ron Paugh of Paughco on some frames. Pro-One are another of the new wave manufacturers of frames and billet parts. A spin-off of the wide availability of sufficient custom parts to build a motorcycle is that companies are building complete bikes for sale to customers. Two such companies are California-based Illusion and Big Dog Motorcycles Inc. from Kansas. This is in addition to the enterprises seeking to relaunch other famous American marques such as Indian and Excelsior.

The style of apehangers and flames has never gone out of fashion for choppers. This is a nineties version of the old theme and uses many high tech parts alongside the traditional styling. CNC-machined components and disc brakes are just some of the modern parts.

SPECIFICATION

Name
Flamin' Ape
Owner
Arlen Ness
Builder
Owner
Location
San Leandro, California

Engine model
H–D Shovelhead
Capacity
74cu. in.
Year
1980
Modifications
Ness covers and aircleaner

Frame model
H–D Rigid
Type
Wishbone
Modifications
None
Forks
Paughco Springers
Front wheel
21in. spoked
Front brake
Disc and Performance Machine caliper
Front fender
None
Rear wheel
18in. spoked
Rear brake
Disc and Performance Machine caliper
Rear fender
Ness Taildragger

Handlebars
Ness Apehangers
Gas tank
Arlen Ness
Seat
Danny Gray

Paint
Arlen Ness
Plating
High Luster

EUROPEAN INFLUENCES

EUROPE HAS ALWAYS had a motorcycle culture; some of the world's most famous makes came from factories in Great Britain, Italy and Germany. As in America, the enthusiast scene was focused around competitive events and in particular road racing. Events such as the Isle of Man TT Races annually attracted thousands of riders to the island to see the racers battling it out on the twisty roads of the mountain circuit. Riders emulated the style of race bikes with race-style seats, tanks and handlebars and congregated around coffee bars – the so called café racers. In 1969 the film **Easyrider** was shown at cinemas across Europe. It was a breath of fresh air that heralded the winds of change, coming as it did in the decade of flower power and a changing world order. If choppers were good enough for Peter Fonda and Dennis Hopper as Captain America and Billy respectively, then they were cool for Europe too. The problem was that, with one exception – the 45 – in Europe Harley–Davidsons were not plentiful. Because of the numbers of ex-army WL models left behind by the the various armies it was possible to ride a chopped Harley. In France, Brigitte Bardot had just such a chopper and she recorded a song about it. In London John Wallace and Ray Leon had a shop building choppers from the then plentiful WL models. If a Harley engine wasn't available, the alternative was to chop one of the plethora of British bikes. The sudden enthusiasm for choppers prompted disapproval from the established and serious sort of motorcyclist. One journalist commented that an Englishman riding a chopper was as unnatural as a Mexican wearing a kilt. Many motorcyclists didn't agree and chopper building continued unabated.

Times moved on and Harleys became more widely available in many European countries. A trickle of custom parts were imported from America but things really took off in the early eighties when two things happened. Ton Pels, a Dutchman, opened Zodiac International BV near Amsterdam which specialized in custom parts from around the world. Harley–Davidson introduced the Evolution engine and sold them in Europe. With the raw material more widely available it was inevitable that the whole custom bike scene would become more Harley–Davidson orientated. That is exactly what happened and in Holland, France, Britain, Sweden, Norway and Germany are to be found huge numbers of Harley riders. The popularity of custom Harleys has spread beyond these countries of course: Italy, Spain and the

Airbrush Willy (far left) is a Belgian who earns his living by custom painting. Completely contrasting styles of show standard custom Harley: a luxury liner (left) and a pair of traditional rigid choppers (right). What they do have in common though is that they were built in Europe, in France and Scotland respectively.

former Eastern Bloc countries are seeing increasing numbers of Harleys on their roads.

The different types of riding conditions experienced in Europe, in terms of weather conditions, more frenetic traffic and, in some cases, stricter legislation, have led to various different types of modifications being made to Harley–Davidsons. For example, the more frequent salting of roads to keep snow and ice at bay means that many custom parts are made from corrosion-resistant stainless steel. The prevailing traffic conditions and the existence of such things as roundabouts has encouraged the uprating of braking equipment. The strictest legislation concerning modifications to motorcycles in Europe is found in Germany where all custom parts have to be approved by a certain government department. This hasn't stopped German customizers but has had a bearing on what they manufacture.

One style of custom Harley that seems almost exclusive to Europe is a combination of a Harley engine and frame but with the front end and wheels from a Japanese sports bike. The idea behind this is that the builder ends up with what can be described as the best of both worlds. He has a Harley–Davidson with a series of performance modifications that enhance both the appearance and abilities of his motorcycle. The complete front end of a Japanese bike that would be utilized features twin discs and high quality calipers as well as cast alloy wheels that can be painted to complement the remainder of the bike. One of the reasons for this type of modification is simply that the parts are more plentiful and less expensive than corresponding performance Harley parts. This situation is changing though as the popularity of Harleys continues to increase in Europe.

With this increasing popularity is coming a much larger market and one that will support a specialist aftermarket for Harleys. As a result, it is now possible to find custom shops, engine builders and tuners, bike restorers and unofficial Harley shops in most European countries.

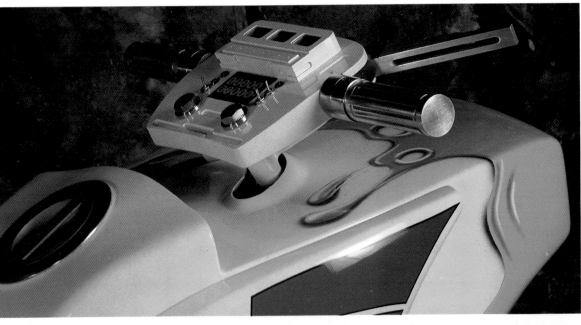

Custom bike building is all about building something different. Hans Boekhoue from Bourne, Holland, has gone one step further and built something totally unique around a Shovelhead engine and transmission. The bodywork is completely hand made from steel sheet and incorporates both oil and gas tanks. The speedo (above) is electronic and has a digital display. The handlebars turn the front wheel through the bodywork that carries the headlamp and flows into the downtubes of the frame. Boekhoue did all the work himself, including the paintwork, with the sole exception of the seat. This is designed to allow room for the travel of the rear suspension. The bike runs and Boekhoue regularly rides it to Harley rallies and shows in Europe.

Left: Richard La Plante, the American martial arts novelist who lives in London, England, had this 1989 FXSTS customized by Battistinis, the British custom shop. The engine was rebuilt by Alan Fisher at Ultimate Performance in London to an increased displacement of 95cu. in.

Below: Englishman and long-standing custom Harley rider Andy Peters built this motorcycle from Harley parts and specially fabricated sheet metal. He emulated the long, low 'luxury-liner' style of custom that has become popular in the USA. Both the induction and exhaust systems are particularly intricate.

Right: Nicolas Chavin from Paris, France, built this spectacular Shovelhead lowrider as a tribute to the blues musician Stevie Ray Vaughan. He did all the work himself including making the frame in which to fit the 1980 engine and transmission. The forks and front wheel are from a Suzuki while the rear wheel is an alloy car item fitted with a specially machined hub. Chavin also sprayed the murals and graphics onto the bike which subsequently won many custom show trophies.

Above and right: In Europe the Swedish are famous for building radical choppers with extremely long front ends. Seen here are two examples of such bikes. Above is Boi Andersson's Panhead. He is from Satrabrunn and his bike club is housed in an old silver mine. Andersson did all of the custom work himself including converting the frame to a hardtail in his spare time. The green chopper (right) belongs to Peter Koij from Falun in Sweden. He built it in six months. It is based around a 96cu. in. Evo engine and Sputhe transmission. The rigid frame has been fitted with a Sportster tank and Tolle forks that are 24in. over stock. Careful attention to rake and trail means that such bikes are rideable; indeed, Koij and Andersson ride their bikes at least 1500 kliks each summer on a two week run.

Above: Bill from Bristol, England, built this chopped Shovelhead along traditional lines. It features a rigid frame, apehangers, solo seat, fishtail exhaust pipes and a Sparto tailight as well as a traditional scallop paint job. The valanced rear fender probably owes more to Indian's styling than Harley's. Attention to detail shows in the fact that the plug leads, air filter and Derby covers and even the valve caps on the wheels have been color coordinated yellow to match the fenders and gas tank.

The high tech approach to custom Harley building that is popular in Europe is clearly demonstrated by this Evo, built by Technoplus, a French custom shop from Aiguillon in southwest France. While this bike is based around a Softail frame, much of the remainder was specifically made by Technoplus with the aid of a CNC-milling machine. The wheels, fork legs, brake calipers, hand and foot controls were all made in France. The combined seat and tank unit, known as the Monobody, which brings to mind both traditional fatbob tanks and modern sportsbikes, was also manufactured by Technoplus.

Left and below: Rick James from Cleethorpes, England, is a relative newcomer to the custom bike building scene but has been turning out show standard Harleys for the last couple of years. This 1986 FXST (below) was completely rebuilt in his workshop for a customer, Sue Barnes, from Guernsey. Many of the modifications are very subtle and are aimed at cleaning up the overall appearance of the Softail. Japanese wheels and forks add a high tech look to the bike which is further enhanced by the use of a Ness fairing and rear fender. As much as possible of the Harley was painted black by Rick's brother, Paul.

Right: The combination of a Harley engine and frame with Japanese wheels, forks and brakes is a popular one in Europe. This lime green Evo, built by The Legend Bike Shop from Belgium, is another example of such a bike. It uses Kawasaki wheels, brakes and fork legs although the latter items have been fitted to wideglide yokes. The contemporary paint scheme was sprayed by Airbrush Willy who is in his second year as a professional.

Below right: Dave King, a member of the Outlaws MC from the English Midlands, constructed another variation around an Evolution engine in a Santee custom rigid frame. The forks are the 'upside down' style ones and were made by Suzuki for a GSX-R. Using the complete front end gave him twin discs and four pot calipers on a three-spoke cast alloy wheel.

The advent of the CNC milling machine has certainly revolutionized the art of custom bike building around the globe. This lowrider from France is a good example; it is the product of a specialist custom shop based in southwest France called Technoplus.

SPECIFICATION

Name
Technoplus Lowrider
Owner
Technoplus
Builder(s)
Michel Galmiche/Claude Babot
Location
Aiguillon, France

Engine model
H–D Evolution
Capacity
80cu. in.
Year
Unknown
Modifications
STD cases
Mega-four heads
S&S carb

Frame model
Custom Rigid
Type
Chopper Guys
Modifications
None
Forks
Technoplus
Front wheel
17in. billet aluminum
Front brake
Technoplus caliper and disc
Front fender
Technoplus
Rear wheel
17in. billet aluminum
Rear brake
Technoplus caliper and disc
Rear fender
Monobody

Handlebars
Technoplus billet
Gas tank
Monobody
Seat
custom

Paint
Stevy, Lyon, France
Plating
Technoplus

UNSUNG HEROES

BIKERS ON HARLEYS haven't always been as popular as they seem to be today when every actor, actress or singer who wants to be someone is slipping on a black leather jacket and throwing a leg over a Harley. For a long time, riders of motorcycles were treated as second-class citizens for a variety of reasons. Maybe it was the fashion for long hair and beards; maybe it was the wild reputation bikers had; maybe it was the bad publicity generated by occasional violent incidents; or maybe it was just the worry that your daughter would ride into the sunset behind some 'scooter trash on a chopper'. The bad publicity was a two-way thing – movies like **The Wild One** vastly exaggerated an incident that happened at the AMA sanctioned races at Hollister, California, in 1947 that was reported in **Life** magazine and a few years later there were a succession of what have become known as biker-exploitation movies. Club wars and general mayhem at some of the long established events such as Laconia, Sturgis and Daytona didn't help and attracted a heavy police presence at these events and threats of their being ended. Despite all this the custom bike scene thrived thanks in no small way to magazines including **Easyriders**, **Choppers** and **Iron Horse**, a network of bike shops and clubs who continued to put on events and shows and of course those who lived for the thrill of being 'in the wind'. They truly were the unsung heroes of custom biking.

Another reason why things didn't look so bright for those aboard Harleys was that the market share of motorcycle sales held by the Milwaukee factory was shrinking annually. During the seventies Harley–Davidson was under the control of American Machine & Foundry. Quality control wasn't what it might have been and the last American motorcycle manufacturer was facing devastating competition from the Japanese makers (A similar situation with regard to competition had existed earlier from the British manufacturers but Harley had brought out the Sportster to compete.) The Japanese were producing cheaper, faster and more reliable motorcycles, the first Japanese win at the Daytona 200 was in 1970 and with one exception it has been that way ever since. Honda really stuck the knife in with their advertising slogan, 'You meet the nicest people on a Honda', the clear implication being, of course, that you don't on a Harley. Despite this, a lot of bikers stuck with Harley–Davidson, tolerating unreliable machines and discrimination. The

Dark Star (far left) riding his rigid framed Evo chopper built from parts. (Above left) Bill Bultz's Shovelhead chop required the electric starter cutting off the primary case to make room for the jockey shift linkage. (Above right) Steve Mastine on the 1984 Shovelhead that he bought new that year.

custom scene continued although a surprisingly large percentage of the custom shops made, or stocked, parts for Japanese bikes.

Somewhere it all began to turn around. It is hard to define why, when or exactly where it started. The movie **Mask**, starring Cher and based on a true story, showed a more compassionate, caring side of bikers, The Harley–Davidson Company official campaign on behalf of the Muscular Dystrophy Association, Harley's return to private ownership and better quality control, the introduction of the Evolution engine all helped to improve the public's perception of the Harley rider. Even the formation of the Vietnam Veterans' Motorcycle Club was seen by many as a statement that bikers were proud Americans who did their duty, too. On a similar but slightly different note, the Hells Angels MC ran a campaign whose slogan was 'Hells Angels are Americans too' after some of their members faced discriminatory legal action through the courts. Bikers around the world formed pressure groups to protect their rights to ride: ABATE – A Brotherhood Against Totalitarian Enactments, in America; MAG – Motorcycle Action Group, in England; and FEM – Federation of European Motorcyclists, in Europe.

The other type of unsung hero is the biker who doesn't have a huge and well-equipped workshop and has only one bike. He spends the grocery money to get the custom bike on the road. He works on it during evenings and weekends with the limited facilities of a domestic garage and the assistance of his riding buddies. Despite all this, or possibly because of it, he wheels out a show standard chopper. Not for him the glitz of Hollywood and its weekend riders but nights at the local biker bar, local toy runs and helmet protests, scouring the swap meets for parts, shows and parties and runs with his riding buddies with perhaps occasional rides to the annual events in Sturgis, Daytona or Laconia. At these he's the guy with bedroll strapped on the forks and a tent on the cissy bar rather than the one with a Harley in a pickup bed.

Left and top right: Robby Tomlinson from Jacksonville, Florida, astride the Panhead he built up himself after just buying the engine. The Panhead engine was rebuilt by Michael's Cycle of Mayport Beach who increased the displacement to 86cu. in. The frame forks and rear fender (right) are new custom items from Paughco but are styled after forties' and fifties' Harley parts, giving the whole bike the look of a classic chopper. Up to date touches include the Jaybrake calipers and disc brakes and the vibrant paint.

Right: Similarly vibrant paint adorns Jeff Lorimer's chop. The resident of Omaha, Nebraska, seen here partially rebuilds his bike – which is another variation on the chopped Panhead theme – each winter in preparation for the next year's riding. It uses a swingarm frame and a dresser strutless rear fender.

Right: The Hog Farm is typical of many independent, unauthorized Harley shops that exist around the world carrying out performance, custom and restoration work. The Hog Farm from New York has been run by Ruth Grottanelli and her husband Grott since 1969. It takes its name from the old slang term for a Harley – a Hog. Custom Harleys were referred to as chopped hogs. The Hog Farm built this big twin for Ruth using mostly custom and aftermarket parts. It is a 98cu. in. Shovelhead in an Arlen Ness frame and swingarm. This and a wideglide front end have been fitted with solid cast S&S wheels. A custom rear fender and seat sit behind the fatbob gas tank which features a dash with a digital Cyberdyne speedo. Other custom parts include the drag bars, mirror, grips, tail lights and license plate frame.

Above and right: Shane Ferguson from Minnesota wheelying his café race Sportster. He used parts and technology from high tech sports and race bikes to build this custom Harley himself. It features carbon-Kevlar panels, a race-type fairing, a British JMC alloy swingarm, Works Performance shock absorbers, 43mm Showa forks, cast alloy wheels, a D&D Muffler and (right) a performance engine rebuilt by Carl's Speed Shop from Santa Fe Springs, California. The engine was increased in capacity from 883cc to 1200 and now features S&S pistons, ported heads, a hot cam, S&S carbs and Screamin' Eagle coil and ignition module.

Left and below left: Clive Maye from Chester, England, riding his custom Panhead. The Harley is based around a genuine and rare '55–'57 straightleg Harley frame. Its straight lines give a neat and uncluttered appearance to the finished bike. A custom flat rear fender is supported on specially fabricated struts that flow into the tail light. At the front are a pair of early '80s FX custom wideglide forks that allow mounting of brake calipers and a 21in. front wheel.

Right and below: Steve Mastine riding his 1984 Shovelhead chop at Daytona. He has owned it since it was new and describes it as 'just a good running bike'. It has been rebuilt by Trik Cycles from Florida where Steve works, using a lot of custom parts including CCI fishtail exhausts, Trik oil cooler, Ness pushrod covers, a digital oil pressure gauge and a Corbin seat.

Above: Custom painter, Dark Star, at Sturgis on the rigid Harley–Davidson Evolution chopper that he built from parts then painted in a traditional style of flames.

Below and right: From Wahoo, Nebraska, Bill Bultz and his chopped '75 Shovelhead (right) – it has been like this since 1982. The downtubes of the frame have been lengthened to raise the headstock while it has been lowered at the rear. This means that the rider sits in the classic disdainful 'chopper' pose: arms straight, feet forward (below).

Above and left: Typical of many of the unsung heroes of custom biking are Ken and Jo Schultz from Mead, Nebraska. They have owned this Shovelhead since they bought it new as a stock 1974 FX and have been riding it and modifying it ever since. They've also been riding with the same crowd they met at a Helmet Law Protest in 1974 in Lincoln, Nebraska. Owning a bike for more than two decades means that they were riding a Harley long before it became fashionable. They also stuck by the brand through the troubled years of AMF ownership.

Right: Neilson Miller from Newcastle, England, riding his custom Softail. He rebuilt the Harley from a fire damaged wreck using a combination of genuine Harley and custom aftermarket parts. The forks, frame and rear fender are original while the gas tank, bars, mirrors and forward controls are custom items. The heavy front forks fitted with a minimal front fender and drag-style bars echoes the early 'bobber' idea of cutting down heavy Harleys to make them go faster.

Below: Neilson chose parts to enhance the triangular shape of the Softail frame. The bars and risers flow into the dash. The lines of the dash and tank flow into the seat which is contoured to follow the line of the rear fender out of which curves the Sparto taillight. The bike was photographed in the amusement arcade known as Spanish City and made famous by rock band Dire Straits.

At a glance, this Harley (left) could be mistaken for a completely nostalgic ride – a new old chopper. However, underneath the flamed paint, the apehangers and upswept fishtail pipes it is remarkably modern.

SPECIFICATION

Name
Outlaw Bike
Owner
Flint
Builder
Owner
Location
Coventry, England

Engine model
Evolution
Capacity
80cu. in.
Year
Unknown
Modifications
Mikuni carb

Frame model
Modified HD
Type
Softail
Modifications
Welded on hardtail
Forks
ZXR 'upside-downies'
Front wheel
ZXR cast alloy
Front brake
Kawasaki ZXR
Front fender
Kawasaki ZXR
Rear wheel
ZXR cast alloy
Rear brake
Kawasaki ZXR
Rear fender
Flat custom

Handlebars
Apehangers
Gas tank
King sportster
Seat
Solo seat and P-pad

Paint
Jay, Nuneaton, England
Plating
Custom Chrome, Nuneaton, England

RIDDEN NOT HIDDEN

A SHOWROOM stock motorcycle might be just a means of transportation but a custom bike is always something more. Whether it is daring to be different, simply the rider showing off, built to attract the girls or simply give its owner the satisfaction of riding a handbuilt motorcycle, it is always going to be more than a bike for getting from A to B. It is the sort of bike that will get from A to B but probably by a far more scenic backroad.

Custom Harleys represent different things to different people too; for some a bike is a toy to be ridden on a Sunday but to others it is almost the sole reason for living – 'I only ride Harleys on days that end in Y'. For some it is an easy thing to acquire, a bespoke bike bought with the wave of a credit card; for others a custom Harley is the result of hours of hard work, scrimping, saving and spending the grocery money on bike parts. Each way has its rewards. Whether the custom is for cruising Main Street in Daytona, for the annual pilgrimage to the Black Hills, or for parking outside the Club Wannabe, the characters who ride custom Harleys are as diverse as the colors on the bikes they ride. The hard-riding One Percenter is likely to have a different outlook on life to the weekend riding office worker.

A rider's outlook will affect what he or she rides; the newcomers and show-offs often want to ride a bike that is as ostentatious as possible. A veteran of years on the road is more likely to be riding a classy custom that shows its heritage through a careful choice of minimal but classic parts. Those who want to win trophies at custom shows such as The Rat's Hole Show in Daytona or The Oakland Roadster Show will be viewing the concept of custom bike building from an altogether different angle, while the guy who wants to cruise the bars looking for pretty girls is going to make sure that his is a motorcycle built for two. And so it goes on.

Other much more mundane factors, such as weather and geographical location, influence what type of custom Harley a rider is likely to be found on. Bikes without front fenders look as cool as anything until it rains. Then they become a nightmare to ride as a spray of cold, gritty water hits the rider right between the eyes! There are different fashions around the world, too: East and West Coast styles in the USA, a distinct European style and yet another style in Australia where long front ends are in the minority because of the distances that have to be ridden on poor roads. Once all these factors have

English Outlaws, Dave and Flint, on the urban streets of Coventry (far left) contrast with Taz (above left) on the rural roads of Scotland and Paragon Custom Cycles' pro-street bike in Sturgis, South Dakota (above right), but they are all custom Harleys and all being ridden.

been taken into account, often subconciously, and a bike has been built either up from a bare frame or by modifying an already extant machine, it's time to go riding. There are rides for every mood whether it be the lone rider wandering on quiet roads or a pack of Harleys coming on like a thousand-bomber raid. It might be a charity run to help some less fortunate group or it could be that the rider is heading for the mayhem of a big party. It could be that the destination is a protest run to remind (none too subtly) the politicians that bikers are voters; it might just be a run to the mountains.

The rumble of a V-twin, the clunk from the transmission as a gear is selected, the buzz of anticipation as the clutch is let out.

Get your motor runnin' and head out on the highway. Other makes and models of motorcycle may come and go but Harleys simply go on for ever. Occasionally they may be hamstrung by the men who write silly little laws about the position of turn signals or that 'objects in the rearview mirror may appear closer than they are' but, riding down the road, with the sun glinting off the chrome and listening to the backbeat from the pipes, suddenly none of that matters. There are those, particularly among the paternalistic road safety lobby, who see Harley–Davidsons, indeed motorcycles as a whole, as iron dinosaurs and wish they were extinct. Unfortunately for them motorcycles, unlike the dinosaurs, are continually evolving and it is often the custom bike builders who point the way that the evolution will take. Recently Harleys, like all other motor vehicles, had to be manufactured suitable to run on unleaded gas, due to increasingly stringent emissions regulations. The latest heinous crime a motorcycle rider can commit is to make too much noise. It is thought that under the draconian proposals for quieter motorcycles it will be impossible to market an air-cooled machine. Worldwide, many manufacturers already produce liquid-cooled bikes, and Harley–Davidson have been experimenting with a liquid-cooled racer, the VR1000, which might just be the future.

Left: The combination of components is critical so that the finished custom looks exactly right. This is particularly important with the long forks and high handlebars of a classic chopper. Scottish bikers Charlie and Logie have both achieved the archetypal appearance despite using different combinations of parts.

Above: Ken Schultz has also engineered his Harley to create the classic chopper look. The lines of the frame have been enhanced through judicious lengthening of the downtubes while the angle and length of forks mean that the handlebars fall comfortably within reach, allowing the rider that studied air of casualness.

Below: More café-racer in styling is Felix La Fore's rigid Shovelhead but its shape still allows an upright and feet forward riding position through the use of pullback bars which are mostly concealed behind the tinted perspex of the fairing windshield. The triangular shape of the rigid frame remains deliberately uncluttered.

Left and below: Women ride custom Harley–Davidsons too; Jill Stanley (left) regularly rides this heavily modified 1987 Lowrider in the company of partner, Dave Bell. Seen leaving the Hamsters MC picnic in Spearfish, South Dakota, is this lady (below) aboard a beautiful flamed custom Softail. The Hamsters MC are a club dedicated to riding spectacular custom bikes and include Arlen Ness among their members.

Right: This Harley has been modified but still retains many factory parts, including the frame. Although a Softail, it has rear suspension and was designed to look like a triangular early rigid frame. The forks too have a vintage appearance but are fitted to current models. Harley build what are often described as 'factory customs'.

Below: The Sportster chop seen at the Red River Run in New Mexico definitely isn't a factory custom. The frame tubes have been heavily modified to get the high headstock and accommodate the long custom forks as well as giving the upright riding position. The spoked wheels, Mustang gas tank, seat, small cissy bar and flat rear fender are also from a custom parts supplier.

Right: Stefan from Denmark riding his traditional-style Panhead chopper. It is essentially a Hydraglide in that it has telescopic forks and a rigid frame but the apehangers, jockey shift gearchange, Mustang tank and high cissy bar confirm it as a bona fide chopper from the old school. Cissy bars are so-named for passengers who worry about falling off backwards.

Left and below: Two custom Harleys from different eras: a sharp Ironhead Sportster at the Red River Run (left) and a more contemporary customized FLSTC (below) that belongs to Todd Tumminello. From Michigan, Tumminello bought it as a stock second-hand bike and reworked it to suit his requirements. It is a combination of old style FL and new style paint and parts.

Left and below: Bill Bultz riding his chopped Shovelhead at Sturgis. The absence of a helmet law in South Dakota is just one of the event's attractions. Also taking advantage of this in the August sunshine are the staff and friends of La Fore's Motorcycle Shop (below) who had traveled to the Black Hills from Lakewood, Colorado. They are seen here riding through Deadwood toward Sturgis. During the week-long rally and races all the towns for miles around Sturgis itself are filled with bikers who come to see such attractions as Mt Rushmore.

Right: This bike may at first glance appear to be a stock Harley from the fifties but it is typical of a nostalgia-type custom bike. It is a current model Evolution Harley–Davidson dressed up with numerous aftermarket custom parts to look like a fifties bike. Parts added include the exhaust pipes, seat, saddlebags and, of course, the whitewall tires.

the food of
THAILAND

the food of
THAILAND

Photography by Alan Benson
Text by Lulu Grimes
Recipes by Oi Cheepchaiissara

MURDOCH
BOOKS

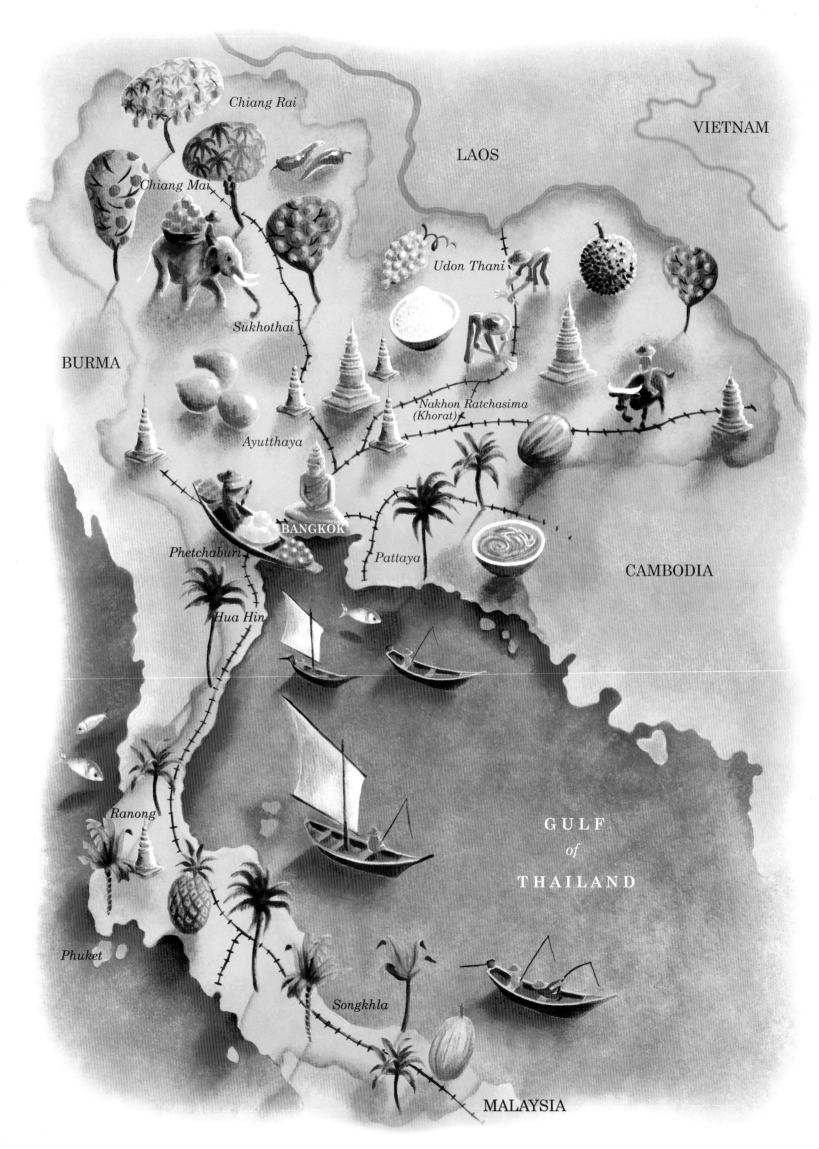

CONTENTS

FOOD JOURNEYS IN THAILAND

the food of
THAILAND

THAILAND, FOR CENTURIES A STOP-OFF FOR THE TRADERS MOVING BETWEEN SOUTH-EAST ASIA, INDIA, CHINA AND BEYOND, HAS VERY SKILFULLY ASSIMILATED INFLUENCES FROM OTHER COUNTRIES INTO ITS OWN DISTINCTIVE CUISINE WITHOUT COMPROMISING LOCAL CULTURE AND RITUALS.

Despite acting as a trade conduit throughout its history, Thailand, unlike many other Asian nations, has never been ruled by a European power. Mystical and exotic, Siam, as Thailand was once known, managed simultaneously to charm, manipulate and resist her European visitors. Closer neighbours were not so easily rebuffed and Thailand was periodically invaded, most notably by Burma. Despite these incursions, Thailand's remarkably stable religious (Buddhist) and cultural history, coupled with an abundance of locally grown food, is reflected in its historic cuisine. Buddhism permeates all aspects of Thai life. Most men spend at least three months of their young lives as a monk and, as monks are fed by everyone else in the community as a mark of respect, so food and religion are bound together.

The basic tenets of Thai cuisine are ancient in origin and were upheld for centuries by the royal kitchens while being supplemented by many outside influences. Even though they are worlds apart in terms of wealth, the underlying ingredients and recipes used, as well as styles of cooking, were, and still are, not much different between court and country. Presentation, with intricate artistry employed, and, to a certain extent, the superior quality of ingredients available to the court, were what elevated the cuisine of the royal kitchens above that of the common people. Palaces put much effort into teaching culinary skills and crafts in order to maintain their proud reputations.

Rice is central to Thai culture and cuisine. Banana leaves are used as receptacles for snacks sold on the streets. Young monks ride on river boats along the Chaophraya in Bangkok. Bananas are seen growing all over Thailand. Delicious street food is available at night markets. A woman keeps cool in a traditional hat. Ornate architecture on Wat Saen Fang in Chiang Mai.

7

Dried seafood is a popular
ingredient, the fish caught
from waters such as these
around Phang-nga. Fresh
produce such as rambutans
and green mango is sold
whole, or, like the preserved
lotus root, ready to eat. The
charming wai greeting is
used as a logo. Sugar,
chillies with vinegar, chilli
sauce and fish sauce are
used as seasonings. Herbs
are an essential flavouring.

INFLUENCES

Geographically, culinary ideas have seeped into Thailand through the permeable borders with Malaysia, Laos, Cambodia and Burma. China, who had a far reaching influence on the entire region, has also made her mark on Thai cuisine. As would be expected, influences are strongest nearest the borders. The dishes found along the Mekong River have close affiliations to Laos, Cambodia and Vietnam. Around Chiang Mai there are Burmese-style curries and soups, and close to Malaysia, Muslim recipes such as massaman and roti are common.

The most significant addition to Thai cuisine came not from Asia but from South America, via Europe. In the sixteenth century the Portuguese introduced what was to become one of the hallmarks of the cuisine, the chilli. Thai cuisine, like that of other cultures which accepted the chilli so readily, had long included an element of heat by way of fresh green peppercorns, dried white peppercorns and galangal. As well, foreign *(farang)* vegetables and fruit have been cultivated for the last couple of centuries: tomatoes, eggplants (aubergines), asparagus, carrots (known as orange long turnips), snow peas (mangetout) and corn are common.

EATING THAI FOOD

With the exception of snacks such as noodles, green papaya salad, or a single portion of curry over rice, Thai food is, on the whole, made to be shared. Portions are served on platters and meant for at least two people. Everything on the table is an accompaniment to rice, the most important component of the meal. Generally the rice is served with a curry, a fish dish, a stir-fry, a salad, a soup and vegetables. All the food is served at once. Unlike European tradition, soups come in a large bowl and are eaten with the meal, not before it. Meals begin when the host says *kin khao* or 'eat rice'. The food is not necessarily eaten piping hot.

ETIQUETTE

Thai people eat with a spoon and fork, the fork being used to push food onto the spoon or to pick up pieces of meat or sliced fruit. Chopsticks are only used with noodles, and sticky rice and its accompaniments are eaten using the right hand. When eating in Thailand there are further subtle areas of etiquette to be observed. Platters of food are left on the table, and not passed around, as stretching is not considered rude and someone on the other side of the table will always be happy to spoon things onto your plate. You should only take a couple of spoonfuls of each dish at a time as an accompaniment to rice.

THE FOOD OF THE NORTH-EAST

This region is known as Isaan and the food of the region is identified by the same name. Most of the area is a high plateau divided by the Phu Phan mountains. Divided from the rest of Thailand by more mountains, Laos and Cambodia, just over the border, have had a strong culinary influence, with much of the cuisines overlapping. The Mekong River flows along the border with both countries and has been the main means of trade for centuries.

North-Eastern Thailand was one of the first areas in Asia to grow rice. Rice is cultivated over much of the plateau but, unlike in other areas of Thailand, rain is less reliable, thus making the yield patchy. Sticky rice is preferred in the countryside and long-grain rice in the cities. As much of the area is poorer than the rest of the country, food reflects this. Rice is a staple and dishes that are served with it are small in quantity but very pungent in flavour. Unfermented fish sauce and chillies are the main seasonings. Commonly used pickled and preserved foods are another symptom of an unreliable food supply and also add more flavour to a diet of rice in this form than their original fresh state.

Kai yang or *kai ping*, grilled chicken, is found all over the area, often sold by roadside vendors. The chicken skin is rubbed with garlic, fish sauce, coriander (cilantro) root or lemon grass and black pepper, then the chicken is usually flattened and pinned on a bamboo skewer before being barbecued over coals and served with a chilli dipping sauce. Chicken is also made into *laap*, a minced meat salad made with lime juice, fish sauce, lemon grass, chillies or chilli powder and *khao khua pon*, roasted rice. Duck, fish and buffalo are also used to make *laap*, and *neu naam tok*, grilled strips of beef, are used for similar salads.

Som tam, a green papaya salad with chillies, peanuts, cherry tomatoes and dried shrimp, is a popular snack. Individual portions are pounded together by hand and eaten with sticky rice. The addition of pickled crabs transforms *som tam* into a Laotian-style dish. Soups are hot and sour style *tom*, or spicy style, *sukii*. *Sukii* are served in steamboats and each person dips in and cooks their own set of ingredients. The very south of the region has some coconut milk in soups.

Insects and frogs are popular, and red ants are used as a souring agent in some dishes. Fish are freshwater, the Mekong River being famous for the giant catfish caught from it, mainly in the months of April and May.

Roast chicken is a popular
street food. Cooked frogs
and insects are eaten in the
North. The sun sets over the
Mekong River with Thailand
in the distance. Rickshaws
are a popular form of
transport in Udon Thani.
Common street snacks
include freshly prepared
bamboo shoot salad and
green papaya salad, as well
as sticky rice, often served
on banana leaves.

Stalls and markets are prevalent in Thailand: roasted vegetables are beautifully laid out on a vegetable stall, cut fresh fruit is sold in plastic bags, and prepared *naam phrik* can be bought at Warorot market in Chiang Mai. Workers in the paddy fields near Chiang Rai. A typical Akha tribal headdress. Corn is grown in the hills near Mae Salong in the northern regions.

THE FOOD OF THE NORTH

Northern Thailand, which is the area bordered by Burma to the west and Laos to the east, has always had a strong regional identity that is distinctively different from the Thailand of the South and of the Centre. Hill tribes farm the hillsides, growing corn and rice, and families work as collectives, helping each other during the planting and harvest time. The cooler climate of the hills means that many types of European fruit grow well there, so peaches, apples and strawberries are found growing alongside lychees. Non-indigenous vegetables such as asparagus, snow peas (mangetout) and corn are also cultivated.

Above all the other dishes of the area, Northern Thai curries have Burmese influences. Made without coconut milk, they are fiery and thinner in consistency. *Kaeng hangleh muu*, Chiang Mai pork curry, is the most famous. *Naam phrik*, chilli dips, are also popular, served with cooked or raw vegetables and crunchy pieces of deep-fried pork rind.

Pork is more popular in this region, eaten both in its natural state and made into sausages. *Naem maw*, fermented sausages made with pork rind and sticky rice, are common, as are *sai ua*, bright red sausages made with pork and chillies. German-style frankfurters appear in salads and this is just one of the influences that American soldiers, stationed in the area during the Vietnam war, had on the cuisine.

Khao niaw, sticky rice, is the preferred rice, eaten with dishes such as *naam phrik*, *som tam* or pomelo salad and with *kaeng hangleh muu*. Many dishes are always served with sticky rice. Sticky rice can be bought ready-cooked wrapped in banana leaves, or in plastic bags, at markets.

Noodles are popular due to the large amounts of Chinese (Shan and Yunnanese) and Burmese people who live in the area. *Khao sawy*, flat egg noodles with curry, is a speciality of Chiang Mai, sold by Yunnanese noodle vendors near the mosques. *Khanom jiin* and *kuaytiaw* (types of rice noodles) are also popular and *wun sen*, mung bean noodles, are used in salads and soups as well as being wrapped in rice paper rolls in the same way as Vietnamese spring rolls.

Formal meals are served in small bowls on a *khao niaw*, teak platter. This is a revival of old-style serving that has become popular once again. Another speciality of the area is insects. Deep-fried bamboo worm, water beetles and various other insects are sold as snacks.

13

THE FOOD OF THE CENTRE AND BANGKOK

Central Thailand runs upwards from the Isthmus of Kra and encompasses the plains north of Bangkok. To the East it stretches to the Cambodian border, and to the West as far as Burma. Much of this area, which is watered by many rivers, constitutes the rice-bowl of Thailand. A network of canals further irrigates the region, as well as providing a means of transport. Paddy fields cover most of the area, but fruit, sugar cane, maize, peanuts and taro are also cultivated on a large scale.

Though most of this area has no access to the sea, the waterways provide a host of freshwater fish, prawns (shrimp) and crabs. Crabs and fish even live amongst the paddy as do the frogs and water beetles that are commonly eaten. Chicken, pork and beef feature in the cuisine, alongside the fish. The fertility of these regions means many vegetables grow easily and cultivated vegetables include the popular Thai eggplants (aubergines), *cha-om* (a bitter green vegetable that resembles a fern), and bamboo shoots, as well as snake beans and European vegetables like tomatoes. Vegetables grown in or alongside the waterways include *phak bung* (water spinach) and lotus shoots.

The cuisine of the Centre is what is generally considered to be 'classic Thai' and includes what are probably the most recognizable Thai dishes. Curries include red, green and *phanaeng* (panaeng). Soups are *tom khaa kai*, *tom yam* and *kaeng jeut* (bland soup); *yam* (salads) are popular as are stir-fries. Dishes influenced by the Chinese include those baked in clay pots, various noodle dishes as well as some braised dishes flavoured with Chinese spices. Japanese-style *sukii* (similar to sukiyaki) is also available.

Seasonings are classic, designed to give the typical hot, sour, salty and sweet combination. The use of palm sugar makes many recipes sweeter than their southern counterparts. Si Racha on the Gulf of Thailand is famous for the chilli sauce made there and it appears as a condiment on virtually every table.

Bangkok, or Krung Thep, to use the abbreviated Thai name, is the modern home of royal Thai cuisine. In 1960, King Bhumibol allowed the court cookbooks to be opened to everyone and dishes such as roast duck curry became accessible. Restaurants specialize in these dishes and are the best place to sample such delights.

Fresh rice noodles are sold at Aw Taw Kaw market in Bangkok. An endearing girl looks curiously at the camera in Bangkok. A giant gold Buddha dominates the scene on the road to Khorat. Vegetables on sale at Aw Taw Kaw market. Frantic Bangkok, Thailand's capital, contrasts with the serenity of transport boats used around the quiet khlongs of Damnoen Saduak.

Lunch at a beachside cafe
includes fresh local fish.
Palm trees line roads and
waterways. Fishermen in
longtail boats fish near
Phang-nga. Coconuts
are ubiquitous in the South:
seen growing, being cracked
for meat, and young
coconuts being sold for their
liquid. Lemon grass is one
of the main flavours in Thai
cooking. Fish is displayed
at Ranong fish market.

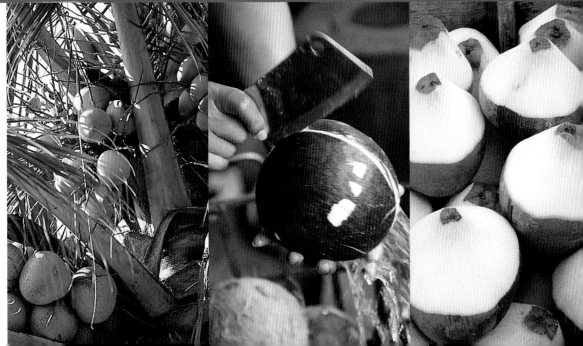

THE FOOD OF THE SOUTH

The fourteen provinces that make up the area between the Isthmus of Kra (the narrowest point in Thailand) and the Malaysian border have always been culturally different from the rest of the country. Once under the influence of the ancient Indonesian Sriwijaya empire along with areas of Malaysia, Malay-Indonesian culture and religion is still apparent in the life and language of the South.

The provinces closest to Malaysia have large numbers of Muslims, mostly concentrated around the coast and on surrounding islands where they make their living by fishing. Buddhist Thai people farm the inland regions and a Chinese minority mainly live and work in the cities.

Seafood and fish are the predominate feature of southern cuisine and are acceptable to all, both culturally and in regard to religion. With the advantage of two long coastlines, fresh fish and seafood is eaten in abundance. It is grilled over charcoal, used in stir-fries or curries, and even more of it is preserved by drying. Racks of dried squid and cottonfish line many coastal roads. Locally made shrimp paste and fish sauce are used in quantity.

The South is also the land of the palm tree. Coconut and oil palms are 'farmed' in plantations as well as growing wild, fringing the beaches on both coasts. Further up the Isthmus, sugar palms are grown for their sweet sap. Phuket is home to many pineapple plantations and rice is cultivated wherever it can be persuaded to grow.

There are three main styles of cooking. Thai (Buddhist) curries and soups are often tempered and enriched by the addition of coconut milk or cream. Spices include turmeric and pepper, and chillies are used with abandon. 'Yellow' curries are popular. Muslim dishes use ghee and oil rather than coconut and use a larger range of fragrant spices including cardamom, cumin and cloves. *Kaeng matsaman*, an Indian-style curry, is at its best in the South. Indo-Malay dishes such as satay are popular as are Indian-style roti. Chinese-style dishes include *khanom jiin* (Chinese-style rice noodles), barbecued meats, various deep-fried snacks, steamed buns, and dumplings.

Coffee shops sell *kopi* (filtered coffee), and this, served with *khao yam* (cooked dry rice, toasted coconut, makrut (kaffir) lime leaves, bean sprouts and lemon grass), makes a typical breakfast in the southern areas of Thailand.

17

SNACKS &
STREET FOOD

Using wet hands makes the fish mixture less likely to stick to your hands and also easier to handle.

FRIED FISH CAKES WITH GREEN BEANS

FISH CAKES ARE JUST ONE OF MANY DELICIOUS SNACKS SOLD AS STREET FOOD IN THAILAND. BATCHES ARE FRIED ON REQUEST AND SERVED IN A PLASTIC BAG, ALONG WITH A BAMBOO SKEWER FOR EATING THEM AND A SMALL BAG OF SAUCE FOR ADDITIONAL FLAVOUR.

450 g (1 lb) firm white fish fillets
1 tablespoon red curry paste
    (page 276) or bought paste
1 tablespoon fish sauce
1 egg
50 g (2 oz) snake beans,
    finely sliced
5 makrut (kaffir) lime leaves,
    finely shredded
peanut oil, for deep-frying
sweet chilli sauce (page 284),
    to serve
cucumber relish (page 287),
    to serve

MAKES 30

REMOVE any skin and bone from the fish and roughly chop the flesh. In a food processor or a blender, mince the fish fillets until smooth. Add the curry paste, fish sauce and egg, then blend briefly until smooth. Spoon into a bowl and mix in the beans and makrut lime leaves. Use wet hands to shape the fish paste into thin, flat cakes, about 5 cm (2 inches) across, using about a tablespoon of mixture for each.

HEAT 5 cm (2 inches) oil in a wok or deep frying pan over a medium heat. When the oil seems hot, drop a small piece of fish cake into it. If it sizzles immediately, the oil is ready.

LOWER five or six of the fish cakes into the oil and deep-fry them until they are golden brown on both sides and very puffy. Remove with a slotted spoon and drain on paper towels. Keep the cooked fish cakes warm while deep-frying the rest. Serve hot with sweet chilli sauce and cucumber relish.

FOR a variation make up another batch of the fish mixture but leave out the curry paste. Cook as above and serve both types together.

SOM TAM MALAKAW

GREEN PAPAYA SALAD

THIS DISH FROM THE NORTH-EAST IS NOW POPULAR THROUGHOUT THAILAND. SOM MEANS 'SOUR', AND TUM MEANS 'POUND' (WITH A PESTLE AND MORTAR). MULTIPLY THE INGREDIENTS BY THE NUMBER OF PORTIONS BUT MAKE JUST ONE SERVE AT A TIME OTHERWISE IT WON'T FIT IN YOUR MORTAR.

120 g (4 oz) small hard, green, unripe papaya
1½ tablespoons palm sugar
1 tablespoon fish sauce
1–2 garlic cloves
25 g (1 oz) roasted peanuts
25 g (1 oz) snake beans cut into 2.5 cm (1 inch) pieces
1 tablespoon ground dried shrimp
2–6 bird's eye chillies, stems removed (6 will give a very hot result)
50 g (2 oz) cherry tomatoes, left whole, or 2 medium tomatoes, cut into 6 wedges
half a lime
sticky rice (page 280), to serve

SERVES 1

PEEL the green papaya with a vegetable peeler and cut the papaya into long, thin shreds. If you have a mandolin, use the grater attachment.

MIX the palm sugar with the fish sauce until the sugar has dissolved.

USING a large, deep pestle and mortar, pound the garlic into a paste. Add the roasted peanuts and pound roughly together with the garlic. Add the papaya and pound softly, using a spoon to scrape down the sides, and turning and mixing well.

ADD the beans, dried shrimp and chillies and keep pounding and turning to bruise these ingredients. Add the sugar mixture and tomatoes, squeeze in the lime juice and add the lime skin to the mixture. Lightly pound together for another minute until thoroughly mixed. As the juice comes out, pound more gently so the liquid doesn't splash. Discard the lime skin. Taste the sauce in the bottom of the mortar and adjust the seasoning if necessary. It should be a balance of sweet and sour with a hot and salty taste.

SPOON the papaya salad and all the juices onto a serving plate. Serve with sticky rice.

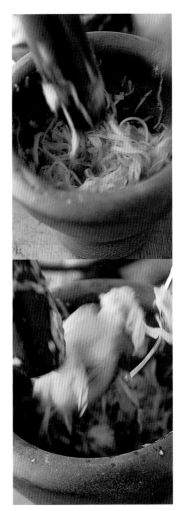

Only one portion of the salad at a time will fit into your mortar.

Cooking satay at Aw Taw Kaw market in Bangkok.

Mixing the marinade into the chicken with your fingers will help ensure all the pieces are coated.

CHICKEN SATAY

ORIGINATING IN INDONESIA, SATAY HAS MADE ITS WAY NORTH AND HAS BEEN ADAPTED TO SUIT LOCAL TASTE. SATAY SHOULD BE COOKED QUICKLY OVER HOT CHARCOALS. TRADITIONALLY SERVED WITH PEANUT SAUCE, IT IS ALSO DELICIOUS WITH CUCUMBER RELISH OR SWEET CHILLI SAUCE.

1 kg (2 lb 4 oz) skinless chicken
   breast fillets

MARINADE
2–3 Asian shallots, roughly chopped
4–5 garlic cloves, roughly chopped
4 coriander (cilantro) roots,
   finely chopped
2.5 cm (1 inch) piece of ginger,
   sliced
1 tablespoon roasted ground
   coriander
1 tablespoon roasted ground cumin
1 tablespoon roasted ground
   turmeric
1 teaspoon Thai curry powder
   (page 287) or bought Thai
   curry powder
2 tablespoons light soy sauce
4 tablespoons vegetable oil
410 ml (1⅔ cups) coconut milk
   (page 279)
2 tablespoons palm sugar
1½ teaspoons salt
40 bamboo sticks, about 18–20 cm
   (7–8 inches) long
peanut sauce (page 284) or
   cucumber relish (page 287),
   to serve

MAKES 40 STICKS

CUT the chicken fillets into strips 4 cm (1½ inches) wide x 10 cm (4 inches) long x 5 mm (¼ inch) thick and put them in a bowl.

USING a food processor, blender or pestle and mortar, blend or pound the shallots, garlic, coriander roots and ginger to a paste.

ADD the paste to the chicken, along with the ground coriander, cumin, turmeric, curry powder, light soy sauce, vegetable oil, coconut milk, sugar and salt. Mix with your fingers or a spoon until the chicken is well coated. Cover with plastic wrap and marinate in the refrigerator for at least 5 hours, or overnight. Turn the chicken occasionally.

SOAK the bamboo sticks in water for 1 hour to prevent them from burning during cooking.

THREAD a piece of the marinated chicken onto each stick as if you were sewing a piece of material. If the pieces are small, thread two pieces onto each stick.

HEAT a barbecue or grill (broiler) to high. If using the grill, line the tray with foil.

BARBECUE the satay sticks for 5 to 7 minutes on each side, or grill (broil) for 10 minutes on each side, until the chicken is cooked through and slightly charred. Turn frequently and brush the marinade sauce over the meat during cooking. If using the grill, cook a good distance below the heat. Serve hot with peanut sauce or cucumber relish.

KHAO NIAW NA KUNG
STICKY RICE WITH SHRIMP OR COCONUT TOPPING

SHRIMP TOPPING
2 garlic cloves, roughly chopped
4 coriander (cilantro) roots, cleaned
¼ teaspoon ground black pepper
1 tablespoon vegetable oil
200 g (7 oz) minced (ground) shrimp
    or very small raw prawns (shrimp)
25 g (1 oz) grated coconut
1 teaspoon fish sauce
3 tablespoons sugar

OR

COCONUT TOPPING
150 g (5 oz) grated coconut or
    desiccated coconut
150 g (5 oz) palm sugar

1 quantity of sticky rice with
    coconut milk (page 280)
3 makrut (kaffir) lime leaves,
    finely sliced, for garnish

SERVES 4

TO MAKE the shrimp topping, use a pestle and mortar to pound the garlic, coriander roots and pepper to a smooth paste. Alternatively, chop with a sharp knife until smooth. Heat the oil in a wok or frying pan and stir-fry the garlic mixture over a medium heat until fragrant. Add the minced shrimp or prawns, coconut, fish sauce and sugar and stir-fry for 3 to 4 minutes or until the minced shrimp is cooked. Taste, then adjust the seasoning if necessary. The flavour should be sweet and lightly salty.

TO MAKE the coconut topping, mix the coconut, sugar, 125 ml (½ cup) water and a pinch of salt in a saucepan and stir over a low heat until the sugar is dissolved. Do not let it thicken to a point where it will harden. Remove from the heat.

SERVE by filling a small, wet bowl with the sticky rice and turning it out on a small dessert plate. Top with shrimp or coconut topping and a sprinkle of lime leaves. You can use half of each topping if you like.

KAI TUN
STEAMED EGGS

2 large eggs
2 teaspoons light soy sauce
1 spring onion (scallion), finely sliced
a pinch of ground white pepper
1½ tablespoons vegetable oil
3–4 garlic cloves, finely chopped
a few coriander (cilantro) leaves,
    for garnish
1–2 long red chillies, thinly sliced,
    for garnish

SERVES 2

BEAT the eggs in a bowl with a fork. Mix in 170 ml (⅔ cup) water and the soy sauce, spring onion and pepper. Divide between two small heatproof bowls.

FILL a wok or steamer pan with water, cover, bring to a boil, then reduce the heat to medium. Taking care not to burn your hands, place the bowls on the rack of a bamboo steaming basket or on a steamer rack in the wok or pan. Cover the steamer and leave over the simmering water for 13 to 15 minutes or until the eggs set. Test with a skewer or fork. If it comes out clean the eggs are cooked.

HEAT the oil and stir-fry the garlic until golden. Serve the eggs hot or warm, sprinkled with the garlic. Garnish with coriander leaves and chillies.

STEAMED EGGS

KRA PAO TONG

GOLD PURSES

THESE DEEP-FRIED SNACKS ARE AN EXAMPLE OF THE INFLUENCE CHINESE CUISINE HAS HAD IN THAILAND. GOLD PURSES ARE GOOD TO SERVE WITH DRINKS BUT ARE ALSO A NICE WAY TO START A MEAL. THEY CAN BE SERVED WITH A SWEET OR A HOT CHILLI SAUCE, OR SOY SAUCE.

Put a small amount of filling in the centre of the won ton sheet and gently gather up into a dainty little purse.

110 g (4 oz) minced (ground) raw
   prawns (shrimp)
80 g (½ cup) water chestnuts,
   drained and roughly chopped
1 garlic clove, finely chopped
1 spring onion (scallion),
   finely chopped
1 tablespoon oyster sauce
¼ teaspoon salt
¼ teaspoon pepper
30–35 won ton sheets 7.5 cm
   (3 inches) square
peanut oil, for deep-frying
sweet chilli sauce (page 284),
   or other chilli sauce, to serve

MAKES ABOUT 30

COMBINE the prawns with the water chestnuts, garlic and spring onion in a bowl. Mix in the oyster sauce, salt and pepper. Spoon about ½ teaspoon of mixture into the middle of each won ton sheet. Gather up, squeezing the corners together to make a little purse. Place on a tray. Continue until you have used up all the sheets and filling.

HEAT 5 cm (2 inches) oil in a wok or deep frying pan over a medium heat. When the oil seems hot, drop a small piece of won ton sheet into the oil. If it sizzles immediately, the oil is ready. Don't have the oil too hot or the purses will burn.

LOWER five purses into the oil. After 2 to 3 minutes they will start to go hard. Lower another four to five purses into the oil and deep-fry them all together. To help cook the tops, spoon some of the oil over the tops. Deep-fry for another 3 to 4 minutes or until golden brown and crispy. As each batch cooks, lift out the purses with a slotted spoon and add some more in their place. Drain on paper towels. Keep warm while deep-frying the remaining purses. Transfer to a serving plate. Serve with chilli sauce.

CURRY PUFFS

FILLING

1½ tablespoons vegetable oil
2–3 garlic cloves, finely chopped
1 small onion, finely chopped
5 coriander (cilantro) roots,
    finely chopped
200 g (7 oz) minced (ground)
    chicken, pork or raw prawns
    (shrimp)
1 small red capsicum (pepper),
    finely diced
50 g (⅓ cup) peas
350 g (12 oz) potatoes, peeled,
    cooked and cut into small dice
3 tablespoons fish sauce
2 tablespoons sugar
1 teaspoon Thai curry powder
    (page 287) or bought Thai
    curry powder
peanut oil, for deep-frying

PASTRY A

340 g (2¾ cups) self-raising flour
2 teaspoons sugar
½ teaspoon salt
80 ml (⅓ cup) vegetable oil

PASTRY B

185 g (1½ cups) self-raising flour
80–125 ml (⅓–½ cup) vegetable oil

MAKES 30

HEAT the oil in a wok or frying pan and stir-fry the garlic. Add the onion and coriander roots and cook over a medium heat for 2 to 3 minutes. Stir in the chicken, breaking it up until it is separated and cooked. Add the capsicum and peas and stir for 1 to 2 minutes. Stir in the potatoes, fish sauce, sugar and curry powder. Adjust the seasoning.

TO MAKE pastry A, combine the flour, sugar and salt in a bowl. Make a well and add the oil. Gradually mix in 125–170 ml (½–⅔ cup) water and gently knead until the dough is smooth. Make 15 balls, place them on a tray and cover with plastic wrap. To make pastry B, lightly mix the flour and oil until the dough just holds together. Make 15 balls, place on a tray and cover.

ROLL a ball of pastry A into a disc, wrap it around a ball of pastry B, then squeeze together. Roll out a 5 x 15 cm (2 x 6 inch) rectangle. Take the short edge and roll it up tightly into a tube. Using a rolling pin, flatten the pastry lengthways to form a rectangle. Repeat one more time, rolling and flattening the pastry. Roll into a tube and cut in half. You should see the different layers of pastry in the cross section. To use, take one half, turn it vertically so it rests on the cut section and roll it into a round sheet. Place a sheet on the work surface and spoon 1–1½ tablespoons of filling onto the middle. Brush the pastry edge with water and fold over to form a semicircle. Press the edges to seal. Make repeated folds on the rounded edge by folding a little piece of the pastry over as you move around the edge. Place on a tray and repeat with the remaining pastry and filling.

HEAT 7.5 cm (3 inches) oil in a wok or deep frying pan over a medium heat. Drop a small piece of pastry into the oil. If it sizzles immediately, the oil is ready. Don't have the oil too hot. Lower in three or four puffs. After 2 minutes they will rise. Lower in another two to three and deep-fry them all together. To help cook the tops, splash oil over the tops. Deep-fry for 3 to 4 minutes until they puff up. As each batch cooks, lift out with a slotted spoon and add more puffs to the oil. Drain on paper towels. Serve hot, warm or cold.

The pastry for these morsels takes a little while to make but the end result is an absolutely delicious crunchy curry puff.

Traditionally, Thais use spring onion greens for tying these bags but you may find it easier to use chives.

GOLD BAGS

THIS DELICATE CHINESE-STYLE STARTER OR SNACK LOOKS EXACTLY AS IT IS DESCRIBED — A TINY GOLD BAG. BLANCHED CHIVES WILL ALSO WORK AS TIES FOR THE TOPS OF THE BAGS. IF YOU LIKE YOU CAN USE HALF PRAWNS AND HALF CHICKEN OR PORK FOR THE FILLING.

280 g (10 oz) raw prawns (shrimp), peeled, deveined and roughly chopped, or skinless chicken or pork fillet, roughly chopped
225 g (8 oz) tin water chestnuts, drained and roughly chopped
3–4 garlic cloves, finely chopped
3 spring onions (scallions), finely sliced
1 tablespoon oyster sauce
1 teaspoon ground white pepper
1 teaspoon salt
2–3 bunches of spring onions (scallions), or 40 chives, for ties
2 tablespoons plain (all-purpose) flour
40 spring roll sheets 13 cm (5 inches) square
peanut oil, for deep-frying
a chilli sauce, to serve

MAKES 40

USING a food processor or blender, whiz the prawns, chicken or pork to a fine paste. In a bowl, combine the minced prawn or meat, water chestnuts, garlic, spring onions, oyster sauce, white pepper and salt.

TO MAKE spring onion ties, cut each into 4 to 6 strips, using only the longest green parts, then soak them in boiling water for 5 minutes or until soft. Drain, then dry on paper towels.

MIX the flour and 8 tablespoons cold water in a small saucepan until smooth. Stir and cook over a medium heat for 1 to 2 minutes or until thick.

PLACE 3 spring roll sheets in front of you and keep the remaining sheets in the plastic bag to prevent them drying out. Spoon 2 teaspoons of filling into the middle of each sheet. Brush around the filling with flour paste, then pull up into a bag and pinch together to enclose the filling. Place on a tray that is lightly dusted with plain (all-purpose) flour. Repeat until you have used all the filling and sheets. Tie a piece of spring onion twice around each bag and tie in a knot. Use chives if you prefer.

HEAT 7.5 cm (3 inches) oil in a wok or deep frying pan over a medium heat. When the oil seems hot, drop a small piece of spring roll sheet into it. If it sizzles immediately, the oil is ready. It is important not to have the oil too hot or the gold bags will cook too quickly and brown. Lower four bags into the oil and deep-fry for 2 to 3 minutes until they start to go hard. Lower another three or four bags into the oil and deep-fry them all together. To help cook the tops, splash the oil over the tops and deep-fry for 7 to 10 minutes or until golden and crispy. As each batch is cooked, lift the bags out with a slotted spoon and add another batch. Drain on paper towels. Keep the gold bags warm while deep-frying the rest. Serve with a chilli sauce.

KHAO PHOHT THAWT
SWEET CORN CAKES

400 g (2 cups) corn kernels
1 egg
3 tablespoons rice flour
1 tablespoon yellow curry paste
(page 275)
2 tablespoons chopped Asian
shallots
1 tablespoon fish sauce
25 g (½ cup) roughly chopped
coriander (cilantro)
1 large red chilli, chopped
peanut oil, for shallow-frying
cucumber relish (page 287), to serve

MAKES 8

COMBINE the corn kernels, egg, rice flour, curry
paste, shallots, fish sauce, coriander and chilli in
a bowl. Shape the mixture into small patties,
adding more rice flour, if necessary, to combine
into a soft mixture.

HEAT the oil and fry the corn cakes for 3 to
4 minutes, turning once, until golden brown.
Serve hot with cucumber relish.

Akah girl.

KHANOM BANG NA KUNG
SESAME PRAWNS ON TOASTS

280 g (10 oz) raw prawns (shrimp),
peeled and deveined
2 teaspoons light soy sauce
1 egg
4–5 large garlic cloves,
roughly chopped
7–8 coriander (cilantro) roots,
roughly chopped
¼ teaspoon ground white pepper
½ teaspoon salt
7 slices day-old white bread,
crusts removed, each slice
cut into two triangles
3 tablespoons sesame seeds
peanut oil, for deep-frying
cucumber relish (page 287), to serve

MAKES 14

USING a food processor or blender, whiz the
prawns into a smooth paste. Transfer to a bowl,
add the light soy sauce and egg and mix well.
Leave for about 30 minutes to firm.

USING a pestle and mortar, pound the garlic,
coriander roots, white pepper and salt into a
smooth paste. Add to the prawns. (Using a pestle
and mortar gives the best texture but you can also
whiz the garlic, coriander roots, pepper, light soy
sauce and egg with the prawns.) Heat the grill
(broiler) to medium. Spread the bread on a baking
tray and put under the grill for 3 to 4 minutes or
until the bread is dry and slightly crisp. Spread the
prawn paste thickly on one side of each piece.
Sprinkle with sesame seeds and press on firmly.
Refrigerate for 30 minutes.

HEAT the oil in a wok or deep frying pan over a
medium heat. Drop in a small cube of bread. If it
sizzles immediately, the oil is ready. Deep-fry a few
toasts at a time, paste-side down, for 3 minutes or
until golden. Turn with a slotted spoon. Drain
paste-side up on paper towels. Serve with relish.

SESAME PRAWNS ON TOASTS

Keep the spring roll sheets in their plastic bag so they don't dry out while you are rolling the rest.

PAW PIA THAWT

SPRING ROLLS

THESE SAVOURY ROLLS ARE POPULAR THROUGHOUT SOUTH-EAST ASIA. THE THAI VERSION IS A DELICATE CROSS BETWEEN CHINESE AND VIETNAMESE STYLES. THAI SPRING ROLLS ARE DEEP-FRIED UNTIL LIGHT GOLDEN BROWN AND CRISPY. THEY CAN BE SERVED WITH CHILLI OR LIGHT SOY SAUCE.

50 g (2 oz) vermicelli, cellophane
  or wun sen noodles
15 g (½ oz) dried black fungus
  (about half a handful)
2 tablespoons plain (all-purpose)
  flour
1½ tablespoons vegetable oil
3–4 garlic cloves, finely chopped
100 g (3½ oz) minced (ground)
  chicken or pork
1 small carrot, finely grated
140 g (1⅔ cups) bean sprouts
1 cm (½ inch) piece of ginger,
  finely grated
1½–2 tablespoons fish sauce
1½ tablespoons oyster sauce
¼ teaspoon ground white pepper
25 spring roll sheets 13 cm
  (5 inches) square
peanut oil, for deep-frying
a chilli sauce, to serve

MAKES 25 SMALL SPRING ROLLS

SOAK the vermicelli in hot water for 1 to 2 minutes or until soft. Drain, then cut into small pieces. Soak the dried mushrooms in hot water for 2 to 3 minutes or until soft. Drain, then finely chop. To make a paste, stir the flour and 2 tablespoons of water together in a small bowl until smooth.

HEAT the oil in a wok or frying pan and stir-fry the garlic until golden brown. Add the chicken or pork and using a spoon, break the meat until it separates into small bits and is cooked. Add the vermicelli, mushrooms, carrot, bean sprouts, ginger, fish sauce, oyster sauce and white pepper. Cook for another 4 to 5 minutes. Taste, then adjust the seasoning. Allow to cool.

PLACE 3 spring roll sheets on a work surface and spread some flour paste around the edges. Keep the remaining sheets in the plastic bag. Spoon 2 teaspoons of filling onto a sheet along the side nearest to you, about 2.5 cm (1 inch) from the edge. Bring the edge up, then roll it away from you a half turn over the filling. Fold the sides into the centre to enclose the filling, then wrap and seal the join tightly with the flour paste. Repeat with the rest of the filling and wrappers. (At this stage, the rolls can be frozen. If freezing, wrap each roll with another spring roll sheet.)

HEAT 5 cm (2 inches) oil in a wok or deep frying pan over a medium heat. When the oil seems hot, drop a small piece of spring roll sheet into the oil. If it sizzles immediately, the oil is ready. Don't have the oil too hot. Lower five rolls into the oil and deep-fry for 2 to 3 minutes. When they start to go hard, lower another four rolls into the oil and deep-fry them all together. To help cook the tops, splash oil over the tops. Deep-fry for 6 to 8 minutes or until crispy. As the spring rolls cook, lift out one at a time with a slotted spoon and add another. Drain on paper towels. Serve with a chilli sauce.

CHICKEN WRAPPED IN PANDANUS LEAF

PANDANUS LEAVES ACT AS BOTH A WRAPPING AND A FLAVOURING IN THIS DISH. LEAVING A LONG TAIL ON THE PARCELS WILL MAKE THEM PRETTIER AND EASIER TO HANDLE SO DON'T TRIM THE LEAVES. TO EAT, CAREFULLY UNWRAP THE PARCELS AND DIP THE CHICKEN IN THE SAUCE.

5 coriander (cilantro) roots, cleaned and roughly chopped
4–5 garlic cloves
1 teaspoon ground white pepper
¼ teaspoon salt
600 g (1 lb 5 oz) skinless chicken breast fillets, cut into 25 cubes
2 tablespoons oyster sauce
1½ tablespoons sesame oil
1 tablespoon plain (all-purpose) flour
25 pandanus leaves, cleaned and dried
vegetable oil, for deep-frying
plum sauce (page 284) or a chilli sauce, to serve

MAKES 25

USING a pestle and mortar or a small blender, pound or blend the coriander roots, garlic, white pepper and salt into a paste.

IN a bowl, combine the paste with the chicken, oyster sauce, sesame oil and flour. Cover with plastic wrap and marinate in the refrigerator for at least 3 hours, or overnight.

FOLD one of the pandanus leaves, bringing the base up in front of the tip, making a cup. Put a piece of chicken in the fold and, moving the bottom of the leaf, wrap it around to create a tie and enclose the chicken. Repeat until you have used all the chicken.

HEAT the oil in a wok or deep frying pan over a medium heat.

WHEN the oil seems hot, drop a small piece of leaf into it. If it sizzles immediately, the oil is ready. Lower some parcels into the oil and deep-fry for 7 to 10 minutes or until the parcels feel firm. Lift out with a slotted spoon and drain on paper towels. Keep the cooked ones warm while deep-frying the rest. Transfer to a serving plate. Serve with plum sauce or a chilli sauce.

Pandanus leaves are used to enclose the chicken in an attractive tie shape.

KUNG HOM PAR
PRAWNS IN A BLANKET

THESE PRAWNS, WHICH ARE PREPARED IN CHINESE STYLE, ARE AN APPEALING CANAPE. CHOOSE PLUMP BIG PRAWNS AND LEAVE THE TAILS ON FOR ATTRACTIVE PRESENTATION. YOU CAN MARINATE THE PRAWNS OVERNIGHT IN THE REFRIGERATOR IF YOU WANT TO PREPARE AHEAD.

12 raw large prawns (shrimp), peeled and deveined, tails intact
1 tablespoon plain (all-purpose) flour
2 garlic cloves, roughly chopped
3 coriander (cilantro) roots, finely chopped
1 cm (½ inch) piece of ginger, roughly sliced
1½ tablespoons oyster sauce or, for a hotter flavour, ½ teaspoon red curry paste (page 276)
a sprinkle of ground white pepper
12 frozen spring roll sheets or filo sheets, 12 cm (5 inches) square, defrosted
peanut oil, for deep-frying
a chilli sauce, or plum sauce (page 284), to serve

SERVES 4

TO make the prawns easier to wrap, you can make 3 or 4 shallow incisions in the underside of each, then open up the cuts to straighten the prawns.

MIX the flour and 3 tablespoons water in a small saucepan until smooth. Stir and cook over a medium heat for 1 to 2 minutes or until thick. Remove from the heat.

USING a pestle and mortar or a small blender, pound or blend the garlic, coriander roots and ginger together.

IN a bowl, combine the garlic paste with the prawns, oyster sauce, pepper and a pinch of salt. Cover with plastic wrap and marinate in the refrigerator for 2 hours, turning occasionally.

PLACE a spring roll or filo sheet on the work surface and keep all the remaining sheets in the plastic bag to prevent them drying out. Fold the sheet in half, remove a prawn from the marinade and place it on the sheet with its tail sticking out of the top. Fold the bottom up and then the sides in to tightly enclose the prawn. Seal the joins tightly with the flour paste. Repeat with the rest of the prawns and wrappers.

HEAT the oil in a wok or deep frying pan over a medium heat. When the oil seems hot, drop a small piece of spring roll sheet into it. If it sizzles immediately, the oil is ready. Deep-fry four prawns at a time for 3 to 4 minutes or until golden brown and crispy. Remove with a slotted spoon and drain on paper towels. Keep the prawns warm while deep-frying the rest.

TRANSFER to a serving plate. Serve hot with chilli sauce or plum sauce.

Large prawns are best for making these little bites. The attractive tails make them easier to pick up.

Sausages are a popular snack.

PORK SAUSAGES

KUNG PHAT BAI PHAK CHII LAE PHRIK

PRAWNS WITH CORIANDER LEAVES AND CHILLI

350 g (12 oz) raw prawns (shrimp)
1 garlic clove, finely chopped
1 tablespoon coriander (cilantro)
  leaves, finely chopped
½–1 long red chilli, seeded and
  finely chopped
2 teaspoons lime juice
2 teaspoons vegetable oil
1 teaspoon sesame oil
1½ teaspoons light soy sauce
1 tablespoon oyster sauce
¼ teaspoon ground white pepper
4 bamboo sticks

SERVES 4

PEEL and devein the prawns and cut each prawn along the back so it opens like a butterfly (leave each prawn joined along the base and at the tail).

PUT the garlic, coriander, chilli, lime juice, both oils, light soy sauce, oyster sauce and ground pepper in a shallow dish and mix well. Add the prawns to the marinade and mix to coat the prawns. Cover with plastic wrap and marinate in the refrigerator for at least 30 minutes, or overnight.

SOAK the bamboo sticks in water for 1 hour to help prevent them from burning during cooking. Thread the prawns onto the skewers.

HEAT a barbecue or grill (broiler) to a high heat. If using a grill, line the tray with foil. Grill (broil) the prawns a good distance below the high heat for 8 to 10 minutes on each side. If you cook them directly on a barbecue plate they will cook more quickly, about 4 to 5 minutes. Turn the prawn sticks frequently until the prawns turn pink and are cooked through. You can brush the marinade sauce over the prawns during the cooking. Serve hot.

SAI UA

PORK SAUSAGES

THIS KIND OF PORK SAUSAGE IS USUALLY ENCASED IN SKIN. HOWEVER, THIS RECIPE WITHOUT SKIN IS MUCH EASIER. IN THAILAND SOME SAUSAGES ARE LEFT TO FERMENT BEFORE COOKING BUT THEY TASTE JUST AS GOOD WHEN FRESH. SERVE WITH RAW VEGETABLES SUCH AS CABBAGE WEDGES.

3 coriander (cilantro) roots
1 lemon grass stalk, white part only,
  chopped
4 garlic cloves, chopped
½ teaspoon ground white pepper
1 small red chilli, chopped
2 teaspoons fish sauce
2 teaspoons sugar
300 g (10 oz) minced (ground) pork

SERVES 4

USING a pestle and mortar or food processor, pound or blend the coriander, lemon grass, garlic and pepper to a fine paste.

ADD the chilli, fish sauce, sugar and pork to the paste mixture and combine well. Form into sausage shapes.

HEAT a barbecue or grill (broiler) and cook the sausages for 4 to 5 minutes each side until cooked through.

KHAI LUK KOEI

SON-IN-LAW EGGS

A TRADITIONAL CELEBRATION DISH, THESE EGGS ARE ENJOYED ON NEW YEAR'S DAY OR AT WEDDING FEASTS, AND ARE TAKEN AS AN OFFERING TO THE MONKS WHEN THAI PEOPLE VISIT THEIR LOCAL TEMPLE. THEY MAKE GOOD SNACKS. DEEP-FRYING GIVES THE SKINS A UNIQUE TEXTURE.

2 dried long red chillies, about
    13 cm (5 inches) long
vegetable oil, for deep-frying
110 g (4 oz) Asian shallots,
    finely sliced
6 large hard-boiled eggs, shelled
2 tablespoons fish sauce
3 tablespoons tamarind purée
5 tablespoons palm sugar

SERVES 4

CUT the chillies into 5 mm (¼ inch) pieces with scissors or a knife and discard the seeds. Heat 5 cm (2 inches) oil in a wok or deep frying pan over a medium heat. When the oil seems hot, drop a slice of the Asian shallot into the oil. If it sizzles straight away, the oil is ready. Deep-fry the chillies for a few seconds, being careful not to burn them, to bring out the flavour. Remove them with a slotted spoon, then drain on paper towels.

IN the same wok, deep-fry the Asian shallots for 3 to 4 minutes until golden brown. Be careful not to burn them. Remove with a slotted spoon, then drain on paper towels. Use a spoon to slide one egg at a time into the same hot oil. Be careful as the oil may splash. Deep-fry for 10 to 15 minutes or until the whole of each egg is golden brown. Remove with a slotted spoon, then drain on paper towels. Keep warm.

IN a saucepan over a medium heat, stir the fish sauce, tamarind purée and sugar for 5 to 7 minutes or until all the sugar has dissolved.

HALVE the eggs lengthways and arrange them with the yolk upwards on a serving plate. Drizzle the tamarind sauce over the eggs and sprinkle the crispy chillies and shallots over them.

When the eggs are golden, they are ready. Carefully remove with a slotted spoon and drain on paper towels.

MIANG KHAM
BETEL LEAVES WITH SAVOURY TOPPING

2 tablespoons peanut oil
4 Asian shallots, finely sliced
2 garlic cloves, smashed with the
   side of a cleaver
150 g (5 oz) minced (ground)
   chicken or pork
2 tablespoons fish sauce
1 tablespoon tamarind purée
1 tablespoon dried shrimp, chopped
2 tablespoons palm sugar
1 cm (½ inch) piece of ginger, grated
2 bird's eye chillies, finely chopped
1 tablespoon roasted peanuts,
   chopped
1 tablespoon chopped coriander
   (cilantro) leaves
16 betel leaves
lime wedges, for squeezing

MAKES 16

HEAT the oil in a wok and fry the shallots and garlic for a minute or two until they brown. Add the chicken and fry it until the meat turns opaque, breaking up any lumps with the back of a spoon. Add the fish sauce, tamarind purée, shrimp and palm sugar and cook everything together until the mixture is brown and sticky. Stir in the ginger, chillies, peanuts and coriander leaves.

LAY the betel leaves out on a large plate and top each with some of the mixture. Serve with the lime wedges to squeeze over the mixture.

GALLOPING HORSES

MAR HOR
GALLOPING HORSES

1½ tablespoons vegetable oil
2–3 garlic cloves, finely chopped
225 g (8 oz) minced (ground) pork
1 spring onion (scallion), finely sliced
½ tablespoon coriander (cilantro)
   leaves, finely chopped
25 g (1 oz) unsalted cooked
   peanuts, roughly ground
2 tablespoons light soy sauce
3 tablespoons palm sugar
a pinch of ground white pepper
16 small segments of pineapple,
   or tangerine, mandarin
   or orange segments
a few coriander (cilantro) leaves,
   for garnish
1 red chilli, very finely sliced,
   for garnish

SERVES 4

HEAT the oil in a saucepan or wok and stir-fry the garlic until golden brown. Add the pork and cook over a medium heat. With a spoon, break up the meat until it has separated and is almost dry. Add the spring onion, coriander leaves, ground peanuts, light soy sauce, sugar and pepper. Stir together for 4 to 5 minutes or until the mixture is dry and sticky.

IF YOU are using pineapple, spoon some mixture onto each segment.

IF USING citrus fruit, cut each segment from top to bottom, around the outer curve, and open each up like a butterfly. Remove any pips.

ARRANGE the segments on a serving plate and, with a teaspoon, transfer a little pork mixture onto each piece. Place a coriander leaf and a slice of chilli on top of each.

HAWY THAWT
FRIED MUSSEL PANCAKE

2 kg (4 lb 8 oz) large mussels
  in their shells (yielding around
  350 g/12 oz meat)

CHILLI SAUCE
1 long red chilli, seeded and
  finely chopped
2½ tablespoons white vinegar
½ teaspoon sugar

50 g (2 oz) tapioca or plain
  (all-purpose) flour
40 g (⅓ cup) cornflour (cornstarch)
1 tablespoon fish sauce
1 teaspoon sugar
6 garlic cloves, finely chopped
350 g (4 cups) bean sprouts
4 spring onions (scallions), sliced
8 tablespoons vegetable oil
4 large eggs
a few coriander (cilantro) leaves
1 long red chilli, seeded and
  finely sliced
a sprinkle of ground white pepper
4 lime wedges

SERVES 4

SCRUB the mussels and remove their hairy
beards. Discard any open mussels and any that
don't close when tapped on the work surface.
Preheat the oven to 180°C/350°F/Gas 4. Spread
the mussels over a baking tray and bake for
5 minutes or until the shells open slightly. Discard
any unopened mussels. When the shells return to
a comfortable temperature, prise them open,
scoop out the meat from each and put it in a
colander to drain out out any juices.

TO MAKE the chilli sauce, mix the chilli, vinegar,
sugar and a pinch of salt in a small serving bowl.

COMBINE the flours with 6 to 8 tablespoons water
using a fork or spoon until the mixture is smooth
and without lumps. Add the fish sauce and sugar.
Divide among four bowls and add some mussels
to each bowl.

SEPARATE the garlic, bean sprouts and spring
onions into equal portions for each serving.

MAKE one pancake at a time. Heat 1 tablespoon
oil in a small frying pan and stir-fry one portion of
garlic over a medium heat until golden brown.
Stir one portion of the mussel mixture with a
spoon and pour it into the frying pan, swirling the
pan to ensure that the mixture spreads evenly.
Cook for 2 to 3 minutes or until it is brown
underneath. Turn with a spatula and brown the
other side. Make a hole in the centre and break
an egg into the hole. Sprinkle a half portion of
bean sprouts and spring onion over the top.
Cook until the egg sets, then flip the pancake
again. Turn the pancake onto a serving plate.

SPRINKLE each pancake with coriander leaves,
sliced chilli and ground pepper. Place a lime
wedge, bean sprouts and spring onions on the
plate. Serve with the chilli sauce.

Choose small black mussels for
these pancakes rather than the
large green-lipped variety.

อาหารตามสั่ง

หมู–

หมูแดงราดข้าว

ข้าวผัด

ปู–กุ้ง–หมู–เนื้อ–ไก่ - 20.

ข้าวผัดพริกแกง - 20.

ข้าวผัดกะเพรา - 20.

ข้าวไก่ผัดเม็ดมะม่วง - 20.

ข้าวปูผงกะหรี่ - 20.

ข้าวผัดเปรี้ยวหวาน - 20

STREET STALLS Virtually every dish in Thai cuisine can be bought from one type of stall or another, the exception being royal cuisine. From full-blown meals, often a choice of two or three dishes with rice (top left) to simple snacks like grilled bananas (bottom left), mussel pancakes (centre) and satay (right) can be bought at any time of the day or night. Dishes like curries are pre-cooked but everything else is freshly made.

STREET FOOD

THAIS LIKE TO EAT AT ALL HOURS OF THE DAY. STREET OR HAWKER FOOD IS A SUBCULTURE THAT THRIVES ALL OVER THE COUNTRY. *ROT KHEN* (VENDOR CARTS) ARE PARKED BY THE ROADSIDE IN EVEN THE SMALLEST VILLAGE. MOSTLY FOUND NEAR MARKETS DURING THE DAY, HAWKER FOOD COMES INTO ITS OWN AT DUSK AND INTO THE NIGHT.

WHERE TO FIND STREET FOOD

Hawker stalls are allowed to set up virtually wherever they like. They can be found around the edge of markets, beside busy roads, down back streets or close to bus stops and stations. Stalls can be simple carts, which are pushed home every night, or they can be more permanent. Those that have a good reputation last for years, decades, and even generations on the same spot.

TYPES OF STREET FOOD

There are five basic types of street food identifiable by the type of stall that sells them. Look out for the right type of cart and it will have the dish you are looking for. Carts with glass showcases sell dishes like *som tam* (green papaya salad),

Pieces of roast pork are popular (top left), sold with two types of dipping sauce. Corn on the cob (top right) is a relatively new introduction. Corn grows in areas where rice can't be cultivated. Chinese-style soups are popular at lunchtime (bottom left) and insects of various types, such as these deep-fried cockroaches with a chilli dipping sauce (bottom right), are common in the northern part of Thailand.

noodle dishes and soups, roast pork and chicken and Chinese chicken rice. Stalls with charcoal barbecues sell satay, barbecued chicken and pork, Thai sausages, dried squid and grilled bananas. Steamer domes indicate red braised pork, Chinese dumplings and buns, pumpkin custard and sticky rice in banana leaves. Carts fitted with a large hotplate make mussels in batter, omelettes, pancakes and fried noodles. Woks mean spring rolls, won tons, fish cakes and dough sticks. Ready-cooked food comes from vendors with prepared dishes such as fish curry in banana cups, pork-rind soups and lots of different puddings such as sticky rice. Drinks carts sell fruit juices and sweets served over crushed ice. Other specialist carts sell fresh fruit, preserved fruit and seafood, including boiled clams or cockles.

53

PALM SUGAR PARCELS

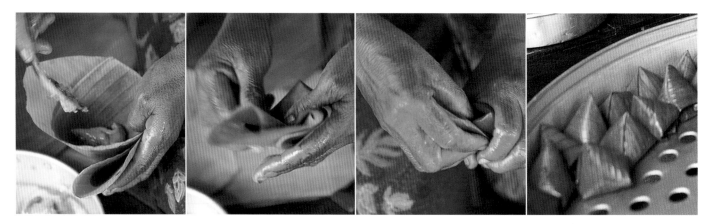

PALM SUGAR AND PEANUT PARCELS These steamed sweet snacks are made by wrapping peanut paste in a flour and sugar paste and then spooning the filling into banana leaves. Deft hands and plenty of practice are needed to fold the banana leaves into neat triangles before steaming them in a large steamer. The vendor makes the same amount of parcels daily and keeps the stall open until everything sells out.

SOM TAM

MAKING SOM TAM Not quite a salad and not quite anything else either, *som tam* is made in single portions and served as a snack with sticky rice. The bulk of the dish is green papaya that has been finely shredded, to which tomatoes, palm sugar, peanuts, chilli and lime juice, fish sauce, dried prawns, garlic, snake beans and herbs are added. The customer tastes the *som tam* and adjusts the flavour as it is made.

ROTI

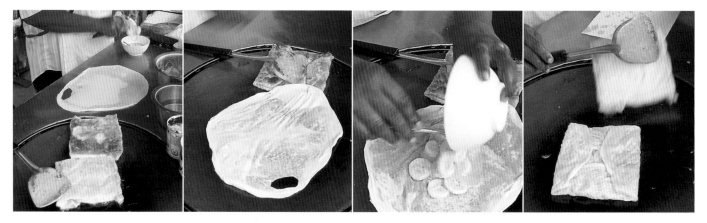

MAKING BANANA ROTI Roti are Indian-style pastries that are cooked on a flat hotplate. The name means bread but the finished dish resembles a pancake or pastry rather than anything doughy. The roti are made by spreading a fine, stretchy dough on a hotplate and then adding sweet fillings like bananas and condensed milk and folding the dough over them. The result is a crispy pastry with a soft, sweet filling.

NOODLE SOUP Noodles are generally sold as a snack in Thailand. These are *khanom jiin*, rice noodles, made in the North-Eastern style, served with fennel.

BARBECUED CHICKEN Roadside rotisseries provide a constant supply of chickens cooked over charcoal. They are chopped into pieces on request.

DRIED SQUID Grilled dried squid is a popular night-time snack in Thailand. The dried squid are rolled to soften them before they are grilled over hot coals.

THAI SAUSAGES Spicy pork sausages are very popular in Thailand. These are made from pork with glutinous rice and seasonings and are sold grilled.

FRIED FISH Fish are eaten all over Thailand and are often fried whole. They are commonly served over rice with a chilli sauce of some sort.

THAI OLIVES This is a snack sold in small plastic bags, along with a seasoning of chilli sugar, combining opposing flavours, which is common in Thailand.

GRILLED BANANAS Eaten in many ways, small sugar bananas are often grilled over coals until the outside browns and the inside is soft, then eaten as a snack.

STEAMED STICKY RICE Steamed sticky rice wrapped in banana leaves has added flavourings such as coconut, mashed taro or black beans.

COCONUT PUDDINGS These are made by pouring batter and sweet coconut milk into a mould, sometimes with flavouring, then baking over charcoal or gas.

DEEP-FRIED PORK BELLY Large pieces of this pork are cut into slices and sold with little bags of chilli dipping sauce. Smaller pieces are fried as they are.

CHINESE-STYLE SOUP *(kaeng jeut),* or bland soup, is steamed in individual bowls. Soups are eaten with meals except, as here, when a snack.

CHINESE STEAMED BUNS A fluffy dough is filled with barbecued or minced pork, or yellow mung beans, to make a Chinese dim sum speciality.

SOUPS

The delicious flavour of this soup comes from the melding of prawn, chicken and vegetables.

A huge woven basket used for threshing rice.

RICE SOUP WITH PRAWNS AND CHICKEN

ALTHOUGH DERIVED FROM CHINESE-STYLE 'CONGEE, THAI RICE SOUPS USE WHOLE RICE GRAINS RATHER THAN THE BROKEN GRAINS PREFERRED BY THE CHINESE. RICE SOUPS ARE ENJOYED AS A SNACK AT NIGHT OR AS A BREAKFAST DISH. THEY ARE SUSTAINING ENOUGH TO BE A MEAL.

110 g (4 oz) raw prawns (shrimp)
2 tablespoons vegetable oil
3–4 large garlic cloves,
    finely chopped
1 coriander (cilantro) root,
    finely chopped
1 garlic clove, extra, roughly
    chopped
a pinch of ground white pepper,
    plus extra, to sprinkle
75 g (3 oz) minced (ground) chicken
    or pork
1 spring onion (scallion),
    finely chopped
935 ml (3¾ cups) chicken or
    vegetable stock
2 tablespoons light soy sauce
2 teaspoons preserved radish
325 g (1¾ cups) cooked jasmine
    rice
1 tablespoon finely sliced ginger
1 Chinese cabbage leaf, roughly
    chopped
2 spring onions (scallions), finely
    chopped, for garnish
a few coriander (cilantro) leaves,
    for garnish

SERVES 4

PEEL and devein the prawns and cut each prawn along the back so it opens like a butterfly (leave each prawn joined along the base and at the tail, leaving the tail attached).

HEAT the oil in a small wok or frying pan and stir-fry the finely chopped garlic until light golden. Remove from the heat and discard the garlic.

USING a pestle and mortar or a small blender, pound or blend the coriander root, roughly chopped garlic, pepper and a pinch of salt into a paste. In a bowl, combine the coriander paste with the chicken or pork and spring onion. Using a spoon or your wet hands, shape the mixture into small balls about 1 cm (½ inch) across.

HEAT the stock to boiling point in a saucepan. Add the light soy sauce, preserved radish and rice. Lower the meatballs into the stock over a medium heat and cook for 3 minutes or until the chicken is cooked. Add the prawns, ginger and Chinese cabbage to the stock. Cook for another 1 to 2 minutes or until the prawns open and turn pink. Taste, then adjust the seasoning if necessary.

GARNISH with spring onions and coriander leaves. Sprinkle with ground white pepper and the garlic oil.

KAENG JEUT PLAA MEUK SAI MUU

STUFFED SQUID SOUP

KAENG JEUT ARE ONE OF THE THREE MAIN TYPES OF SOUP COMMONLY FOUND IN THAILAND. THE NAME MEANS BLAND SOUP. THIS SOUP IS ANOTHER THAI DISH WITH A CHINESE INFLUENCE. THESE SOUPS ARE NOT HIGHLY FLAVOURED SO YOU SHOULD USE THE BEST QUALITY STOCK POSSIBLE.

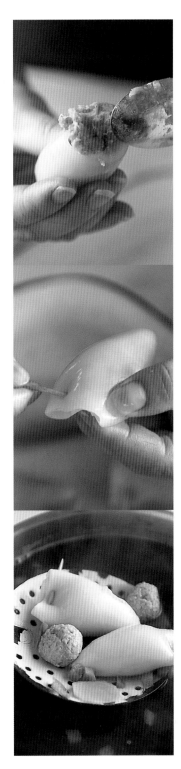

280 g (10 oz) small squid
2 coriander (cilantro) roots,
 finely chopped
3–4 large garlic cloves, roughly
 chopped
280 g (10 oz) minced (ground) pork
 or chicken
¼ teaspoon salt
¼ teaspoon ground white pepper
2 litres (8 cups) vegetable stock
2.5 cm (1 inch) piece of ginger,
 sliced
4 tablespoons light soy sauce
1 tablespoon preserved radish,
 sliced
5 spring onions (scallions), slivered,
 for garnish
a few coriander (cilantro) leaves,
 for garnish
ground white pepper, for sprinkling

SERVES 4

TO CLEAN each squid, grasp the squid body in one hand and pull away the head and tentacles from the body. Cut the head off the tentacles just above the eyes and discard the head. Clean out the body. Pull the skin off the squid and rinse well. Drain well.

USING a pestle and mortar, pound the coriander roots and garlic into a paste. In a bowl, combine the coriander paste with the pork or chicken and the salt and pepper. Spoon some mixture into a squid sac until two-thirds full, being careful not to overfill it as the filling will swell during cooking. Squeeze the squid tube closed at the end. With a bamboo stick or sharp toothpick, prick several holes in the body of the squid. Place on a plate and repeat with the rest. Use a spoon or your wet fingers to shape the remaining meat mixture into small balls about 1 cm (½ inch) across.

HEAT the stock to boiling point in a saucepan. Reduce the heat to low and add the ginger, light soy sauce and preserved radish. Lower the meatballs into the stock, then gently drop in the stuffed squid and cook over a low heat for 4 to 5 minutes or until the meatballs and squid are cooked. Taste the broth and adjust the seasoning if necessary.

GARNISH with spring onions and coriander leaves. Sprinkle with ground white pepper.

Don't stuff too much of the mixture into the squid sac as it will swell during cooking.

Soup flavourings are often sold ready-made in bundles.

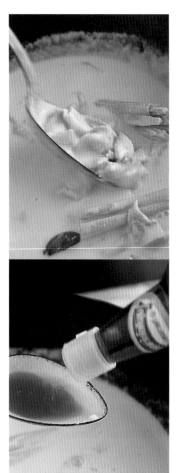

It is best to carefully measure ingredients such as fish sauce as the flavour is quite strong.

CHICKEN, COCONUT AND GALANGAL SOUP

THIS IS ONE OF THE CLASSIC SOUPS OF THAILAND. THE THAI NAME MEANS 'BOILED GALANGAL CHICKEN'. ALTHOUGH USUALLY MADE WITH CHICKEN, YOU CAN MAKE THIS RECIPE USING PRAWNS, FISH OR VEGETABLES. DON'T WORRY WHEN THE COCONUT MILK SPLITS — IT IS SUPPOSED TO.

750 ml (3 cups) coconut milk
(page 279)
2 lemon grass stalks, white part
only, each cut into a tassel
or bruised
5 cm (2 inch) piece of galangal,
cut into several pieces
4 Asian shallots, smashed with
the flat side of a cleaver
400 g (14 oz) skinless chicken
breast fillets, cut into slices
2 tablespoons fish sauce
1 tablespoon palm sugar
200 g (7 oz) baby tomatoes, cut
into bite-sized pieces if large
150 g (5 oz) straw mushrooms
or button mushrooms
3 tablespoons lime juice
6 makrut (kaffir) lime leaves,
torn in half
3–5 bird's eye chillies, stems
removed, bruised, or 2 long red
chillies, seeded and finely sliced
a few coriander (cilantro) leaves,
for garnish

SERVES 4

PUT the coconut milk, lemon grass, galangal and shallots in a saucepan or wok over a medium heat and bring to a boil.

ADD the chicken, fish sauce and palm sugar and simmer, stirring constantly for 5 minutes or until the chicken is cooked through.

ADD the tomatoes and mushrooms and simmer for 2 to 3 minutes. Add the lime juice, makrut lime leaves and chillies in the last few seconds, taking care not to let the tomatoes lose their shape. Taste, then adjust the seasoning if necessary. This dish is not meant to be overwhelmingly hot, but to have a sweet, salty, sour taste. Serve garnished with coriander leaves.

TOM YAM KUNG

HOT AND SOUR PRAWN SOUP

THIS SOUP IS PROBABLY THE MOST WELL KNOWN THAI DISH OF ALL. ALTHOUGH IT IS USUALLY MADE WITH PRAWNS, IT WORKS EQUALLY WELL WITH FISH. TO ACHIEVE THE FAMOUS DISTINCTIVE AROMA AND FLAVOURS, USE ONLY THE FRESHEST GOOD-QUALITY INGREDIENTS.

350 g (12 oz) raw prawns (shrimp)
1 tablespoon oil
3 lemon grass stalks, white part
  only, bruised
3 thin slices of galangal
2 litres (8 cups) chicken stock
  or water
5–7 bird's eye chillies, stems
  removed, bruised
5 makrut (kaffir) lime leaves, torn
2 tablespoons fish sauce
70 g (2 oz) straw mushrooms,
  or quartered button mushrooms
2 spring onions (scallions), sliced
3 tablespoons lime juice
a few coriander (cilantro) leaves,
  for garnish

SERVES 4

PEEL and devein the prawns, leaving the tails intact and reserving the heads and shells. Heat the oil in a large stockpot or wok and add the prawn heads and shells. Cook for 5 minutes or until the shells turn bright orange.

ADD one stalk of lemon grass to the pan with the galangal and stock or water. Bring to the boil, then reduce the heat and simmer for 20 minutes. Strain the stock and return to the pan. Discard the shells and flavourings.

FINELY slice the remaining lemon grass and add it to the liquid with the chillies, lime leaves, fish sauce, mushrooms and spring onions. Cook gently for 2 minutes.

ADD the prawns and cook for 3 minutes or until the prawns are firm and pink. Take off the heat and add the lime juice. Taste, then adjust the seasoning with extra lime juice or fish sauce if necessary. Garnish with coriander leaves.

VERMICELLI SOUP WITH MINCED PORK

THIS IS A LIGHT, CLEAR SOUP FROM THE NORTH OF THAILAND. UNLIKE OTHER NOODLE RECIPES THIS ONE IS ALWAYS EATEN WITH RICE. IT IS A WARMING 'COMFORT FOOD' AND IS VERY EASY TO PREPARE. THE NOODLES CONTINUE TO SOAK UP LIQUID AS THEY SIT, SO SERVE THE SOUP STRAIGHT AWAY.

15 pieces of dried black fungus
50 g (2 oz) mung bean vermicelli
2 tablespoons vegetable oil
3–4 large garlic cloves, finely
    chopped
450 g (1 lb) minced (ground) pork
20 coriander (cilantro) leaves,
    finely chopped
¼ teaspoon salt
¼ teaspoon ground white pepper
625 ml (2½ cups) vegetable or
    chicken stock
2 tablespoons light soy sauce
1 tablespoon preserved radish
a few coriander (cilantro) leaves,
    for garnish

SERVES 4

SOAK the mushrooms in hot water for 5 minutes or until soft, then drain them and cut into smaller pieces if necessary.

SOAK the mung bean vermicelli in hot water for 5 to 7 minutes or until soft, then drain it well and cut it into small pieces.

HEAT the oil in a small wok or frying pan and stir-fry the garlic until light golden. Remove from the heat, lift out the garlic with a slotted spoon and drain on paper towels.

IN a bowl, combine the pork with the coriander leaves, salt and pepper. Use a spoon or your wet hands to shape the mixture into small balls about 1 cm (½ inch) across.

HEAT the stock to boiling point in a saucepan. Add the light soy sauce and preserved radish. Lower the pork balls into the stock and cook for 2 minutes over a medium heat. Add the mushrooms and noodles and cook for another 1 to 2 minutes, stirring frequently. Taste, then adjust the seasoning if necessary. Sprinkle with crispy garlic, garlic oil and coriander leaves.

Pedal power competes with cars in Chiang Mai.

TOM YAM TAO-HUU
FRAGRANT TOFU AND TOMATO SOUP

TOFU, OR BEAN CURD, COMES IN SEVERAL DIFFERENT VARIETIES, FROM SOFT TO QUITE FIRM. THE SOFTEST, CALLED SILKEN TOFU, HAS THE BEST TYPE OF TEXTURE FOR THIS RECIPE. THE STRONG FLAVOURINGS USED IN THE RECIPE ARE A PERFECT CONTRAST FOR THE TOFU.

PASTE
½ teaspoon dried shrimp paste
1 teaspoon small dried prawns
    (shrimp)
4 Asian shallots, roughly chopped
½ teaspoon white peppercorns
2 coriander (cilantro) roots
1 garlic clove, chopped
2 teaspoons grated ginger

1 tablespoon vegetable oil
750 ml (3 cups) chicken stock
    or water
3 tablespoons tamarind purée
1 tablespoon palm sugar
2 tablespoons fish sauce
3 cm (1¼ inch) piece of ginger,
    julienned
3 Asian shallots, smashed with the
    flat side of a cleaver
300 g (10 oz) silken tofu
    (bean curd), cut into 2 cm (¾ inch)
    cubes
2 tomatoes, each cut into 8 wedges
1 tablespoon lime juice
2 tablespoons coriander (cilantro)
    leaves, for garnish

SERVES 4

TO MAKE the paste, use a pestle and mortar or food processor to pound or blend the shrimp paste, dried prawns, shallots, peppercorns, coriander roots, garlic and ginger together.

HEAT the oil in a saucepan over a low heat, add the paste and cook for 10 to 15 seconds, stirring constantly. Add the stock or water, tamarind purée, palm sugar, fish sauce and ginger. Simmer for 5 minutes to soften the ginger.

ADD the shallots, tofu, tomatoes and lime juice to the pan and cook for 2 to 3 minutes to heat through. Garnish with coriander leaves.

Pound the ingredients in a pestle and mortar to make a paste, then mix with the chicken and shape into small balls.

KAENG JEUT PHRAK KAI

VEGETABLE SOUP WITH CHICKEN AND PRAWN

A BLAND SOUP THAT IS BEST SERVED WITH A MEAL, TO BE EATEN ALONGSIDE THE OTHER MAIN DISHES. BLAND SOUPS HELP TAKE THE HEAT OUT OF CHILLI DISHES. THE CHICKEN BALLS IN THIS SOUP ARE EASILY MADE BUT YOU COULD USE CUBES OF CHICKEN INSTEAD. USE GOOD-QUALITY STOCK.

175 g (6 oz) raw prawns (shrimp)
2 coriander (cilantro) roots, cleaned
    and finely chopped
2 garlic cloves, roughly chopped
pinch of ground white pepper,
    plus extra, to sprinkle
150 g (5 oz) minced (ground)
    chicken
½ spring onion (scallion), finely
    chopped
935 ml (3¾ cups) chicken or
    vegetable stock
2 tablespoons light soy sauce
2 teaspoons preserved radish
175 g (6 oz) marrow or pumpkin
    (squash), cut into 2.5 cm (1 inch)
    cubes
175 g (6 oz) Chinese cabbage,
    roughly chopped
a few coriander (cilantro) leaves,
    for garnish

SERVES 4

PEEL and devein the prawns and cut each prawn along the back so it opens like a butterfly (leave each prawn joined along the base and at the tail, leaving the tail attached).

USING a pestle and mortar or a small blender, pound or blend the coriander roots, garlic, pepper and a pinch of salt into a paste. In a bowl, combine the coriander paste with the chicken and spring onion. Use a spoon or your wet hands to shape the chicken mixture into small balls about 1 cm (½ inch) across.

HEAT the stock to boiling point in a saucepan. Add the light soy sauce and preserved radish. Lower the chicken balls into the stock and cook over a medium heat for 1 to 2 minutes or until the balls are cooked.

ADD the marrow to the pan and cook for 2 to 3 minutes. Add the prawns and Chinese cabbage and cook for another 1 to 2 minutes. Taste, then adjust the seasoning if necessary. Garnish with coriander leaves. Sprinkle with ground white pepper.

KAENG SOM PLA KUP PHAK BUNG
SOUR FISH SOUP WITH WATER SPINACH

THIS SOUP IS A POPULAR ADDITION TO A MAIN MEAL IN THAILAND. YOU CAN SUBSTITUTE MEAT FOR

THE FISH IF YOU PREFER. WATER SPINACH IS ALSO KNOWN AS MORNING GLORY AND ONG CHOY.

SOUR CURRY PASTE
3 garlic cloves, roughly chopped
3 bird's eye chillies, stems removed
1 Asian shallot, chopped
1 teaspoon grated galangal
1 teaspoon grated turmeric
  (or a pinch of dried)
1 teaspoon shrimp paste

175 g (6 oz) skinless white fish fillets
3 tablespoons tamarind purée
175 g (6 oz) water spinach, cut into
  pieces, leaves separated
1 tablespoon fish sauce
1 tablespoon sugar

SERVES 4

TO MAKE the sour curry paste, use a pestle and mortar or food processor to pound or blend all the ingredients together until smooth.

REMOVE any remaining bones from the fish using tweezers, then cut the fish fillets into 5 cm (2 inch) pieces.

IN a saucepan, bring 625 ml (2½ cups) water to the boil. Stir in the sour curry paste and reduce the heat to medium. Add the tamarind, water spinach stems, fish sauce and sugar and cook for 2 to 3 minutes. Add the fish fillets and cook for another 1 to 2 minutes. Add the water spinach leaves and gently mix. Taste, then adjust the seasoning if necessary. Spoon into a serving bowl and serve hot with rice.

KHAO TOM PLAA
RICE SOUP WITH FISH FILLET

RICE SOUP WITH FISH FILLET

2 tablespoons vegetable oil
3–4 large garlic cloves, finely chopped
1.25 litres (5 cups) vegetable,
  chicken or fish stock
2½ tablespoons light soy sauce
2 teaspoons preserved radish,
  sliced
245 g (1⅓ cups) cooked jasmine
  rice
280 g (10 oz) skinless white fish
  fillets, cut into bite-sized pieces
1 tablespoon finely sliced ginger
1 spring onion (scallion), finely
  chopped, for garnish
a few coriander (cilantro) leaves,
  for garnish
ground white pepper, for sprinkling

SERVES 4

HEAT the oil in a small wok or frying pan and stir-fry the garlic until light golden. Remove from the heat and discard the garlic.

HEAT the stock to boiling point in a saucepan. Add the light soy sauce, preserved radish and rice and cook over a medium heat for 2 to 3 minutes. Add the fish and ginger and cook for another 1 to 2 minutes or until the fish is cooked. Season well, taste, then adjust the seasoning again if necessary.

GARNISH with spring onion and coriander leaves and sprinkle with ground pepper and the garlic oil.

Put the lemon grass, coriander roots, fish sauce, curry paste, chillies and stock in the pan.

TOM YAM THELAH

HOT AND SOUR SOUP WITH MIXED SEAFOOD

YOU CAN USE YOUR FAVOURITE COMBINATION OF SEAFOOD FOR THIS SOUP BUT MAKE SURE IT IS ALL ABSOLUTELY FRESH TO ENSURE A DELICIOUS TASTE. THE CURRY PASTE WILL MAKE THE SOUP BROTH CLOUDIER THAN IF USING DRIED CHILLIES BUT IT WILL RESULT IN A MORE COMPLEX FLAVOUR.

600 g (1 lb 5 oz) mixed fresh seafood such as raw prawns (shrimp), squid tubes, mussels, white fish fillets and scallops
1 litre (4 cups) vegetable stock
3 x 4 cm (1½ inch) lemon grass stalks, white part only, each cut into a tassel or bruised
6 coriander (cilantro) roots, bruised
2–2½ tablespoons fish sauce
1½–2 tablespoons Chiang Mai curry paste (page 272), according to taste, or 2 dried red chillies, soaked, drained and finely chopped
2–3 bird's eye chillies, bruised
2 Asian shallots, smashed with the flat side of a cleaver
110 g (4 oz) straw or mixed mushrooms, left whole if small, or quartered if large
150 g (5 oz) baby tomatoes (about 12, cut in half if large) or medium tomatoes, each cut into 6 pieces
8 makrut (kaffir) lime leaves, torn
3 tablespoons lime juice

SERVES 4

PEEL and devein the prawns and cut each prawn along the back so it opens like a butterfly (leave each prawn joined along the base and at the tail).

PEEL off any skin from the squid tubes, rinse the insides and cut the tubes into 5 mm (¼ inch) rings. If the squid are very big, cut them in half, open the tubes and slightly score the inside of each squid with diagonal cuts to make a diamond pattern. Cut the tubes into pieces about 2 cm (¾ inch) square. Remove any dark veins from the scallops.

SCRUB the mussels and remove their hairy beards. Discard any open mussels and any that don't close when tapped on the work surface. Cut the fish into 2 cm (¾ inch) cubes.

PUT the stock, lemon grass, coriander roots, fish sauce, curry paste and chillies in a large saucepan and bring to a boil.

REDUCE the heat to medium, add the seafood and cook for 2 to 3 minutes. (If using cooked mussels, add them after the tomatoes.) Add the shallots, mushrooms, baby tomatoes, makrut lime leaves and cook for another 2 to 3 minutes, taking care not to let the tomatoes lose their shape. Taste, add the lime juice, then adjust the seasoning if necessary. Spoon into a serving bowl.

KAENG JEUT TAO-HUU SAI KUNG
STUFFED TOFU SOUP WITH PRAWNS

THIS RECIPE IS QUITE FIDDLY BUT WELL WORTH THE EFFORT. DON'T OVERSTUFF THE TOFU OR IT MIGHT EXPLODE OUT AS IT COOKS. AS WITH OTHER 'BLAND' SOUPS, USE A GOOD-QUALITY STOCK. THE STUFFED TOFU CAN ALSO BE FRIED AND EATEN ON ITS OWN.

275 g (10 oz) raw prawns (shrimp)
2–3 coriander (cilantro) roots, roughly chopped
2 garlic cloves, roughly chopped
¼ teaspoon salt
1 tablespoon cornflour (cornstarch)
¼ teaspoon ground white pepper
320 g (11 oz) firm tofu (bean curd)
1.5 litres (6 cups) vegetable stock
2.5 cm (1 inch) piece of ginger, sliced
4 tablespoons light soy sauce
1 tablespoon preserved radish
5 spring onions (scallions), cut into slivers, for garnish

SERVES 4

PEEL and devein the prawns. Set aside about 80 g (3 oz) of the prawns and cut the rest of them along their backs so they open like a butterfly (leave each prawn joined along the base and at the tail).

USING a food processor or blender, whiz the coriander roots and garlic until as smooth as possible. Add the prawns that are not butterflied, along with the salt, cornflour and white pepper, then blend until as smooth as possible. If you prefer, you can use a pestle and mortar to pound the coriander roots and garlic into a paste before processing with the prawns. This gives a slightly better flavour.

DRAIN the tofu and cut it into 16 triangles. Cut a pocket into the long side of each piece of tofu with a knife. Spoon some prawn mixture into each pocket and gently press down on top. Repeat until you have used all the tofu and the mixture.

HEAT the stock to boiling point in a saucepan. Reduce the heat to low and add the ginger, light soy sauce and preserved radish. Lower the tofu envelopes into the stock and cook for 4 to 5 minutes or until cooked. Add the butterflied prawns and cook for another 1 to 2 minutes or until the prawns open and turn pink. Taste, then adjust the seasoning if necessary. Serve garnished with spring onions.

Spoon some of the prepared prawn mixture into each tofu pocket, then carefully lower them into the stock.

A spirit house in Damnoen Saduak.

SALADS

Slice off a section from the top of the pomelo before cutting it into sections and segmenting it.

Peeling pomelo in Pattaya.

PRAWN AND POMELO SALAD

THIS NORTHERN THAI SALAD USES POMELO TO GIVE IT A SWEET/TART FLAVOUR. DIFFERENT VARIETIES OF POMELO ARE AVAILABLE IN THAILAND: SOME HAVE PINK FLESH AND OTHERS HAVE YELLOW. SERVE THE SALAD WITH STICKY RICE AND EAT IT AS SOON AS IT IS READY.

1 large pomelo
1 tablespoon fish sauce
1 tablespoon lime juice
1 teaspoon sugar
1 tablespoon chilli jam (page 283)
300 g (10 oz) raw medium prawns
　(shrimp), peeled and deveined,
　tails intact
3 tablespoons shredded fresh
　coconut, lightly toasted until
　golden (if fresh unavailable, use
　shredded desiccated)
3 Asian shallots, finely sliced
5 bird's eye chillies, bruised
20 g (1 cup) mint leaves
10 g (⅓ cup) coriander (cilantro)
　leaves
1 tablespoon fried Asian shallots

SERVES 4

TO PEEL a pomelo, first, slice a circular patch off the top of the fruit, about 2 cm (¾ inch) deep (roughly the thickness of the skin). Next, score four deep lines from top to bottom, dividing the skin into four segments. Peel away the skin, one quarter at a time. Remove any remaining pith and separate the segments of the fruit. Peel the segments and remove any seeds. Crumble the segments into their component parts, without squashing them or releasing the juice.

TO MAKE the dressing, combine the fish sauce, lime juice, sugar and chilli jam in a small bowl and stir.

BRING a large saucepan of water to the boil. Add the prawns and cook for 2 minutes. Drain and allow the prawns to cool.

IN a large bowl, gently combine the pomelo, prawns, toasted coconut, shallots, chillies, mint and coriander. Just before serving, add the dressing and toss gently to combine all the ingredients. Serve sprinkled with fried shallots.

YAM PLAA

CRISPY FISH SALAD

THE FISH (TRADITIONALLY CATFISH) IN THIS RECIPE IS TURNED INTO AN ALMOST UNRECOGNIZABLE FLUFFY, CRUNCHY AFFAIR THAT IS THEN FLAVOURED WITH A SWEET, HOT AND SOUR DRESSING. PINK SALMON IS SUITABLE TO USE AS A SUBSTITUTE FOR THE WHITE FISH.

This tasty salad is made using a colourful combination with flavours that contrast well.

DRESSING
1 lemon grass stalk, white part
    only, roughly chopped
4 bird's eye chillies,
    stems removed
1 garlic clove, chopped
1 tablespoon fish sauce
2 tablespoons lime juice
2 teaspoons palm sugar
¼ teaspoon ground turmeric

300 g (10 oz) skinless firm white
    fish fillets
1 tablespoon sea salt
peanut oil, for deep-frying
3 tomatoes or large cherry
    tomatoes, each cut into
    4 or 6 wedges
2 Asian shallots, thinly sliced
1 small red onion, sliced into
    thin wedges
15 g (½ cup) coriander (cilantro)
    leaves
18–24 mint leaves
2 tablespoons roasted peanuts,
    roughly chopped

SERVES 4

TO MAKE the dressing, use a pestle and mortar or food processor to pound or blend the lemon grass, chillies and garlic to a paste. Transfer to a bowl and add the fish sauce, lime juice, sugar and turmeric. Stir until the sugar dissolves.

PREHEAT the oven to 180°C/350°F/Gas 4. Pat dry the fish fillets, then toss them in the sea salt. Place them on a rack in a baking tray and bake for 20 minutes. Remove, allow to cool, then transfer to a food processor and chop until the fish resembles large breadcrumbs.

HALF fill a wok with oil and heat over a high heat. Drop a small piece of fish into the oil. If it sizzles immediately, the oil is ready. Drop a large handful of the chopped fish into the hot oil. The fish will puff up and turn crisp. Cook for 30 seconds and carefully stir a little. Cook for another 30 seconds until golden brown. Remove with a slotted spoon and drain on paper towels. Repeat to cook all the fish.

PUT the tomatoes, shallots, red onion, coriander leaves, mint leaves and peanuts in a bowl with about half of the dressing. Transfer the salad to a serving plate. Break the fish into smaller pieces if you wish and place on the salad. To ensure that the fish stays crispy, pour the remaining dressing over the salad just before serving.

Pound the chilli paste ingredients together in a pestle and mortar, or if you prefer, use a blender.

YAM KAI

CHICKEN AND PAPAYA SALAD

ONE OF THAILAND'S MANY HOT AND TANGY SALADS, THIS VERSION HAS COCONUT RICE INCLUDED, BUT YOU COULD SERVE IT ON ITS OWN IF YOU PREFER. MAKE SURE THE PAPAYA IS GREEN, AND NOT RIPE, OR THE SALAD WON'T TASTE AT ALL RIGHT.

250 ml (1 cup) coconut cream
  (page 279)
200 g (7 oz) skinless chicken breast
  fillet, trimmed
200 g (1 cup) jasmine rice
350 ml (1⅓ cups) coconut milk
  (page 279)
2 garlic cloves, chopped
3 Asian shallots, chopped
3 small red chillies
1 teaspoon small dried shrimp
2 tablespoons fish sauce
8 cherry tomatoes, cut in halves
150 g (5 oz) green papaya,
  grated
2 tablespoons lime juice
30 g (1½ cups) mint leaves,
  roughly chopped
20 g (⅔ cup) coriander (cilantro)
  leaves, roughly chopped

SERVES 4

BRING the coconut cream to a boil in a small saucepan. Add the chicken breast and simmer over a low heat for 5 minutes. Turn off the heat and cover the pan for 20 minutes. Remove the chicken from the pan and shred it.

WASH the rice under cold running water until the water runs clear. Put the rice and coconut milk in a small saucepan and bring to the boil. Reduce the heat to low, cover the pan with a tight-fitting lid and simmer for 20 minutes. Remove from the heat and leave the lid on until ready to serve.

USING a pestle and mortar or blender, pound or blend the garlic, shallots and chillies together. Add the shrimp and fish sauce and pound to break up the dried shrimp. Add the tomatoes and pound all the ingredients together to form a rough paste.

IN a bowl, combine the shredded chicken and chilli paste mixture with the grated papaya, lime juice, mint and coriander leaves. Serve with the hot coconut rice.

YAM HUA PLII

SHREDDED CHICKEN AND BANANA BLOSSOM

BANANA BLOSSOMS LOOK LIKE VERY LARGE PURPLE FLOWER BUDS. MOST OF THE BLOSSOM IS
DISCARDED DURING PREPARATION AND ONLY THE SLIGHTLY BITTER CORE IS EATEN. THEY DISCOLOUR
IN SECONDS SO WORK QUICKLY OR YOU WILL END UP WITH BLACKENED SHREDS.

3 tablespoons lime juice
1 large banana blossom
250 ml (1 cup) coconut cream
  (page 279)
200 g (7 oz) skinless chicken breast
  fillet, trimmed
1 tablespoon chilli jam (page 283)
1 tablespoon fish sauce
1 tablespoon palm sugar
2 teaspoons lime juice
12 cherry tomatoes, cut in halves
20 g (1 cup) mint leaves
10 g (⅓ cup) coriander (cilantro)
  leaves
1 makrut (kaffir) lime leaf, finely
  shredded, for garnish

SERVES 4

PUT the lime juice in a large bowl of cold water.
Using a stainless steel knife, remove the outer
leaves of the banana blossom until you reach
the creamy pale centre. Cut the heart or centre
into quarters and remove the hard cores and
stamens from each. Finely slice the fleshy heart
on an angle and place the slices in the lime water
until ready to use.

RESERVE 2 tablespoons of the coconut cream
and pour the rest into a small saucepan and bring
to a boil. Add the chicken breast, return to a boil,
then reduce the heat and simmer for 5 minutes.
Remove from the heat and cover the pan with a
tight lid for 20 minutes. Remove the chicken from
the pan and discard the cream. Allow the chicken
to cool, then shred it into bite-sized pieces.

IN a small bowl, combine the reserved coconut
cream with the chilli jam, fish sauce, palm sugar
and lime juice.

JUST before serving, drain the banana blossom
and put it in a large bowl with the shredded
chicken, tomato halves, and mint and coriander
leaves. Add the dressing and gently toss to
combine the ingredients. Garnish with the
shredded makrut lime leaf.

Remove the outer leaves of the
banana blossom until you come
to the pale centre.

YAM PUU MAMUANG
CRAB AND GREEN MANGO SALAD

2 tablespoons fish sauce
2 tablespoons lime juice
2 teaspoons palm sugar
2 green bird's eye chillies, chopped
2 red bird's eye chillies, chopped
1 teaspoon ground dried shrimp
300 g (10 oz) fresh crab meat
30 g (⅔ cup) chopped mint leaves
20 g (⅓ cup) chopped coriander
  (cilantro) leaves
4 Asian shallots, finely sliced
1 green mango, flesh finely shredded
1 tomato, cut in half lengthways and
  thinly sliced
1 large green chilli, thinly sliced on
  an angle

SERVES 4

TO make a dressing, put the fish sauce, lime juice, palm sugar, bird's eye chillies and dried shrimp in a small bowl and stir to dissolve the sugar.

JUST before serving, put the crab meat, mint and coriander leaves, shallots, mango and tomato in a large bowl and toss gently.

POUR the dressing over the salad, then toss to combine and serve with the sliced chilli on top.

YAM PLAA YAANG
HOT AND SOUR GRILLED FISH SALAD

2 mackerel or whiting (about
  400 g/14 oz each fish), cleaned
  and gutted, with or without head,
  or firm white fish fillets
2 lemon grass stalks, white part
  only, finely sliced
2 Asian shallots, finely sliced
1 spring onion (scallion), finely sliced
2.5 cm (1 inch) piece of ginger,
  finely sliced
5 makrut (kaffir) lime leaves,
  finely sliced
20 g (1 cup) mint leaves
5 tablespoons lime juice
1 tablespoon fish sauce
4–5 bird's eye chillies, finely sliced
a few lettuce leaves
1 long red chilli, seeded and finely
  sliced, for garnish

SERVES 4

HEAT a barbecue or grill (broiler) to medium. If using a grill, line the tray with foil. Cook the fish for about 20 minutes on each side or until the fish is cooked and light brown. You can use a special fish-shaped griddle that opens out like tongs to make it easier to lift and turn on the barbecue.

USE your hands to remove the fish heads, backbone and other bones. Break all the fish, including the skin, into bite-sized chunks and put them in a bowl.

ADD the lemon grass, shallots, spring onion, ginger, makrut lime leaves, mint leaves, lime juice, fish sauce and chillies to the fish. Mix well, then taste and adjust the seasoning if necessary.

LINE a serving plate with lettuce leaves, then spoon the salad over the leaves. Sprinkle with chilli slices.

HOT AND SOUR GRILLED
FISH SALAD

LAAP PET

SPICY GROUND DUCK

LAAP MEANS 'GOOD FORTUNE'. THIS VERSION USING DUCK IS A SPECIALITY FROM AROUND UBON

RACHATHANI BUT YOU CAN USE MINCED CHICKEN INSTEAD OF DUCK. LAAP IS SERVED WITH RAW

VEGETABLES SUCH AS SNAKE BEANS, CABBAGE AND FIRM, CRISP LETTUCE.

Pound the dry-fried rice in a pestle and mortar until it forms a powder. Alternatively, you can use a small blender.

1 tablespoon jasmine rice
280 g (10 oz) minced (ground) duck
3 tablespoons lime juice
1 tablespoon fish sauce
2 lemon grass stalks, white part
    only, finely sliced
50 g (2 oz) Asian shallots,
    finely sliced
5 makrut (kaffir) lime leaves,
    finely sliced
5 spring onions (scallions),
    finely chopped
¼–½ teaspoon roasted chilli powder,
    according to taste
a few lettuce leaves
a few mint leaves, for garnish
raw vegetables such as snake
    beans, cut into lengths, cucumber
    slices, thin wedges of cabbage,
    halved baby tomatoes, to serve

SERVES 4

DRY-FRY the rice in a small pan over a medium heat. Shake the pan to move the rice around, for 6 to 8 minutes, or until the rice is brown. Using a pestle and mortar or a small blender, pound or blend the rice until it almost forms a powder.

IN a saucepan or wok, cook the duck with the lime juice and fish sauce over a high heat. Crumble and break the duck until the meat has separated into small pieces. Cook until light brown. Dry, then remove from the heat.

ADD the rice powder, lemon grass, shallots, makrut lime leaves, spring onions and chilli powder to the duck and stir together. Taste, then adjust the seasoning if necessary.

LINE a serving plate with lettuce leaves. Spoon the duck over the leaves, then garnish with mint leaves. Arrange the vegetables on a separate plate.

Add the mung bean vermicelli and mushrooms to the seafood, then the flavourings.

Unloading mussels in Pattaya.

YAM WUN SEN THALEH

HOT AND SOUR VERMICELLI WITH MIXED SEAFOOD

ONE OF THE MILDER CLASSIC SALADS FOUND ALL OVER THAILAND, OFTEN MADE JUST WITH PRAWNS, BUT HERE MADE WITH SEAFOOD. THE VERMICELLI USED BECOMES ALMOST TRANSLUCENT WHEN SOAKED. AS THE DRESSING IS ABSORBED QUICKLY, DON'T MAKE THE SALAD TOO FAR AHEAD.

110 g (4 oz) mung bean vermicelli
175 g (6 oz) mixed raw medium
   prawns (shrimp), squid tubes and
   scallops
8 mussels
15 g (½ oz) dried black fungus
   (about half a handful)
1½ tablespoons vegetable oil
4–5 garlic cloves, finely chopped
3 tablespoons lime juice
1 tablespoon fish sauce
2 lemon grass stalks, white part
   only, finely sliced
3 Asian shallots, finely sliced
¼–½ teaspoon chilli powder
   or 2–3 bird's eye chillies,
   finely sliced
3 spring onions (scallions),
   finely chopped
a few lettuce leaves
1 long red chilli, seeded and
   finely sliced, for garnish

SERVES 4

SOAK the mung bean vermicelli in boiling water for 1 to 2 minutes, or until soft, then drain and roughly chop.

PEEL and devein the prawns and cut each prawn along the back so it opens like a butterfly (leave each prawn joined along the base and at the tail, leaving the tail attached).

PEEL off the skin from the squid tubes, rinse the insides and cut the tubes into 5 mm (¼ inch) rings. Remove any dark vein from the scallops.

SCRUB the mussels and remove their hairy beards. Discard any open mussels and any that don't close when tapped on the work surface.

SOAK the black fungus in boiling water for 2 to 3 minutes or until soft, then drain and roughly chop them.

HEAT the oil in a small wok or frying pan and stir the garlic over a medium heat until light brown. Transfer the fried garlic to a small bowl.

IN a saucepan or wok, cook the prawns, squid rings and mussels over a medium heat with the lime juice and fish sauce for 1 to 2 minutes or until the prawns open and turn pink. Add the scallops and cook for 1 minute. Discard any unopened mussels. Add the vermicelli and mushrooms to the pan and cook for another 2 minutes or until the vermicelli is cooked. Remove from the heat.

ADD the lemon grass, shallots, chilli powder or chillies, and spring onions and mix well. Taste, then adjust the seasoning if necessary.

LINE a serving plate with lettuce leaves, then spoon the seafood over the leaves. Sprinkle with chilli slices and the fried garlic.

YAM NEUA YANG NAHM TOKE

SLICED STEAK WITH HOT AND SOUR SAUCE

YAM NEUA YANG NAHM TOKE LITERALLY MEANS 'BEEF GRILLED ON BURNING HOT CHARCOAL TILL THE JUICES FALL'. THIS NORTHERN SALAD IS EATEN WITH STICKY RICE AND IS PERFECT WITH BEER, THAI WHISKY OR WINE. SERVE THE SALAD WITH RAW VEGETABLES SUCH AS GREEN CABBAGE.

350 g (12 oz) lean sirloin, rump
   or fillet steak
2 tablespoons fish sauce
4 tablespoons lime juice
1 teaspoon sugar
¼ teaspoon roasted chilli powder
3–4 Asian shallots, finely sliced
a few lettuce leaves, to serve
20 g (⅓ cup) roughly chopped
   coriander (cilantro) leaves,
   for garnish
15 g (¼ cup) roughly chopped mint
   leaves, for garnish

SERVES 4

HEAT a barbecue or grill (broiler) to medium. If using a grill, line the tray with foil. Put the beef on the grill rack and sprinkle both sides with salt and pepper. Cook for 5 to 7 minutes on each side, turning occasionally. Fat should drip off the meat and the meat should cook slowly enough to remain juicy and not burn. Using a sharp knife, slice the cooked beef crossways into strips.

MIX the fish sauce, lime juice, sugar and chilli powder in a bowl. Add the Asian shallots and the slices of beef. Taste, then adjust the seasoning if necessary.

LINE a serving plate with lettuce leaves, then spoon the mixture over the leaves. Sprinkle with coriander and mint leaves.

Heat the barbecue to medium before adding the meat.

Paddy fields in Phetchaburi.

TROPICAL FRUIT Thai fruit is sold whole, or completely prepared, usually cut into segments ready to eat. In either case the fruit is sold by weight. Jackfruit (kha-nun), (top left), have a flavour like fruit salad and a slightly rubbery texture. The tough, spiky, outer skin is peeled away to reveal segments of flesh (bottom left) which are then seeded. Rambutan (ngaw), above, have a bright red coating with soft, green spikes.

FRUIT

A WONDERFUL ARRAY OF TROPICAL FRUIT (PHON-LA-MAI) IS TAKEN FOR GRANTED AS PART OF EVERYDAY LIFE IN THAILAND. FRUIT IS EATEN AT BREAKFAST, AS A SNACK, INSTEAD OF DESSERT, AND APPEARS IN MANY RECIPES. IT IS ALSO JUICED, DRIED, PICKLED AND SALTED. IT IS SOLD ON EVERY STREET CORNER OF EVERY CITY, TOWN AND VILLAGE.

Tropical fruit grows well throughout Thailand. A drive around the countryside reveals rows of fruit trees, and not just in orchards. Even in town, every spare scrap of land has a banana tree or two, a papaya tree and possibly a mango tree. Fresh fruit is often sold prepared. You can buy a plastic bag full of fruit pieces with a wooden skewer for picking them up. Most bags come with a little bag of seasoning. Thais like a balance of flavours and fruit is no exception. Salt, sugar and a little chilli powder perk up fruit and bring out the flavour.

Fruit is used extensively in Thai cuisine. Jackfruit, carambola (starfuit), mangosteen, green mango and lychees are all used in curries. Salads are made from green mango, papaya or pieces of pomelo. Bananas are steamed in their skins and

BANANAS *(kluay)* There are more than 20 varieties of banana in Thailand, each with individual characteristics and taste. All are used in cooking. Bananas are sold at floating markets and green bananas hang ripening from the eaves of houses. Medium *kluay naam waa* are the typical banana. Egg bananas *(kluay khai)* are referred to as 'lady fingers' elsewhere. Sugar bananas are small and sweet.

served for breakfast, or speared on skewers and roasted over hot coals to be eaten as a roadside snack. Desserts include the ubiquitous banana fritters, as well as bananas simmered in coconut milk, sticky rice with mango, macerated fruit and grilled bananas. Modern cuisine has embraced ice creams and sorbets made in every imaginable fruit flavour.

FRUIT DRINKS

Fresh fruit juices *(naam pan)* often come as something of a shock to the visitor to Thailand. Just as fresh fruit is eaten with a special seasoning of chilli, sugar and salt, fruit juices are 'seasoned' with salt. Juices are usually chopped fruit, water and ice whizzed in a blender with a pinch of salt. Most vendors have a couple of blenders on the go at once.

CARVED FRUIT is one of the main forms of table decoration in smart hotels and restaurants in Thailand. Large fruit such as papaya, pomelo and melons are carved into intricate open flower patterns and smaller fruit or half fruit are carved into smaller flowers. Leaves are carved out of pieces of skin and the whole lot arranged in sumptuous displays. One melon takes an experienced carver just 20 minutes to complete.

PRESERVED FRUIT (phon-la-mai chaei im)

In Thailand, as many types of fruit as possible are preserved by dry-salting, pickling, candying or drying. Bags of preserved fruit are sold at stalls and are as common as bags of sweets in the West.

DURIAN

The infamous durian (thurian) is the most anticipated fruit in the Thai calendar. Although 'tasting like heaven but smelling like hell', durian has a reputation second to none. The putrid smell lingers but is not enough to deter enthusiasts from loving the rich pulp. Different varieties are available throughout the year but, when not in season, a desire for it can be satisfied by products such as freeze-dried chips or deep-fried slices.

FRUIT SEASONS

Bananas, guavas, jackfruit, limes, watermelons, oranges, papayas, pomelos and pineapples are always present. European fruit is now grown in cooler uplands, especially in the hill area north-west and north of Chiang Mai. Orchards of peaches, cherries and apples, as well as hothouses with strawberries growing, are seen alongside lychees.

March sees the arrival of mangoes, followed by mangosteens in April and lychees in May. The following five months are the best time for fruit: custard apples, longans, rambutans, rose apples, sapodilla, carambola, jujube, langsat, santol and sala come into season and then go again. The colder winter months are the time for year-round and non-indigenous fruit.

CUSTARD APPLE *(nauy naa)* Also known as sugar apple, these have a sweet flavour and a soft creamy texture. They have hard black seeds.

DRAGON FRUIT *(keow mang korn)* An extraordinary bright fruit, pink and green on the outside, these have a crisp, sweet, watery white flesh and tiny black seeds.

GUAVA *(farang)* Guava have a perfumed flesh that is astringent when unripe. Pink- or white-fleshed, they will overpower other fruit when ripe.

MANGOSTEEN *(mang-khut)* These have a hard casing and a soft, white, sweet flesh that comes in segments. There are about two seeds per fruit.

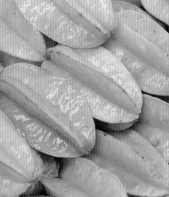

DURIAN *(thurian)* Banned from airlines, hotel rooms and public places, durian inspires love or hate. Without its rotten smell the sweet flesh would be better liked.

CARAMBOLA *(ma feuang)* Also known as starfruit because of their cross-sectional appearance. Eaten with both savoury and sweet dishes.

GREEN MANGO *(mamuang)* Used in savoury dishes for their souring properties. Shredded into salads *(yam)* or added to curries and soups.

SAPODILLA *(lamut)* Soft fruit with a fuzzy yellow-brown skin. Each has three or four flat black seeds. The flesh browns and sweetens as it ripens.

ROSE APPLE *(chom-phuu)* Crisp fruit eaten more for their texture than flavour. Often served with dips like *naam phrik* and alongside savoury food.

LONGKONG These grow in clusters like a bunch of grapes. The skins cover segments of translucent white flesh and green seeds.

POMELO *(som-oh)* Giant citrus fruit with a sweet juicy flesh. Eaten out of the hand or sometimes broken into segments and used in salads *(yam)*.

MAKRUT LIME *(luk ma-krut)* Also kaffir limes, these knobbly limes are used for their zest rather than for their bitter juice. Peel off the zest in sections.

FISH & SHELLFISH

Whether you are using chillies or capsicums, remove all the seeds and membrane.

Fishing in Phang-nga.

HAW MOK THALEH PHRIK YUAK

CURRIED FISH STEAMED IN BANANA CHILLIES

A SMOOTH CURRIED CUSTARD WITH FISH FILLS THESE CHILLIES. CHOOSE A SELECTION OF COLOURS FOR A VERY STRIKING DISH. RED, YELLOW AND ORANGE CHILLIES KEEP THEIR COLOUR BETTER THAN GREEN ONES. YOU CAN ALSO USE SMALL CAPSICUMS OF VARIOUS COLOURS.

FISH FILLING
4–5 dried long red chillies
3 garlic cloves, roughly chopped
1–2 Asian shallots, roughly chopped
4 coriander (cilantro) roots,
    roughly chopped
1 lemon grass stalk, white part only,
    finely sliced
1 cm (½ inch) piece of galangal,
    finely chopped
1 teaspoon makrut (kaffir) lime zest
    or 2 makrut (kaffir) lime leaves,
    finely sliced
1 teaspoon shrimp paste
¼ teaspoon salt
275 g (10 oz) firm white fish fillets,
    cut into 1 cm (½ inch) pieces,
    or small raw prawns (shrimp)
    or small scallops
400 ml (1⅔ cups) coconut milk
    (page 279)
2 eggs
2 tablespoons fish sauce

10 banana chillies,
    or small capsicums (peppers),
    preferably elongated ones
2 handfuls of Thai sweet basil
    leaves
2 tablespoons coconut cream
3–4 makrut (kaffir) lime leaves,
    finely sliced, for garnish
1 long red chilli, seeded, finely
    sliced, for garnish

SERVES 4

TO MAKE the fish filling, using a pestle and mortar or blender, pound or blend the chillies, garlic, shallots and coriander roots together. Add the lemon grass, galangal, makrut lime zest, shrimp paste and salt, one ingredient at a time, until the mixture forms a curry paste.

IN a bowl, combine the curry paste, fish, coconut milk, eggs and fish sauce. Keep stirring in the same direction for 10 minutes, then cover and refrigerate for 30 minutes to set slightly.

IF USING chillies, or if the capsicums are the long ones, make a long cut with a sharp knife, or if they are the round ones, cut a small round slice from the tops. Remove the seeds and membrane, then clean the chillies or capsicums and pat them dry. Place a few basil leaves in the bottom of each. Spoon in the fish mixture until it nearly reaches the top edge.

FILL a wok or a steamer pan with water, cover and bring to a rolling boil over a high heat. Place the chillies or capsicums on a plate. Use a plate that will fit on the rack of a traditional bamboo steamer basket or on a steamer rack inside the wok or pan. Taking care not to burn your hands, set the basket or rack over the water and put the plate on the rack. Reduce the heat to a simmer. Cover and cook for 15 to 20 minutes. Check and replenish the water after 10 minutes.

TURN off the heat and transfer the chillies or capsicums to a serving plate. Spoon the coconut cream on top and sprinkle with makrut lime leaves and sliced chilli.

HAW MOK

FISH STEAMED IN BANANA LEAF

THE DELICIOUS AROMATIC CURRIED FISH CUSTARD FILLING FOR THIS DISH IS THE SAME ONE AS ON
THE PRECEDING PAGE. IN THIS RECIPE THE FISH CUSTARD IS STEAMED IN INDIVIDUAL BANANA LEAF
CUPS AND THIS RESULTS IN A DELIGHTFUL EXOTIC PRESENTATION.

banana leaves
2 handfuls of Thai sweet basil
　leaves
fish filling (page 104)
2 tablespoons coconut cream
3–4 makrut (kaffir) lime leaves,
　finely sliced
1 long red chilli, seeded and finely
　sliced, for garnish

MAKES 6 banana cups

Use a bowl or plate as a guide
when cutting the banana leaves.
Pin together with toothpicks.

TO SOFTEN the banana leaves and prevent them
splitting, put them in a hot oven for about 10 to
20 seconds, or blanch them briefly. Cut the leaves
into 12 circles 15 cm (6 inches) in diameter with
the fibre running lengthways. Place one piece with
the fibre running lengthways and another on top
with the fibre running across. Make a 1 cm (½ inch)
deep tuck 4 cm (1½ inches) long (4 cm in from the
edge and no further) and pin securely with a small
sharp toothpick. Repeat at the opposite point
and at the two side points, making four tucks
altogether. Flatten the base as best you can.
Repeat to make 6 square-shaped cups. Place a
few basil leaves in the bottom of each cup and
spoon in fish filling until three-quarters full.

FILL a wok or a steamer pan with water, cover and
bring to a boil over a high heat. Place the banana
cups on a plate. Use a plate that will fit on the rack
of a traditional bamboo steamer basket or on a
steamer rack inside the wok or pan. (If your wok or
pan has a special steaming plate that will hold the
cups flat, you may not need to put them on a
separate plate.) Taking care not to burn your
hands, set the rack or basket over the water and
put the plate on the rack. Reduce the heat to a
simmer. Cover and cook for 15 to 20 minutes.
Check and replenish the water after 10 minutes.

WHEN the cups are cooked the filling will puff and
rise slightly. Turn off the heat and carefully transfer
the cups to a serving plate. Spoon a little coconut
cream on top and sprinkle with lime leaves and
sliced chilli.

Cut the crab into quarters, leaving the legs attached. Add the coconut milk mixture and onion after 5 minutes.

Snack seller in Bangkok.

PUU PHAT PHONG KARII

CRACKED CRAB WITH CURRY POWDER

THIS CRAB RECIPE IS ONE OF THE FEW THAI DISHES TO USE CURRY POWDER AS A MAIN FLAVOURING. BOUGHT CURRY POWDER (LOOK FOR A THAI BRAND) IS USUALLY VERY GOOD AND THIS IS WHAT THAI COOKS WOULD USE BUT THERE IS A RECIPE ON PAGE 287 IF YOU NEED TO MAKE YOUR OWN.

1 live crab, 500 g (1 lb 2 oz)
170 ml (⅔ cup) coconut milk
　(page 279)
1 tablespoon light soy sauce
½ tablespoon oyster sauce
2 teaspoons Thai curry powder
　(page 287) or bought Thai
　curry powder
¼ teaspoon sugar
2 tablespoons vegetable oil
3–4 garlic cloves, finely chopped
1 small onion, cut into 3 wedges
2 spring onions (scallions),
　finely sliced
½ long red chilli, seeded and
　finely sliced, for garnish
a few coriander (cilantro) leaves,
　for garnish

SERVES 4

PUT the crabs in the freezer for 1 hour. Leaving the legs attached, cut the crab in half through the centre of the shell from head to rear. Cut in half again from left to right (quartering the crab), with legs attached to each quarter. Twist off and remove the upper shell pieces. Discard the stomach sac and the soft gill tissue. Using crackers or the back of a heavy knife, crack the crab claws to make them easier to eat. If the claws are too big, cut them in half.

MIX the coconut milk, light soy sauce, oyster sauce, curry powder and sugar in a bowl.

HEAT the oil in a wok or frying pan. Stir-fry the garlic over a medium heat until light brown. Add the crab and stir-fry for about 4 to 5 minutes. Add the coconut mixture and onion and continue stir-frying for another 5 to 7 minutes or until the crab meat is cooked through and the sauce is reduced and very thick. Add the spring onions. Taste, then adjust the seasoning if necessary. Spoon onto a serving plate and sprinkle with sliced chilli and coriander leaves.

NEUNG HAWY LAI KRA-CHAI

CLAMS AND MUSSELS WITH CHINESE KEYS

450 g (1 lb) mixed clams and
    mussels in the shell
75 g (3 oz) Chinese keys,
    finely sliced
2.5 cm (1 inch) piece of galangal,
    cut into 7–8 slices
1 long red chilli, seeded and
    finely chopped
2 teaspoons fish sauce
½ teaspoon sugar
a few sprigs of basil leaves,
    for garnish

SERVES 2

SCRUB the clams and mussels and remove any hairy beards from the mussels. Discard any open mussels or clams and any that don't close when tapped on the work surface. Wash them all in several changes of cold water until the water is clear, then put them in a large bowl, cover with cold water and soak for 30 minutes. This helps remove the sand from the clams.

PUT the clams and mussels, Chinese keys, galangal and chopped chilli in a large saucepan or wok. Cover loosely and cook over a medium heat for 5 minutes, shaking the pan frequently. Add the fish sauce and sugar and toss together. Discard any unopened shells. Serve the clams and mussels in a large bowl. Garnish with basil leaves.

PHAT HAWY MALAENG PHUU TA-KHRAI

MUSSELS WITH LEMON GRASS

450 g (1 lb) mussels or clams
    in the shell
1½ tablespoons vegetable oil
2–3 garlic cloves, finely chopped
1 small onion, finely chopped
3 lemon grass stalks, white part
    only, finely sliced
2.5 cm (1 inch) piece of galangal,
    cut into 7–8 slices
2 long red chillies, seeded and
    finely chopped
1 tablespoon fish sauce
1 tablespoon lime juice
½ teaspoon sugar
25 g (1 cup) holy basil leaves,
    roughly chopped

SERVES 2

SCRUB the mussels or clams and remove any hairy beards from the mussels. Discard any open mussels or clams and any that don't close when tapped on the work surface. If using clams, wash them in several changes of cold water until the water is clear, then put them in a large bowl, cover with cold water and soak for 30 minutes. This helps remove the sand from the clams.

HEAT the oil in a wok and stir-fry the garlic, onion, lemon grass, galangal and chillies over a medium heat for 1 to 2 minutes or until fragrant.

ADD the mussels or clams and stir-fry for a few minutes. Add the fish sauce, lime juice and sugar. Cover loosely and cook over a medium heat for 5 to 7 minutes, shaking the wok frequently. Cook until the shells are open, discarding any unopened shells. Mix in the chopped holy basil. Taste, then adjust the seasoning if necessary.

SERVE the steamed mussels or clams hot in a large bowl.

MUSSELS WITH LEMON
GRASS

DEEP-FRIED FISH WITH SWEET AND SOUR SAUCE

WHEN SERVING WHOLE FISH, LIFT OFF PORTIONS FROM THE TOP FILLETS AND THEN REMOVE THE BONES IN ONE PIECE SO YOU CAN ACCESS THE FILLETS UNDERNEATH. THE FLAVOUR OF SWEET AND SOUR SAUCE WORKS EXTREMELY WELL WITH ALL TYPES OF FISH.

400 g (14 oz) St Peters fish, sea bream, red snapper or grey mullet
3½ tablespoons plain (all-purpose) flour
pinch of ground white pepper
vegetable oil, for deep-frying
225 g (8 oz) tin pineapple slices in juice, each slice cut into 4 pieces (reserve the juice)
1½ tablespoons plum sauce or ketchup
2½ teaspoons fish sauce
1 tablespoon sugar
1½ tablespoons vegetable oil
3–4 garlic cloves, finely chopped
1 medium onion, cut into 8 slices
½ red capsicum (pepper), cut into bite-sized pieces
1 small cucumber (skin left on), cut into bite-sized pieces
1 medium tomato, cut into 8 wedges, or 4 baby tomatoes
a few coriander (cilantro) leaves, for garnish

SERVES 2

CLEAN and gut the fish, leaving the head on. Thoroughly dry the fish and score it three or four times on both sides with a sharp knife. Rub the fish inside and out with a pinch of salt. Put 3 tablespoons of the flour and the pepper on a plate and press the fish lightly into it until coated with flour from head to tail. Shake off any excess.

HEAT 10 cm (4 inches) oil in a large wok or pan big enough to deep-fry the whole fish. Drop a small cube of bread into the oil and if it sizzles straight away, the oil is ready. Lower the heat to medium and gently slide the fish into the oil. Be careful as the hot oil may splash. Deep-fry the fish on just one side (but make sure the oil covers the whole fish) for about 15 to 20 minutes or until the fish is cooked and light brown (if you cook the fish until it is very brown, the fish will be too dry). Drain, then put on paper towels before transferring to a warm plate. Keep warm.

MEANWHILE, mix all the pineapple juice (about 6 tablespoons) with the remaining flour, plum sauce or ketchup, fish sauce and sugar in a small bowl until smooth.

REMOVE the oil from the wok or pan and heat 1½ tablespoons clean oil in the same wok or pan. Stir-fry the garlic over a medium heat for 1 minute or until light brown. Add the onion and capsicum and stir-fry for 1 to 2 minutes. Add the pineapple, cucumber, tomato and pineapple juice mixture. Stir together for another minute. Taste, then adjust the seasoning if necessary. Pour all over the warm fish and garnish with a few coriander leaves.

PLAA NEUNG GEAM BOUI

STEAMED FISH WITH PRESERVED PLUM

BUY AN APPROPRIATELY LARGE STEAMER FOR THIS RECIPE OR USE THE STEAMER RACK OF YOUR WOK. BOTH WILL WORK EQUALLY WELL. PRESERVED PLUMS ARE SOLD IN JARS IN ASIAN SUPERMARKETS AND, ONCE OPENED, THEY WILL KEEP IN THE REFRIGERATOR FOR SOME TIME.

1 tablespoon light soy sauce

½ teaspoon sugar

1 large or 2 smaller pomfret, flounder, or turbot, (total weight about 1 kg/2 lb 4 oz)

50 g (2 oz) mushrooms, roughly sliced

2 small preserved plums, bruised

5 cm (2 inch) piece of ginger, julienned

4 spring onions (scallions), sliced diagonally

2 long red or green chillies, seeded and finely sliced

a few coriander (cilantro) leaves, for garnish

a sprinkle of ground white pepper

SERVES 4

IN a small bowl, mix the light soy sauce and sugar.

CLEAN and gut the fish, leaving the head/s on. Dry the fish thoroughly. Score the fish three or four times on both sides with a sharp knife. Place the fish on a deep plate slightly larger than the fish itself. Use a plate that will fit on the rack of a traditional bamboo steamer basket or on a steamer rack inside the wok. Sprinkle the mushrooms, preserved plums and ginger over the fish. Pour the light soy sauce mixture all over the fish.

FILL a wok or a steamer pan with water, cover and bring to a rolling boil over a high heat. Taking care not to burn your hands, set the rack or basket over the boiling water and put the plate with the fish on the rack. Reduce the heat to a simmer. Cover and steam for 25 to 30 minutes (depending on the variety and size of the fish) or until the skewer will slide easily into the fish. Check and replenish the water every 10 minutes or so. Remove the fish from the steamer. Serve on the same plate. Sprinkle with spring onions, chillies, coriander leaves and pepper.

Deep-fry the basil leaves in two batches until they are crispy.

Pattaya market.

DEEP-FRIED FISH WITH CHILLIES AND BASIL

THIS IS ONE OF THE MOST POPULAR FISH DISHES IN THAILAND AND YOU CAN USE MOST TYPES OF FISH TO MAKE IT. THE FISH HAS A MILDLY SPICY FLAVOUR AND IS GARNISHED WITH DEEP-FRIED CHILLI AND BASIL LEAVES. THE DUSTING OF FLOUR ISN'T TRADITIONAL BUT IT HELPS CRISP THE SKIN.

1 large or 2 smaller red snapper
    (total weight about 1 kg/2 lb 4 oz)
3 tablespoons plain (all-purpose)
    flour
pinch of ground black pepper
1½ tablespoons vegetable oil
½ tablespoon red curry paste
    (page 276) or bought paste
2 tablespoons palm sugar
2 tablespoons fish sauce
vegetable oil, for deep-frying
a handful of Thai sweet basil leaves
1 dried long red chilli, cut into
    5 mm (¼ inch) pieces,
    seeds discarded
3 makrut (kaffir) lime leaves,
    very finely sliced, for garnish

SERVES 4

CLEAN and gut the fish, leaving the head/s on. Thoroughly dry the fish. Score the fish three or four times on both sides with a sharp knife. Rub the fish inside and out with a pinch of salt. Place the flour and ground pepper on a plate and press the fish lightly into it until coated with flour from head to tail. Shake off any excess.

HEAT the oil in a small saucepan, add the red curry paste and stir over a medium heat for 1 to 2 minutes or until fragrant. Add the sugar, fish sauce and 2 tablespoons water and cook for another 1 to 2 minutes or until the sugar has dissolved. Remove from the heat.

HEAT 10 cm (4 inches) oil in a large wok or pan big enough to deep-fry the whole fish. When the oil is hot, drop a few basil leaves into it. If they sizzle immediately, the oil is ready. Deep-fry half of the basil leaves for 1 minute or until they are all crispy. Remove with a slotted spoon and drain on paper towels. Deep-fry the rest.

IN the same wok, deep-fry the dried chilli pieces for a few seconds over a medium heat until light brown. Be careful not to burn them. Remove with a slotted spoon and drain on paper towels. Lower the heat to medium and gently slide the fish into the oil. Be careful as the hot oil may splash. Deep-fry the fish on just one side (but make sure the oil covers the whole fish) for about 5 to 10 minutes or until the fish is cooked and light brown (if you cook the fish until it is very brown, it will be too dry). Drain off the oil and drain the fish on paper towels.

PUT the curry sauce in the wok and gently warm it. Add the fish and coat both sides with the sauce. Transfer the fish to a warm plate with any remaining sauce and sprinkle with crispy basil, fried chilli pieces and the makrut lime leaves.

PLAA PHAO

GRILLED FISH WITH GARLIC AND CORIANDER

BANANA LEAVES ARE USED IN THIS RECIPE TO PROTECT THE FISH FROM DIRECT HEAT AS WELL AS TO ADD A SUBTLE EXTRA FLAVOUR. THE LEAVES WILL CHAR AS THEY COOK. YOU WILL FIND BANANA LEAVES IN ASIAN SUPERMARKETS, OFTEN IN THE FREEZER CABINETS.

4 red tilapa, grey/red mullet, or
    mackerel (about 300 g/
    10 oz each)
8–10 garlic cloves, roughly chopped
6 coriander (cilantro) roots, chopped
1 teaspoon ground white pepper
1 teaspoon salt
1 tablespoon vegetable oil
8 pieces of banana leaf
a chilli sauce, to serve

SERVES 4

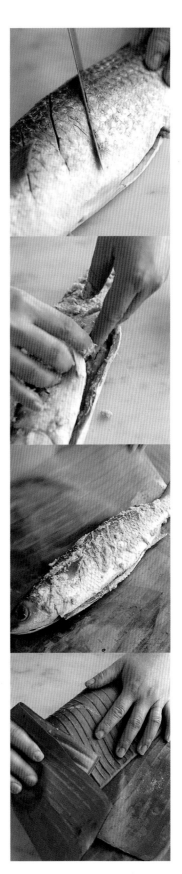

CLEAN and gut the fish, leaving the heads on. Dry the fish thoroughly. Score each fish three or four times on both sides with a sharp knife.

USING a pestle and mortar or a small blender, pound or blend the garlic, coriander roots, ground pepper, salt and oil into a paste. Rub the garlic paste inside the cavities and all over each fish. Cover and marinate in the refrigerator for at least 30 minutes.

TO SOFTEN the banana leaves and prevent them from splitting, put them in a hot oven for 10 to 20 seconds, or blanch them briefly. Using two pieces of banana leaf, each with the grain running at right angles to the other, wrap each fish like a parcel. Pin the ends of the banana leaves together with toothpicks.

HEAT a grill (broiler) or barbecue to medium. Barbecue or grill (broil) the fish for about 15 minutes on each side or until the fish is light brown and cooked. To make the fish easier to lift and turn during cooking, you can place the fish in a fish-shaped griddle that opens out like tongs. Transfer the fish to a serving plate. Serve with a chilli sauce.

Score the fish, then prepare it and wrap in the banana leaves.

Cut the ginger into thin slices
before cutting it into matchsticks.

Dried fish on sale.

PLAA THAWT RAD KHING

DEEP-FRIED FISH WITH GINGER

ALTHOUGH THAI FISH ARE NOT TRADITIONALLY COATED IN FLOUR BEFORE BEING FRIED, IT WILL HELP

GIVE A CRISPER SKIN. MAKE SURE THE FISH IS REALLY WELL COOKED AND CRISP OR THE SAUCE

WILL MAKE IT SOGGY. IF YOU CAN'T GET ONE LARGE FISH, USE SEVERAL SMALLER ONES INSTEAD.

15 g (½ oz) dried black fungus
(about half a handful)
1 large or 2 smaller red snapper,
grey mullet, sea bass or grouper
(total weight about 1 kg/2 lb 4 oz)
3 tablespoons plain (all-purpose)
flour
pinch of ground black pepper
1 tablespoon oyster sauce
1 tablespoon light soy sauce
¼ teaspoon sugar
vegetable oil, for deep-frying
1½ tablespoons vegetable oil
4 garlic cloves, roughly chopped
1 small carrot, cut into matchsticks
2 cm (¾ inch) piece of ginger, cut
into matchsticks
2 spring onions (scallions), finely
sliced, for garnish

SERVES 4

SOAK the black fungus in hot water for 2 to
3 minutes until soft, then drain the fungus
and finely chop.

CLEAN and gut the fish, leaving the head/s on.
Dry the fish thoroughly. Score the fish three or four
times on both sides with a sharp knife. Rub the
fish inside and out with a pinch of salt. Put the
flour and ground pepper on a plate and lightly
press the fish into it until it is coated all over. Shake
off any excess flour.

MIX the oyster sauce, light soy sauce, sugar and
2 tablespoons water in a small bowl.

HEAT 10 cm (4 inches) oil in a large wok or
saucepan big enough to deep-fry the whole fish.
When the oil seems hot, drop a small piece of
spring onion into the oil. If it sizzles straight away,
the oil is ready. Lower the heat to medium and
gently slide the fish into the oil. Be careful as the
hot oil may splash. Deep-fry the fish on just one
side (but make sure the oil covers the whole fish)
for about 5 to 10 minutes or until the fish is
cooked and light brown (if you cook the fish until it
is very brown, the fish will be too dry). Drain on
paper towels before transferring to a warm plate.
Keep warm. Drain off the oil.

HEAT 1½ tablespoons clean oil in the same wok
and stir-fry the garlic over a medium heat until light
brown. Add the carrot, ginger, mushrooms and the
sauce mixture and stir-fry for 1 to 2 minutes. Taste,
then adjust the seasoning if necessary. Pour over
the warm fish and sprinkle with spring onions.

PLAA THAWT SAHM ROT

DEEP-FRIED FISH WITH THREE-FLAVOURED SAUCE

YOU CAN USE LIME JUICE IN THIS DISH IF YOU PREFER A CLEAR SAUCE, OR TAMARIND FOR A THICK
OR DARKER-COLOURED SAUCE. USE TWO OR FOUR SMALLER FISH IF YOU CAN'T FIND ONE FISH
LARGE ENOUGH. GARNISH WITH HOLY BASIL IF YOU CAN FIND IT.

1 x 350 g (12 oz) sea bream, red
  snapper or grey mullet
3 tablespoons plain (all-purpose)
  flour
pinch of ground black pepper
vegetable oil, for deep-frying
4–5 garlic cloves, roughly chopped
5 long red chillies, seeded and
  roughly chopped
4–5 Asian shallots, roughly chopped
3 coriander (cilantro) roots, finely
  chopped
3 tablespoons palm sugar
2 tablespoons fish sauce
3 tablespoon tamarind purée or
  lime juice
a few holy basil or Thai sweet basil
  leaves, for garnish

SERVES 2

CLEAN and gut the fish, leaving the head on. Dry
the fish thoroughly. Score the fish three or four
times on both sides with a sharp knife.

RUB the fish inside and out with a pinch of salt.
Put the flour and ground pepper on a plate or dish
and press the fish lightly into it until coated with
flour from head to tail. Shake off any excess.

HEAT 10 cm (4 inches) oil in a large wok or pan
big enough to deep-fry the whole fish. When the
oil seems hot, drop a piece of shallot into the oil.
If it sizzles straight away, the oil is ready. Lower
the heat to medium and gently slide the fish into
the oil. Be careful as the hot oil may splash. Deep-
fry the fish on just one side (but make sure the oil
covers the whole fish) for about 15 to 20 minutes
or until the fish is cooked and light brown (if you
cook the fish until it is brown, it will be too dry).
Drain, then put on paper towels before transferring
to a warm plate. Keep warm.

WHILE the fish is cooking, use a pestle and mortar
or a small blender to pound or blend the garlic,
chillies, shallots and coriander roots together into
a rough paste.

HEAT 1 tablespoon oil in a wok or frying pan and
stir-fry the chilli paste over a medium heat for 2 to
3 minutes or until fragrant. Add the palm sugar,
fish sauce and tamarind purée or lime juice, and
cook for 2 to 3 minutes or until the sugar has
dissolved. Pour the warm chilli sauce over the fish
and garnish with basil leaves.

Deep-fry the whole floured fish
on one side only, making sure
the oil covers the fish.

Selling vegetables at the floating
market.

FISH Fish caught locally tend to be sold locally, unless caught commercially. The fish market at Ranong deals both in fish caught locally and those found further out to sea. At smaller markets, fresh fish is sold just caught, or even still alive, from buckets and tanks. Market vendors kill and clean the fish as it is sold. Most fish are cooked with the head still on and the cheeks of the fish are considered to be the tastiest parts.

FISH & SEAFOOD

FRESHWATER FISH AND SEAFOOD ARE AN INTEGRAL PART OF THE THAI DIET. AS A FOOD THEY ARE SECOND ONLY TO RICE IN IMPORTANCE. WHILE FRESH SEAFOOD IS EATEN BY MOST PEOPLE ON AN ALMOST DAILY BASIS, FISH SAUCE AND SHRIMP PASTE ARE ALSO PART OF THE THAI LEXICON OF FLAVOURINGS USED IN VIRTUALLY EVERY DISH.

Fish and seafood are caught all over Thailand, along the 2710 kilometres (1685 miles) of coastline, from lakes, inland waterways, ponds and even in amongst rice paddies and in puddles left after storms. Fishing is done by commercial boats, communities and individuals. Wholesale markets at every major port send the catch both abroad and to markets throughout Thailand. Inland, fish is likely to be local freshwater fish, sold at markets with only a tiny amount on offer.

Different areas have particular specialities and marine-based industries. People make their own fish sauce, but commercial operations can be found on the Gulf of Thailand. The Isthmus of Kra and islands are famous for fresh fish and shellfish, grilled (broiled) or barbecued, and Pattaya for crayfish.

Whole cooked fish like these mackerel (top left) can also be bought from most markets. Prawns and shrimp are very popular: tiger prawns (right) are farmed on a large scale and are particularly meaty. Small shrimp are dried and are either ground to a powder or soaked in a liquid before use. Good-quality dried prawns have a deep orange colour, as shown here.

Inland, during April and May, giant catfish are fished from the Mekong in the North. Prawns are farmed in mangroves, though often not to the benefit of the environment or locals.

PRESERVED, DRIED AND FERMENTED SEAFOOD

The majority of what comes out of Thailand's water is dried, preserved or converted to shrimp paste and fish sauce. The sun is used to dry fish, shrimp and squid all along the coast, spread out on mats or on bamboo frames (right). Fish, crabs and shellfish such as mussels are also pickled. Small amounts of preserved or dried fish add lots of flavour and can be used to dress rice or vegetables. Shrimp paste forms the base of dips eaten with fresh vegetables. Dried roast squid, a street snack, is the equivalent of a bag of chips.

FISH SAUCE FACTORY

MAKING FISH SAUCE The Tang Sang Hah factory makes several brands of fish sauce for home and overseas markets. Originally made in ceramic jars (left), fish sauce is now made in concrete tanks. Anchovies are brought to the factory from all over Thailand and mixed with salt before being put into tanks. Each tank is two metres (six feet, six inches) deep and the factory has three thousand tanks. New fish supplies come in every day but the fish shown above (centre) is one month old and has already started to break down. The tanks are covered and the

fish ferments in its own juices, aided by the heat of the sun and preserved by the salt. The fish and juices are mixed as they sit in the tanks and when the fish has fermented for 12 months it has broken down enough for the solids to sink to the bottom of the tank, leaving the fish sauce at the top. The liquid is drawn off from the tanks, then filtered and blended and tested for quality. A small amount of sugar is added to each batch but nothing else. It is then bottled. Fish sauce is sold in different grades and the type of bottle reflects how good it is. Second-

grade fish sauce that is slightly saltier is bottled in larger plastic bottles and, according to the firm, is very popular with noodle vendors who use large amounts of it on a daily basis. Third-grade sauce is also sold in larger plastic bottles. Twelve-month-old premium grade sauce with a good fishy flavour is sold as Tiparos brand and it comes in small glass bottles with gold labels and has a red, blue and white logo (centre right and right). First-grade sauce with a yellow label (left) is the next best.

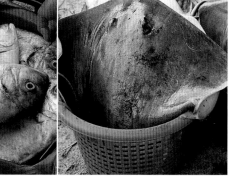

CRABS *(puu)* Crab meat is popular in fried rice dishes and with noodles. Whole crab are often chopped into pieces and fried with curry powder.

SQUID *(plaa meuk kluay)* Squid is eaten both fresh and dried. Fresh squid is usually blanched in boiling water, rather than being fried, to keep it tender.

POMFRET *(plaa-ja-la-met)* This is a good eating fish found all over Asia. Pomfret are particularly good when fried whole and also in curries.

RAY These are caught further off the coast and are not a common fish in Thailand, though they may be found in areas where there is a large fish market.

PRAWNS *(kung)* Tiger prawns are popular in soups, curries and noodle dishes. A prawn (shrimp) dish will be on every Thai menu.

CARP *(plaa tapian)* A favourite in South-East Asia and China, carp are freshwater fish found in local inland markets. Farmed and wild.

TILAPIA *(plaa nin)* Freshwater fish are often farmed, sometimes on a small scale in backyards or ponds. Usually steamed or fried.

CLAMS *(hawy lai)* Clams, eaten in soups and curries, are treated much like oysters with which they share a generic name — *hawy.*

PRESERVED FISH

Salted, dried and pickled fish and seafood are common. As well as keeping efficiently, preserved fish and seafood deliver more flavour. Dried shrimp, often ground, are common. Many varieties are available (far left). Pickled mussels (centre left) are used in stir-fries and salads. Semi-dried fish (centre right) are used in curries, or deep-fried and used in salads. Tiny dried fish (right) are deep-fried and crumbled into dishes.

MEAT & GAME

MUU PING

PORK ON STICKS

JUST LIKE SATAY, PORK ON STICKS IS A POPULAR SNACK AS WELL AS MAKING AN EXCELLENT PARTY FOOD AND IS IDEAL FOR INFORMAL OCCASIONS SUCH AS BARBECUES. IT CAN BE SERVED WITH RICE OR STICKY RICE. NO ADDITIONAL SAUCE IS NECESSARY WITH THIS RECIPE.

The pork is threaded onto skewers using a sewing action.

1 kg (2 lb 4 oz) fillet of pork
250 ml (1 cup) coconut milk
   (page 279)
2 tablespoons coconut sugar
2 tablespoons light soy sauce
2 tablespoons oyster sauce
110 g (4 oz) Asian shallots,
   roughly chopped
4 garlic cloves, roughly chopped
5 coriander (cilantro) roots,
   finely chopped
2.5 cm (1 inch) piece of ginger,
   sliced
1½ teaspoons ground turmeric
¼ teaspoon ground white pepper
25 bamboo skewers, 18–20 cm
   (7–8 inches) long

MAKES 25

CUT the pork into pieces 4 cm (1½ inches) wide x 8 cm (3 inches) long x 5 mm (¼ inch) thick and put them in a bowl.

MIX the coconut milk, sugar, light soy sauce, oyster sauce, shallots, garlic, coriander roots, ginger, turmeric and pepper in a bowl until the sugar has dissolved. Pour over the meat and mix using your fingers or a spoon. Cover with plastic wrap and refrigerate for at least 5 hours, or overnight, turning occasionally.

SOAK the bamboo skewers in water for 1 hour to help prevent them from burning during cooking.

THREAD a piece of the marinated pork onto each skewer as if you were sewing a piece of material. If some pieces are small, thread two pieces onto each stick. Heat a barbecue or grill (broiler) to high heat. If using a grill, line the grill tray with foil.

BARBECUE for 5 to 7 minutes on each side, or grill (broil) the pork for 10 minutes on each side, until cooked through and slightly charred. Turn frequently and brush the marinade sauce over the meat during the cooking. If using the grill, cook a good distance below the heat. Serve hot or warm.

Selling souvenirs in Mae Tang.

MUU YANG

BARBECUED PORK SPARE RIBS

2–3 garlic cloves, chopped
1 tablespoon chopped coriander
  (cilantro) roots or ground coriander
6 tablespoons palm sugar
7 tablespoons plum sauce or
  tomato ketchup
2 tablespoons light soy sauce
2 tablespoons oyster sauce
1 teaspoon ground pepper
½ teaspoon ground star anise
  (optional)
900 g (2 lb) pork spare ribs,
  chopped into 13–15 cm
  (5–6 inch) long pieces (baby
  back, if possible — ask your
  butcher to prepare it)

SERVES 4

USING a pestle and mortar or a small blender, pound or blend the garlic and coriander roots into a paste. In a large bowl, combine all the ingredients and rub the marinade all over the ribs with your fingers. Cover with plastic wrap and marinate in the refrigerator for at least 3 hours, or overnight.

PREHEAT the oven to 180°C/350°F/Gas 4 or heat a barbecue or grill (broiler). If cooking in the oven, place the ribs with all the marinade in a baking dish. Bake for 45 to 60 minutes, basting several times during cooking. If barbecuing, put the ribs on the grill, cover and cook for 45 minutes, turning and basting a couple of times. If the ribs do not go sufficiently brown, grill (broil) them for 5 minutes on each side until well browned and slightly charred. If using a grill, line the grill tray with foil. Cook the pork, turning several times and brushing frequently with the remaining sauce, until the meat is cooked through and slightly charred.

MUU THAWT

DEEP-FRIED PORK SPARE RIBS

5 coriander (cilantro) roots, chopped
3 garlic cloves, finely chopped
1 tablespoon fish sauce
1½ tablespoons oyster sauce
½ teaspoon ground white pepper
900 g (2 lb) pork spare ribs,
  chopped into 4–5 cm
  (1½–2 inch) long pieces (baby
  back, if possible—ask your
  butcher to prepare it)
vegetable oil, for deep-frying
sweet chilli sauce (page 284),
  to serve

SERVES 4

USING a pestle and mortar or a small blender, pound or blend the coriander roots and garlic into a paste. In a large bowl, combine the coriander paste, fish sauce, oyster sauce and ground pepper. Rub the marinade into the pork ribs using your fingertips, then cover and marinate in the refrigerator for at least 3 hours, or overnight.

HEAT 6 cm (2½ inches) oil in a wok or deep frying pan over a medium heat. When the oil seems hot, drop a small piece of garlic into it. If it sizzles immediately, the oil is ready. It is important not to have the oil too hot or the spare ribs will burn. Deep-fry half the spare ribs at a time for 15 to 20 minutes or until golden brown and cooked. Drain on paper towels. Serve with sweet chilli sauce.

DEEP-FRIED PORK SPARE RIBS

BARBECUED PORK SPARE RIBS

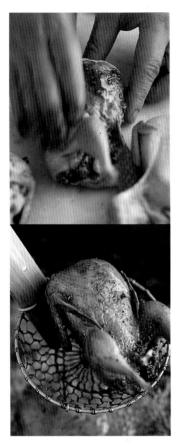

Cover the quails with the paste,
then marinate them. Remove the
cooked quail from the oil with a
slotted spoon.

NOK GRADTAA THAWT
DEEP-FRIED QUAIL

QUAIL WORKS WELL FOR DISHES THAT WOULD PROBABLY TRADITIONALLY HAVE USED PIGEON OR
TURTLE DOVE. CHICKEN PIECES CAN ALSO BE USED BUT THE QUAILS LOOK MORE ATTRACTIVE ON
THE PLATE. SERVE ALONGSIDE VEGETABLE DISHES OR USE AS A STARTER.

5 white peppercorns
5 coriander seeds
¼ teaspoon cumin seeds
1 star anise
2 garlic cloves
2 tablespoons soy sauce
½ teaspoon palm sugar
4 quails
oil, for deep-frying
roasted chilli sauce (page 283) or
    sweet chilli sauce (page 284),
    to serve

SERVES 4

USING a pestle and mortar, pound together the
peppercorns, coriander seeds, cumin seeds, star
anise and a pinch of salt. Add the garlic, soy
sauce and palm sugar and pound to a paste.

RUB the paste all over the quails, cover and
marinate in the refrigerator for at least 3 hours.

HEAT the oil in a wok until a piece of bread
dropped into it sizzles and turns brown. Pat the
quails dry with paper towels. Add the quails and
fry them for about 10 minutes, turning them so
that they cook on all sides. Make sure the oil gets
inside the quails as well.

DRAIN well and sprinkle with a little more salt.
Cut into quarters and serve with roasted chilli
sauce or sweet chilli sauce.

MUU WAAN
CARAMEL PORK

CARAMEL PORK HAS A RELATIVELY SWEET FLAVOUR AND IS BEST SERVED WITH STEAMED JASMINE RICE OR STICKY RICE AND A SHARP-FLAVOURED DISH LIKE GREEN PAPAYA SALAD OR POMELO SALAD. CARAMEL PORK WILL KEEP FOR A FEW DAYS IN THE REFRIGERATOR AND CAN BE MADE IN ADVANCE.

vegetable oil, for deep-frying
75 g (3 oz) Asian shallots, finely sliced
6 garlic cloves, finely chopped
500 g (1 lb 2 oz) shoulder or leg of pork, cut into thin slices
1 tablespoon oyster sauce
1 tablespoon light soy sauce
1 tablespoon fish sauce
4 tablespoons palm sugar
¼ teaspoon ground white pepper

SERVES 4

Palm sugar on sale.

HEAT 5 cm (2 inches) oil in a deep saucepan or wok over a medium heat and deep-fry the shallots until they are golden brown. Be careful not to burn them. Remove them from the wok with a slotted spoon and drain on paper towels.

DRAIN the oil from the saucepan or wok, leaving 2 tablespoons in the pan. Stir-fry the garlic in the oil until light brown, then add the pork and stir-fry for a few minutes. Add the oyster sauce, light soy sauce, fish sauce, sugar and ground pepper and continue cooking for about 5 minutes, or until all the liquid has evaporated and the mixture forms a thick sticky sauce.

SPOON onto a serving plate and sprinkle with the crispy shallots. Serve as required.

MUU PARLOW
BRAISED PORK

1 large pork hock or 2 small ones
oil, for deep-frying
2 coriander (cilantro) roots, chopped
4 garlic cloves, crushed
2 teaspoons ground white pepper
4 slices of ginger
2 star anise
1 cinnamon stick
2 tablespoons palm sugar
2 tablespoons fish sauce
2 tablespoons ketchap manis
1.5 litres (6 cups) chicken stock
4 hard-boiled eggs, shells removed

SERVES 4

BRAISED PORK

PUT the pork hock in a saucepan of salted water and bring to the boil. Drain and repeat, then pat dry with paper towels. Heat a wok one-quarter filled with oil until the oil is very hot. Carefully add the dried pork hock to the wok and fry on all sides until brown. Loosely cover the wok with a lid if the oil spits too much. Remove the hock and drain away all but a tablespoon of the oil.

FRY the coriander roots, garlic and pepper briefly, then add the ginger, star anise and cinnamon stick and fry for a minute. Add the palm sugar, fish sauce, ketchap manis and stock and bring to a boil. Add the hock and cook for 2 hours or until the hock meat starts to fall off the bone. Add the eggs and cook for 10 minutes. Season with salt and serve with jasmine rice.

DRIED BEEF

NEUA HAENG
DRIED BEEF

coriander (cilantro) roots from
  1 bunch, finely chopped
1 teaspoon cumin seeds, roasted
2 teaspoons coriander seeds,
  roasted
4 garlic cloves
1 teaspoon white peppercorns
2 tablespoons palm sugar
2 tablespoons soy sauce
350 g (12 oz) rump steak,
  thinly sliced
oil, for deep-frying
sticky rice (page 280), to serve
a chilli sauce, to serve

SERVES 6

USING a pestle and mortar, pound together the coriander roots, cumin seeds, coriander seeds, garlic, peppercorns and a pinch of salt into a paste. Add the palm sugar and soy sauce and mix until the sugar dissolves. Add the steak and mix. Cover and marinate in the refrigerator overnight.

PREHEAT the oven to its lowest setting. Take the steak strips out of the marinade and drape them over wire cooling racks. Dry the steak strips in the oven for about 4 hours. They should be dry and leathery when they are ready.

IF THE beef is not crisp, heat some oil for deep-frying in a wok. Drop a small piece of steak into the oil and if it sizzles immediately, the oil is ready. Deep-fry the steak in batches until crisp, then drain on paper towels. Serve with sticky rice and chilli sauce.

Chickens spit-roasted by the roadside.

KAI YAANG
GRILLED CHICKEN

IN THAILAND, THESE WHOLE GRILLED CHICKEN ARE SEEN BY THE ROADSIDE ROTATING ON OPEN SPITS. THAI CHICKENS ARE LEANER THAN THOSE FOUND IN WESTERN COUNTRIES BUT THE TASTE WILL BE SIMILAR. THERE ARE MANY FLAVOURING VARIATIONS USED FOR GRILLED CHICKENS.

MARINADE
4 coriander (cilantro) roots,
  finely chopped
4 garlic cloves, finely chopped
1 lemon grass stalk, white part only,
  finely chopped
3 tablespoons fish sauce
¼ teaspoon ground white pepper
1 teaspoon palm sugar

1 chicken, spatchcocked
sweet chilli sauce (page 284),
  to serve
lime wedges, to serve

SERVES 4

USING a pestle and mortar, pound the marinade ingredients together, then spoon into a bowl. Add the chicken and rub the marinade all over the chicken skin. Cover and marinate in the refrigerator for at least 3 hours, or overnight.

HEAT a barbecue, char-grill or grill (broiler) until very hot. Cook the chicken for 20 to 30 minutes, turning it over at regular intervals.

CUT the chicken into pieces and serve with sweet chilli sauce and lime wedges.

CURRIES

The fruit is added towards the end of cooking.

KAENG PLAA KUP KLUAY LAI MAMUANG

SNAPPER WITH GREEN BANANA AND MANGO

GREEN BANANA IS VERY STARCHY, MUCH MORE LIKE A VEGETABLE THAN A FRUIT. HERE IT USED IN A YELLOW CURRY ALONGSIDE ANOTHER FRUIT, GREEN MANGO, WHICH ACTS AS A SOURING AGENT. RAW VEGETABLES ARE OFTEN SERVED AS AN ACCOMPANIMENT TO COUNTERACT THE CHILLI HEAT.

1 teaspoon salt
1 teaspoon ground turmeric
1 small green banana or plantain,
    thinly sliced
60 ml (¼ cup) coconut cream
    (page 279)
2 tablespoons yellow curry paste
    (page 275) or bought paste
1 tablespoon fish sauce
1 teaspoon palm sugar
400 g (14 oz) snapper or other
    white fish fillets, cut into
    large cubes
315 ml (1¼ cups) coconut milk
    (page 279)
1 small green mango, cut into
    thin slices
1 large green chilli, finely sliced
12 Thai sweet basil leaves

SERVES 4

BRING a small saucepan of water to the boil. Add the salt, turmeric and banana slices and simmer for 10 minutes, then drain.

PUT the coconut cream in a wok or saucepan and simmer over a medium heat for about 5 minutes, or until the cream separates and a layer of oil forms on the surface. Stir the cream if it starts to brown around the edges. Add the curry paste, stir well to combine and cook until fragrant. Add the fish sauce and sugar and cook for another 2 minutes or until the mixture begins to darken.

ADD the fish pieces and stir well to coat the fish in the curry mixture. Slowly add the coconut milk until it has all been incorporated.

ADD the banana, mango, green chilli and most of the basil leaves to the pan and gently stir to combine all the ingredients, cooking for a minute or two. Garnish with the remaining basil.

Green mangoes.

KAENG PHANAENG KUNG

PRAWNS WITH THAI SWEET BASIL LEAVES

THE SAUCE FOR THIS DISH SHOULD BE THICK, HOT AND SWEET SO MAKE SURE YOUR WOK IS HOT

ENOUGH TO REDUCE THE COCONUT MILK AS IT HITS THE SURFACE.

600 g (1 lb 5 oz) raw prawns
  (shrimp)
2 tablespoons vegetable oil
2 tablespoons dry curry paste
  (page 272) or bought paste
185 ml (¾ cup) coconut milk
  (page 279)
2 teaspoons fish sauce
2 teaspoons palm sugar
a handful of Thai sweet basil leaves,
  for garnish
1 long red chilli, seeded and finely
  sliced, for garnish

SERVES 4

PEEL and devein the prawns and cut each prawn along the back so it opens like a butterfly (leave each prawn joined along the base and at the tail, leaving the tail attached).

HEAT the oil in a saucepan or wok and stir-fry the dry curry paste over a medium heat for 2 minutes or until fragrant.

ADD the coconut milk, fish sauce and palm sugar and cook for a few seconds. Add the prawns and cook for a few minutes or until the prawns are cooked through. Taste, then adjust the seasoning if necessary. Spoon into a serving bowl and garnish with basil leaves and chillies.

KAENG KUNG

PRAWN AND PINEAPPLE CURRY

SPICE PASTE
4 bird's eye chillies, seeded
6 Asian shallots
2 lemon grass stalks, white part
  only, finely chopped
½ teaspoon shrimp paste
½ teaspoon ground turmeric

2 tablespoons oil
185 ml (¾ cup) coconut milk
  (page 279)
300 g (10 oz) fresh pineapple,
  cut into small wedges
2 tablespoons tamarind purée
3 makrut (kaffir) lime leaves
250 g (9 oz) raw prawns (shrimp),
  peeled and deveined
2 teaspoons fish sauce
1 tablespoon palm sugar

SERVES 4

PUT all the spice paste ingredients in a pestle and mortar and pound to a paste. Alternatively, use a food processor and add 2 tablespoons water. Blend until well combined.

HEAT the oil in a wok or saucepan. Add the spice paste and fry until fragrant. Stir in the coconut milk and cook for 2 minutes. Add the pineapple wedges, tamarind purée and makrut lime leaves and simmer for 5 minutes, or until the pineapple begins to soften.

ADD the prawns and stir well to cover them in the sauce. Simmer for 5 to 6 minutes until the prawns are cooked through. Stir in the fish sauce and sugar before serving.

PRAWN AND PINEAPPLE
CURRY

As soon as the curry paste is fragrant, stir in the pork, Asian shallots, ginger and peanuts.

Songathews and tuk tuks in Chiang Mai.

KAENG HANGLEH MUU

CHIANG MAI PORK CURRY

THIS BURMESE-STYLE CURRY IS TYPICAL OF THE CHIANG MAI AREA. UNLIKE FRAGRANT THAI CURRIES, THIS HAS A SPICIER, ALMOST INDIAN FLAVOUR. NEARLY ALWAYS MADE WITH PORK, YOU WILL OCCASIONALLY FIND IT MADE WITH CHICKEN. THIS CURRY IMPROVES IF MADE IN ADVANCE.

500 g (1 lb 2 oz) pork belly, cut into cubes
2 tablespoons oil
2 garlic cloves, crushed
2 tablespoons Chiang Mai curry paste (page 272) or bought paste
4 Asian shallots, smashed with the blade of a cleaver
4 cm (1½ inch) piece of ginger, shredded
4 tablespoons roasted unsalted peanuts
3 tablespoons tamarind purée
2 tablespoons fish sauce
2 tablespoons palm sugar

SERVES 4

BLANCH the pork cubes in boiling water for 1 minute, then drain well.

HEAT the oil in a wok or saucepan and fry the garlic for 1 minute. Add the curry paste and stir-fry until fragrant. Add the pork, shallots, ginger and peanuts and stir briefly. Add 500 ml (2 cups) water and the tamarind purée and bring to a boil.

ADD the fish sauce and sugar and simmer for about 1½ hours or until the pork is very tender. Add more water as the pork cooks, if necessary. The meat is ready when it is very tender.

KAENG MUU PHRIK THAI ORN

RED PORK CURRY WITH GREEN PEPPERCORNS

PEPPERCORNS ADD A DISTINCTIVE, VERY FRESH AND SPICY, NOT TOO HOT, TASTE TO THIS DISH. YOU CAN USE PORK, AS SUGGESTED, OR FINELY SLICED CHICKEN THIGH FILLETS. COOKED BABY POTATOES AND BAMBOO SHOOTS ARE A POPULAR ADDITION TO THIS CURRY.

60 ml (¼ cup) coconut cream
(page 279)
2 tablespoons red curry paste
(page 276) or bought paste
3 tablespoons fish sauce
1½ tablespoons palm sugar
500 g (1 lb 2 oz) lean pork,
finely sliced
440 ml (1¾ cups) coconut milk
(page 279)
280 g (10 oz) Thai eggplants
(aubergines), cut in halves
or quarters, or 1 eggplant
(aubergine), cubed
75 g (3 oz) fresh green
peppercorns, cleaned
7 makrut (kaffir) lime leaves,
torn in half
2 long red chillies, seeded
and finely sliced, for garnish

SERVES 4

PUT the coconut cream in a wok or saucepan and simmer over a medium heat for about 5 minutes, or until the cream separates and a layer of oil forms on the surface. Stir the cream if it starts to brown around the edges.

ADD the curry paste, stir well to combine and cook until fragrant. Add the fish sauce and palm sugar and cook for another 2 minutes or until the mixture begins to darken. Add the pork and stir for 5 to 7 minutes.

ADD the coconut milk to the saucepan or wok and simmer over a medium heat for another 5 minutes. Add the eggplants and green peppercorns and cook for 5 minutes. Add the makrut lime leaves. Taste, then adjust the seasoning if necessary. Transfer to a serving bowl and sprinkle with the chillies.

Stir-fry the curry paste to bring out the flavour before adding the rest of the ingredients.

KAENG PAA

JUNGLE CURRY WITH PRAWNS

JUNGLE CURRY, A VERY HOT CURRY, IS COMMON TO THE COUNTRYSIDE, PARTICULARLY IN NORTHERN THAILAND. IT IS TRADITIONALLY MADE WITH LOCAL CATFISH BUT WORKS WELL WITH ANY FISH, OR WITH PRAWNS AS IN THIS RECIPE. IT CAN BE MADE WITH PORK AND MOST FRESH VEGETABLES.

JUNGLE CURRY PASTE
8 bird's eye chillies, chopped
2 cm (¾ inch) piece of galangal, chopped
2 lemon grass stalks, white part only, finely chopped
4 Asian shallots, finely chopped
4 garlic cloves, finely sliced
½ teaspoon shrimp paste

400 g (14 oz) raw prawns (shrimp)
1 tablespoon oil
4 baby sweet corn, each cut into half lengthways on an angle
75 g (3 oz) Thai eggplants (aubergines), cut in halves or quarters
50 g (2 oz) pea eggplants (aubergines)
50 g (2 oz) straw or button mushrooms, halved if large
1 tablespoon fish sauce
½ teaspoon palm sugar
2–3 makrut (kaffir) lime leaves, torn into pieces, for garnish
a handful of holy basil or Thai sweet basil leaves, for garnish

SERVES 4

PUT all the jungle curry paste ingredients in a pestle and mortar and pound until smooth. Alternatively, put them in a food processor with 2 tablespoons water and process to a smooth paste.

PEEL and devein the prawns and cut each prawn along the back so it opens like a butterfly (leave each prawn joined along the base and at the tail).

HEAT the oil in a wok or saucepan and stir-fry 2 tablespoons of the curry paste until fragrant. Add 410 ml (1⅔ cups) water and reduce the heat to medium. Add the sweet corn and eggplants and cook for 1 to 2 minutes. Add the mushrooms and prawns, fish sauce and sugar. Cook until the prawns open and turn pink. Taste, then adjust the seasoning if necessary. Sprinkle with the makrut lime leaves and basil leaves before serving.

KAENG MATSAMAN NEUA
MASSAMAN CURRY WITH BEEF

THIS CURRY HAS MANY CHARACTERISTICS OF SOUTHERN THAI COOKING. THE SWEET FLAVOURS AND SPICES DOMINATE, EVEN THOUGH THE CURRY IS MODERATELY HOT. IT ALSO HAS A SOUR TASTE FROM THE TAMARIND. THIS DISH IS ONE OF THE FEW THAI DISHES WITH POTATOES AND PEANUTS.

2 pieces of cinnamon stick
10 cardamom seeds
5 cloves
2 tablespoons vegetable oil
2 tablespoons massaman curry
   paste (page 276) or bought paste
800 g (1 lb 12 oz) beef flank or
   rump steak, cut into 5 cm (2 inch)
   cubes
410 ml (1⅔ cups) coconut milk
   (page 279)
250 ml (1 cup) beef stock
2–3 potatoes, cut into 2.5 cm
   (1 inch) pieces
2 cm (¾ inch) piece of ginger,
   shredded
3 tablespoons fish sauce
3 tablespoons palm sugar
110 g (⅔ cup) ready-made roasted
   salted peanuts, without skin
3 tablespoons tamarind purée

SERVES 4

DRY-FRY the cinnamon stick, cardamom seeds and cloves in a saucepan or wok over a low heat. Stir all the ingredients around for 2 to 3 minutes or until fragrant. Remove from the pan.

HEAT the oil in the same saucepan or wok and stir-fry the massaman paste over a medium heat for 2 minutes or until fragrant.

ADD the beef to the pan and stir for 5 minutes. Add the coconut milk, stock, potatoes, ginger, fish sauce, palm sugar, three-quarters of the roasted peanuts, tamarind purée and the dry-fried spices. Reduce the heat to low and gently simmer for 50 to 60 minutes until the meat is tender and the potatoes are just cooked. Taste, then adjust the seasoning if necessary. Spoon into a serving bowl and garnish with the rest of the roasted peanuts.

Floating vendor.

As with many Thai curries, this one cooks relatively quickly. Keep the meat moving around the wok until you add the liquid.

PANAENG BEEF CURRY

PANAENG CURRY IS A DRY, RICH, THICK CURRY MADE WITH SMALL AMOUNTS OF COCONUT MILK AND A DRY (PANAENG) CURRY PASTE, WHICH HAS RED CHILLIES, LEMON GRASS, GALANGAL AND PEANUTS. IT IS NOT TOO HOT AND HAS A SWEET AND SOUR TASTE. YOU CAN USE ANY TENDER CUT OF BEEF.

2 tablespoons vegetable oil
2 tablespoons dry curry paste
   (page 272) or bought paste
700 g (1 lb 9 oz) beef flank steak,
   sliced into strips
185 ml (¾ cup) coconut milk
   (page 279)
1 tablespoon fish sauce
1 tablespoon palm sugar
3 tablespoons tamarind purée
2 makrut (kaffir) lime leaves, finely
   sliced, for garnish
½ long red chilli, seeded and finely
   sliced, for garnish
cucumber relish (page 287),
   to serve

SERVES 4

HEAT the oil in a saucepan or wok and stir-fry the curry paste over a medium heat for 2 minutes or until fragrant.

ADD the beef and stir for 5 minutes. Add nearly all of the coconut milk, the fish sauce, palm sugar and tamarind purée and reduce to a low heat. Simmer, uncovered, for 5 to 7 minutes. Although this is meant to be a dry curry, you can add a little more water during cooking if you feel it is drying out too much. Taste, then adjust the seasoning if necessary.

SPOON the curry into a serving bowl, spoon the last bit of coconut milk over the top and sprinkle with makrut lime leaves and chilli slices. Serve with cucumber relish.

Busy bustling Bangkok.

KAENG KHIAW-WAAN KAI

GREEN CURRY WITH CHICKEN

THIS FAMILIAR CLASSIC, WHICH SHOULD NEVER BE EXTREMELY HOT, HAS AS ITS BASE A PASTE OF CHILLIES, GALANGAL AND LEMON GRASS. BITTER VEGETABLES SUCH AS THAI EGGPLANT OFFSET THE SWEETNESS OF THE COCONUT CREAM. TENDER STEAK CAN BE USED INSTEAD OF CHICKEN.

60 ml (¼ cup) coconut cream
  (page 279)
2 tablespoons green curry paste
  (page 275) or bought paste
350 g (12 oz) skinless chicken thigh
  fillets, sliced
440 ml (1¾ cups) coconut milk
  (page 279)
2½ tablespoons fish sauce
1 tablespoon palm sugar
350 g (12 oz) mixed Thai eggplants
  (aubergines), cut into quarters,
  and pea eggplants (aubergines)
50 g (2 oz) galangal, julienned
7 makrut (kaffir) lime leaves,
  torn in half
a handful of Thai sweet basil leaves,
  for garnish
1 long red chilli, seeded and finely
  sliced, for garnish

SERVES 4

PUT the coconut cream in a wok or saucepan and simmer over a medium heat for about 5 minutes, or until the cream separates and a layer of oil forms on the surface. Stir the cream if it starts to brown around the edges. Add the curry paste, stir well to combine and cook until fragrant.

ADD the chicken and stir for a few minutes. Add nearly all of the coconut milk, the fish sauce and palm sugar and simmer over a medium heat for another 5 minutes.

ADD the eggplants and cook, stirring occasionally, for about 5 minutes or until the eggplants are cooked. Add the galangal and makrut lime leaves. Taste, then adjust the seasoning if necessary. Spoon into a serving bowl and sprinkle with the last bit of coconut milk, as well as the basil leaves and chilli slices.

Various types of eggplant are used in Thailand and the bitter taste is very popular. They don't take long to cook.

Shrimp paste on sale.

KAENG KARII KAI

YELLOW CHICKEN CURRY WITH PEPPERCORNS

FRESH PEPPERCORNS HAVE A FRAGRANT, PUNGENT QUALITY THAT LIFTS THE FLAVOUR OF ANY CURRY IN WHICH THEY ARE USED. YOU SHOULD BEWARE OF EATING A WHOLE SPRIG IN ONE GO THOUGH AS, JUST LIKE THE PEPPER THEY BECOME, THEY ARE EXTREMELY HOT.

60 ml (¼ cup) coconut cream
  (page 279)
2 tablespoons yellow curry paste
  (page 275) or bought paste
1 tablespoon fish sauce
2 teaspoons palm sugar
¼ teaspoon turmeric
600 g (1 lb 5 oz) chicken thigh
  fillets, cut into thin slices
440 ml (1¾ cups) coconut milk
  (page 279)
100 g (3 oz) bamboo shoots,
  thinly sliced
4 sprigs fresh green peppercorns
4–6 makrut (kaffir) lime leaves
12 Thai sweet basil leaves

SERVES 4

PUT the coconut cream in a wok or saucepan and simmer over a medium heat for about 5 minutes, or until the cream separates and a layer of oil forms on the surface. Stir the cream if it starts to brown around the edges.

ADD the curry paste, stir well to combine and cook until fragrant. Add the fish sauce, palm sugar and turmeric and stir well. Cook for 2 to 3 minutes, stirring occasionally, until the mixture darkens.

ADD the chicken to the pan and stir to coat all the pieces evenly in the spice mixture. Cook over a medium heat for 5 minutes, stirring occasionally and adding the coconut milk a tablespoon at a time to incorporate. Add the bamboo shoots, peppercorns, lime and basil leaves and cook for another 5 minutes.

RED CURRY WITH FISH AND BAMBOO SHOOTS

ALTHOUGH THERE ARE MANY STYLES IN THE LARGE RANGE OF THAI RED CURRIES, ALL HAVE THE DEFINING CHARACTERISTIC RED COLOUR. RED CURRIES ARE QUITE LIQUID COMPARED TO DRY CURRIES SUCH AS PANAENG. BE SURE TO USE A FIRM FISH THAT WON'T FALL APART.

The fish should be cut into bite-sized pieces and the bamboo shoots into matchsticks.

60 ml (¼ cup) coconut cream (page 279)

2 tablespoons red curry paste (page 276) or bought paste

440 ml (1¾ cups) coconut milk (page 279)

1½–2 tablespoons palm sugar

3 tablespoons fish sauce

350 g (12 oz) skinless firm white fish fillets, cut into 3 cm (1¼ inch) cubes

275 g (10 oz) tin bamboo shoots in water, drained, cut into matchsticks

50 g (2 oz) galangal, finely sliced

5 makrut (kaffir) lime leaves, torn in half

a handful of Thai sweet basil leaves, for garnish

1 long red chilli, seeded and finely sliced, for garnish

SERVES 4

PUT the coconut cream in a wok or saucepan and simmer over a medium heat for about 5 minutes, or until the cream separates and a layer of oil forms on the surface. Stir the cream if it starts to brown around the edges. Add the curry paste, stir well to combine and cook until fragrant.

STIR in the coconut milk, then add the sugar and fish sauce and cook for 2 to 3 minutes. Add the fish and bamboo shoots and simmer for about 5 minutes, stirring occasionally, until the fish is cooked.

ADD the galangal and makrut lime leaves. Taste, then adjust the seasoning if necessary. Spoon onto a serving plate and sprinkle with the basil leaves and sliced chilli.

This curry, with its combination of coconut milk, duck and fruit, is very rich. Cook the lychees for only a few minutes.

RED CURRY WITH ROASTED DUCK AND LYCHEES

IN THAILAND, THIS SPECIALITY DISH IS OFTEN SERVED DURING THE TRADITIONAL FAMILY FEASTING THAT ACCOMPANIES CELEBRATIONS INCLUDING THE ORDINATION OF BUDDHIST MONKS, WEDDINGS AND NEW YEAR. THIS IS VERY RICH, SO SERVE IT ALONGSIDE A SALAD TO CUT THROUGH THE SAUCE.

60 ml (¼ cup) coconut cream
  (page 279)
2 tablespoons red curry paste
  (page 276) or bought paste
½ roasted duck, boned and
  chopped
440 ml (1¾ cups) coconut milk
  (page 279)
2 tablespoons fish sauce
1 tablespoon palm sugar
225 g (8 oz) tin lychees, drained
110 g (4 oz) baby tomatoes
7 makrut (kaffir) lime leaves,
  torn in half
a handful of Thai sweet basil leaves,
  for garnish
1 long red chilli, seeded and
  finely sliced, for garnish

SERVES 4

PUT the coconut cream in a wok or saucepan and simmer over a medium heat for about 5 minutes, or until the cream separates and a layer of oil forms on the surface. Stir the cream if it starts to brown around the edges. Add the curry paste, stir well to combine and cook until fragrant.

ADD the roasted duck and stir for 5 minutes. Add the coconut milk, fish sauce and palm sugar and simmer over a medium heat for another 5 minutes. Add the lychees and baby tomatoes and cook for 1 to 2 minutes. Add the makrut lime leaves. Taste, then adjust the seasoning if necessary. Spoon into a serving bowl and sprinkle with the basil leaves and sliced chilli.

KAENG KUNG MANGKAWN
SPICY LOBSTER AND PINEAPPLE CURRY

EVEN THOUGH THIS RED CURRY IS EXPENSIVE BECAUSE OF THE LOBSTER, IT IS EXCELLENT FOR SPECIAL OCCASIONS. YOU CAN USE LARGE PRAWNS OR CRAB HALVES IF YOU LIKE. ALSO, YOU CAN MAKE THE SAUCE AND SERVE IT WITH BARBECUED LOBSTER HALVES.

60 ml (¼ cup) coconut cream
    (page 279)
2 tablespoons red curry paste
    (page 276) or bought paste
1 tablespoon fish sauce
1 tablespoon palm sugar
250 ml (1 cup) coconut milk
    (page 279)
200 g (7 oz) fresh pineapple,
    cut into bite-sized wedges
300 g (10 oz) lobster tail meat
3 makrut (kaffir) lime leaves,
    2 roughly torn and 1 shredded
1 tablespoon tamarind purée
50 g (1 cup) Thai sweet basil
    leaves, for garnish
1 large red chilli, finely sliced,
    for garnish

SERVES 4

PUT the coconut cream in a wok or saucepan and simmer over a medium heat for about 5 minutes, or until the cream separates and a layer of oil forms on the surface. Stir the cream if it starts to brown around the edges.

ADD the curry paste, stir well to combine and cook until fragrant. Add the fish sauce and sugar and stir to combine. Cook for 4 to 5 minutes, stirring constantly. The mixture should darken.

STIR in the coconut milk and the pineapple. Simmer for 6 to 8 minutes to soften the pineapple. Add the lobster tail meat, makrut lime leaves, tamarind purée and basil leaves. Cook for another 5 to 6 minutes until the lobster is firm. Serve with basil leaves and sliced chilli on top.

When the mixture has darkened, stir in the pineapple pieces.

Beaches in Khao Sok National Park.

Use wet hands to roll the fish mixture into balls. Drop them all into the curry at the same time so they cook evenly.

GREEN CURRY WITH FISH BALLS

THIS IS A CLASSIC DISH USING FISH BALLS OR DUMPLINGS RATHER THAN PIECES OF FISH BUT, IF TIME IS SHORT, SLICES OF FISH ARE PERFECTLY ACCEPTABLE. THE FISH IS PROCESSED, THEN POUNDED, TO GIVE IT MORE TEXTURE. SERVE WITH SALTED EGGS, PAGE 287, AND RICE.

350 g (12 oz) white fish fillets,
    without skin and bone,
    roughly cut into pieces
60 ml (¼ cup) coconut cream
    (page 279)
2 tablespoons green curry paste
    (page 275) or bought paste
440 ml (1¾ cups) coconut milk
    (page 279)
350 g (12 oz) mixed Thai eggplants
    (aubergines), quartered, and
    pea eggplants (aubergines)
2 tablespoons fish sauce
2 tablespoons palm sugar
50 g (2 oz) galangal, finely sliced
3 makrut (kaffir) lime leaves,
    torn in half
a handful of holy basil leaves,
    for garnish
½ long red chilli, seeded and
    finely sliced, for garnish

SERVES 4

IN a food processor or a blender, chop the fish fillets into a smooth paste. (If you have a pestle and mortar, pound the fish paste for another 10 minutes to give it a chewy texture.)

PUT the coconut cream in a wok or saucepan and simmer over a medium heat for about 5 minutes, or until the cream separates and a layer of oil forms on the surface. Stir the cream if it starts to brown around the edges. Add the curry paste, stir well to combine and cook until fragrant. Add nearly all of the coconut milk and mix well.

USE a spoon or your wet hands to shape the fish paste into small balls or discs, about 2 cm (¾ inch) across, and drop them into the coconut milk. Add the eggplants, fish sauce and sugar and cook for 12 to 15 minutes, stirring occasionally, until the fish and eggplants are cooked.

STIR in the galangal and makrut lime leaves. Taste, then adjust the seasoning if necessary. Spoon into a serving bowl and sprinkle with the last bit of coconut milk, basil leaves and sliced chilli.

CURRY PASTES (*khreuang kaeng*) are made at home using a granite pestle and mortar. Dry-roasted coriander seeds, black pepper and cumin make up a base. These are finely ground together first. Next, the fresh ingredients are prepared, here by Sompon Nabnian: whole green 'sky-pointing' chillies, chopped galangal, sliced fresh turmeric, sliced lemon grass stalks and Thai sweet basil leaves (stalks removed).

FLAVOURINGS

THAI CUISINE IS BUILT ON A LARGE NUMBER OF HIGHLY FLAVOURED AROMATIC INGREDIENTS. THESE ARE USED, DESPITE THEIR DIVERSITY, TO PRODUCE AN OVERALL EFFECT OF SOME SOPHISTICATION, BALANCE AND SUBTLTY.

Though curry pastes often include dry spices, the majority of Thai seasonings are fresh and pungent. These define the flavour that is 'Thai', as well as being responsible for adding texture to dishes. Thai flavourings are used to give as harmonious effect as possible, the balance of hot, sour, sweet and salty being paramount. Also important is fragrance.

HOT (*phed*) Heat, in nearly all cases, comes from chillies, though it is sometimes supplemented with fresh green peppercorns or black or white pepper. There are about a dozen chillies used in Thai cuisine, each type with a different aroma, flavour, and degree of heat (see page 174). Chillies are used fresh or dried, depending on the recipe.

SOUR (*priaw*) Sour comes from lime juice, the zest and leaves of makrut (kaffir) limes, tamarind, and to a lesser extent, ambarella (a South-East Asian fruit like a small mango). Sour can also come from coconut vinegar or pickles.

SWEET (*waan*) Sweetness is imparted by the use of palm sugar, coconut sugar, cane sugar and coconut milk.

SALTY (*khem*) Fish sauce and shrimp paste add saltiness to a dish. Salt itself is used as an ingredient but never as a condiment, except when sprinkled on fresh fruit.

COMMERCIAL CURRY PASTES These pastes, shown here at the Valcom factory, are made in the same way a homemade paste would be, except on a larger scale. Fresh ingredients such as garlic, shallots, galangal, chillies and lemon grass are peeled and then washed. These are then mixed with spices and herbs in a large bin before being fed into a large mincer. The paste is minced two or three times, depending on

The fresh ingredients are put into a pestle and mortar along with some shrimp paste, coriander (cilantro) root, garlic, makrut (kaffir) lime zest and tamarind, then pounded for about 15 minutes until the paste is smooth. Handmade curry pastes have a more intense flavour than those made by machine because the ingredients are crushed rather than chopped. A heavy Thai granite pestle and mortar makes pounding easier.

FRAGRANCE

The aroma of various herbs, vegetables, rhizomes and leaves add a unique quality to Thai dishes. Robust herbs and roots such as lemon grass, ginger, galangal, turmeric, Chinese keys and coriander (cilantro) roots are used to make pastes and can be cooked for a reasonable length of time. Garlic and shallots are also important and they are often simply smashed with the blade of a cleaver rather then being peeled and finely chopped. Leaf herbs such as coriander (cilantro), Thai sweet basil, lemon and holy basil, and common mint occur frequently. Less well known herbs include long-leaf coriander *(phak chii)*. These are at their most aromatic when eaten raw, or cooked for the bare minimum of time. Sprigs of fresh herbs such as mint *(sa-ra-nae)* and Thai sweet basil *(bai horapha)* are also eaten alongside some dishes. Fragrant pandanus leaves are used as a wrapping and as a flavouring. They are said to have a vanilla flavour, and green pandanus essence is used much like vanilla essence in many sweets.

the label it is to be sold under, and it gets finer each time. The paste is then heated to pasteurize it before being put into sterilized bottles and labelled. Commercial curry pastes such as this are mainly sold abroad though some of them are used within Thailand, especially as supermarket, rather than market, shopping becomes more popular. Valcom make red, green, massaman and tom yam pastes.

CHILLIES *(phrik)* Up to a dozen types of chilli appear in Thai cuisine despite the fact that the plant is not indigenous to the area. Chillies add both colour and flavour to dishes. From left to right, bottom row: red chillies *(phrik chinda)*, named after their growing area; green and red 'bird's eye' or 'mouse dropping' *(phrik khii nuu)* chillies, the hottest chilli available in Thailand; 'sky-pointing' chillies *(phrik chii faa)*, green and red, are used both fresh and dried; orange chillies *(phrik leuang)*, rare outside Thailand, have a hot and sour flavour.

TOM YAM FLAVOURINGS
Bundles of flavourings are sold already portioned out, each geared towards a particular dish, as here for tom yam soup.

GALANGAL *(khaa)* A rhizome with a hot peppery flavour. Young pale galangal can be eaten in pieces. Older redder pieces are best used in curry pastes.

CORIANDER *(phak chii)*
Coriander (cilantro) is sold in bunches with the root on. All parts of the plant, the roots, stalks and leaves, are used.

TURMERIC *(kha-min)* There are three types of turmeric, red (above), zedoary and white. The first two are used as an ingredient. White is eaten raw.

MAKRUT LIME LEAVES
(bai makrut) Makrut (kaffir) limes have double leaves and a knobbly skin. The leaves and zest are used but not the bitter juice.

ASIAN SHALLOTS *(hawm)*
These tiny red shallots are ubiquitous to Thai cuisine. They are often used whole, smashed with a cleaver.

HOLY BASIL *(bai ka-phrao)*
This basil has a hot sharp flavour and comes in both white (above) and red varieties. Used with seafood and stir-fries.

LEMON GRASS *(ta-khrai)*
A popular flavouring, only the tender middle of lemon grass stalks should be used. Peel down to the purple ring.

LEMON BASIL *(bai maeng-lak)*
The least common of the basils, this is used in soups and fish curries. It has a citrus flavour and delicate leaves.

TAMARIND *(ma-khaam)*
Shown here in pod form, more commonly sold as dried pulp which is fibrous. It is soaked and a tart liquid extracted before use.

GARLIC *(kra-tiam)*
Milder, sweeter and smaller than European garlic, Thai garlic is often fried in oil and used as a crisp garnish.

THAI SWEET BASIL
(bai horapha) Used in curries and soups, this has a very intense aniseed fragrance that is instantly recognizable as Thai.

STIR-FRIES

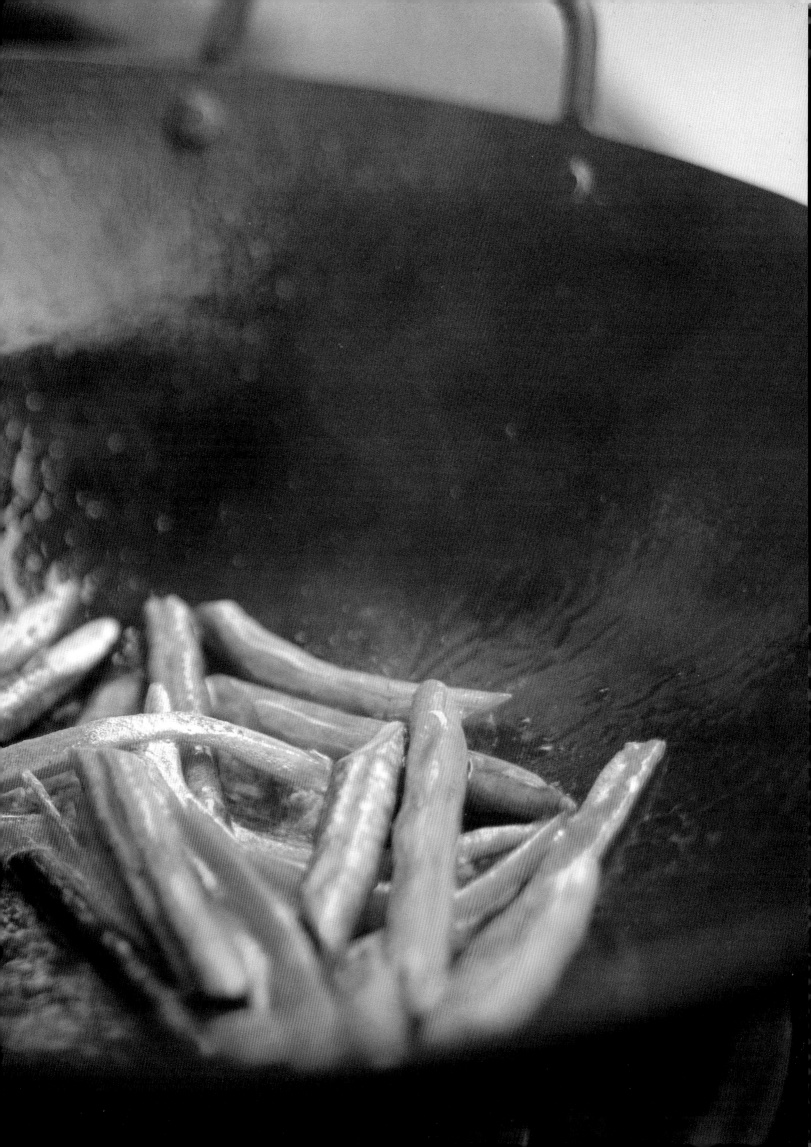

Warorot market.

BEEF WITH THAI SWEET BASIL LEAVES

THAI SWEET BASIL IS ONE OF THE TROPICAL HERBS WITH A DISTINCTIVE FLAVOUR AND PERFUME THAT INSTANTLY EVOKES THAI CUISINE. NO OTHER HERB WILL DO AS A SUBSTITUTE FOR THIS RECIPE. YOUR WOK SHOULD BE VERY HOT AND THE DISH SHOULD TAKE NO MORE THAN 7 OR 8 MINUTES TO COOK.

1 tablespoon fish sauce
3 tablespoons oyster sauce
4 tablespoons vegetable or
    chicken stock, or water
½ teaspoon sugar
2 tablespoons vegetable oil
4 garlic cloves, finely chopped
3 bird's eye chillies, lightly crushed
    with the side of a cleaver
500 g (1 lb 2 oz) tender rump or
    fillet steak, finely sliced
1 medium onion, cut into thin
    wedges
2 handfuls of Thai sweet basil
    leaves

SERVES 4

MIX the fish sauce, oyster sauce, stock and sugar in a small bowl.

HEAT the oil in the wok or frying pan and stir-fry half the garlic over a medium heat until light brown. Add half the crushed chillies and half the meat and stir-fry over a high heat for 2 to 3 minutes or until the meat is cooked. Remove from the wok and repeat with the remaining garlic, chillies and meat. Return all the meat to the wok.

ADD the onion and the fish sauce mixture and stir-fry for another minute.

ADD the basil leaves and stir-fry until the basil begins to wilt. Taste, then adjust the seasoning if necessary. Spoon onto a serving plate.

BEEF WITH BLACK BEAN SAUCE

THIS CHINESE DISH APPEARS IN VARIOUS GUISES IN THAILAND. HERE IT IS MADE WITH SNAKE BEANS AND BEEF. BLACK BEANS ARE OFTEN CALLED FERMENTED OR PRESERVED BLACK BEANS AND ARE SOLD IN JARS OR TUBS IN SHOPS THAT SPECIALIZE IN CHINESE FOOD.

1 tablespoon black beans, rinsed
and roughly mashed
3 tablespoons vegetable or chicken
stock, or water
1 tablespoon fish sauce
1 tablespoon oyster sauce
1 tablespoon sesame oil
½ teaspoon sugar
1 tablespoon vegetable oil
3–4 garlic cloves, finely chopped
250 g (9 oz) tender rump or fillet
steak, finely sliced
½ carrot, cut into fine matchsticks
4 snake beans, cut into 5 cm
(2 inch) lengths
2 spring onions (scallions), cut into
2.5 cm (1 inch) lengths
a few coriander (cilantro) leaves,
for garnish

SERVES 4

MIX the black beans, stock, fish sauce, oyster sauce, sesame oil and sugar in a small bowl.

HEAT the oil in a wok or frying pan and stir-fry half the garlic over a medium heat until light brown. Add half the meat and stir-fry over a medium heat for 3 to 4 minutes or until the meat is cooked. Remove from the wok. Repeat with the remaining garlic and meat. Return all the garlic and meat to the wok.

ADD the carrot, beans and the sauce mixture to the wok and stir-fry for another 1 to 2 minutes. Taste, then adjust the seasoning if necessary. Stir in the spring onions and cook for a few seconds. Spoon onto a serving plate and garnish with coriander leaves.

Mix the black beans with the
stock, sauces, oil and sugar.

CHICKEN WITH CRISPY HOLY BASIL LEAVES

THIS IS ONE OF THE MOST COMMON DISHES YOU WILL COME ACROSS IN THAILAND. HOLY BASIL COMES IN TWO COLOURS, RED AND GREEN. IT HAS A HOT, SLIGHTLY SHARP FLAVOUR AND IS OFTEN USED IN CONJUNCTION WITH CHILLIES IN STIR-FRIES. SERVE WITH PLENTY OF RICE.

500 g (1 lb 2 oz) skinless chicken breast fillets, thinly sliced
4–5 garlic cloves, finely chopped
4–5 small red or green bird's eye chillies, lightly crushed
1 tablespoon fish sauce
2 tablespoons oyster sauce
vegetable oil, for deep-frying
2 handfuls of holy basil leaves
2 tablespoons vegetable or chicken stock, or water
½ teaspoon sugar
1 red capsicum (pepper), cut into bite-sized pieces
1 medium onion, cut into thin wedges

SERVES 4

MIX the chicken, garlic, chillies, fish sauce and oyster sauce in a bowl. Cover with plastic wrap and marinate in the refrigerator for at least 30 minutes.

HEAT 5 cm (2 inches) oil in a wok or deep frying pan over a medium heat. When the oil seems hot, drop a few basil leaves into it. If they sizzle immediately, the oil is ready. Deep-fry three-quarters of the basil leaves for 1 minute or until they are all crispy. Lift out with a slotted spoon and drain on paper towels. Discard the remaining oil.

HEAT 2 tablespoons oil in the same wok or frying pan and stir-fry half the chicken over a high heat for 3 to 4 minutes. Remove from the pan and repeat with the remaining chicken. Return all the chicken to the wok.

ADD the stock and sugar to the wok, then the capsicum and onion, and stir-fry for another 1 to 2 minutes. Stir in the fresh basil leaves. Taste, then adjust the seasoning if necessary. Garnish with the crispy basil leaves.

Floating markets at Damnoen Saduak.

KAI PHAT MET MUANG HIMAPHAAN

CHICKEN WITH CASHEW NUTS

THIS POPULAR DISH IS TYPICALLY CHINESE BUT APPEARS ON MANY THAI RESTAURANT MENUS. THE CASHEWS ARE ACTUALLY A THAI ADDITION. FRYING THE CASHEW NUTS SEPARATELY BRINGS OUT THEIR FLAVOUR AND ADDS A MORE 'NUTTY' TASTE TO THE DISH.

1–2 dried long red chillies
1 tablespoon fish sauce
2 tablespoons oyster sauce
3 tablespoons chicken or vegetable
   stock, or water
½–1 teaspoon sugar
4 tablespoons vegetable oil
80 g (½ cup) cashew nuts
4–5 garlic cloves, finely chopped
500 g (1 lb 2 oz) skinless chicken
   breast fillets, finely sliced
½ red capsicum (pepper), cut into
   thin strips
½ carrot, sliced diagonally
1 small onion, cut into 6 wedges
2 spring onions (scallions), cut into
   1 cm (½ inch) lengths
ground white pepper, to sprinkle

SERVES 4

TAKE the stems off the dried chillies, cut each chilli into 1 cm (½ inch) pieces with scissors or a sharp knife and discard the seeds.

MIX the fish sauce, oyster sauce, stock and sugar in a small bowl.

HEAT the oil in a wok over a medium heat and stir-fry the cashew nuts for 2 to 3 minutes or until light brown. Remove with a slotted spoon and drain on paper towels.

STIR-FRY the chillies in the same oil over a medium heat for 1 minute. They should darken but not blacken and burn. Remove from the pan with a slotted spoon.

HEAT the same oil again and stir-fry half the garlic over a medium heat until light brown. Add half the chicken and stir-fry over a high heat for 4 to 5 minutes or until the chicken is cooked. Remove from the wok and repeat with the remaining garlic and chicken. Return all the chicken to the wok.

ADD the capsicum, carrot, onion and the sauce mixture to the wok and stir-fry for 1 to 2 minutes. Taste, then adjust the seasoning if necessary.

ADD the cashew nuts, chillies and spring onions and toss well. Sprinkle with ground pepper.

Wat Saen Fang in Chiang Mai.

Mangroves in Phang-nga.

PHAT THALEH

MIXED SEAFOOD WITH CHILLIES

THE BIRD'S EYE CHILLIES GIVE THIS DISH QUITE A LOT OF HEAT BUT IF YOU WOULD LIKE IT EVEN HOTTER, JUST ADD A FEW MORE. SERVE WITH PLENTY OF JASMINE RICE AND A COCONUT-BASED CURRY TO HELP TAKE SOME OF THE STING OUT OF THE DISH.

450 g (1 lb) mixed fresh seafood such as prawns (shrimp), squid tubes, small scallops
2 tablespoons vegetable oil
3–4 garlic cloves, finely chopped
1 green capsicum (pepper), cut into bite-sized pieces
1 small onion, cut into thin slices
5 snake beans, cut into 2.5 cm (1 inch) pieces
1 cm (½ inch) piece of ginger, finely grated
4 bird's eye chillies, lightly bruised
1 tablespoon oyster sauce
½ tablespoon light soy sauce
¼ teaspoon sugar
1 long red chilli (optional), seeded and sliced diagonally
1–2 spring onions (scallions), thinly sliced
a few holy basil leaves, or coriander (cilantro) leaves, for garnish

SERVES 4

PEEL and devein the prawns and cut each prawn open along the back so it opens like a butterfly (leave each prawn joined along the base and at the tail). Peel off the outer skin of the squid and rinse out the insides of the tubes. Cut each in half and open the pieces out. Score the inside of each squid with diagonal cuts to make a diamond pattern, then cut into squares. Carefully slice off and discard any vein, membrane or hard white muscle from each scallop. Scallops can be left whole, or, if large, cut each in half.

HEAT the oil in a wok or frying pan and stir-fry the garlic over a medium heat until light brown. Add the capsicum, onion, beans, ginger and chillies and stir-fry for 1 minute.

ADD the seafood in stages, prawns first, then scallops, adding the squid last and tossing after each addition. Add the oyster sauce, light soy sauce and sugar and stir-fry for 2 to 3 minutes, or until the prawns open and turn pink and all the seafood is cooked.

ADD the chilli and spring onions and toss together. Taste, then adjust the seasoning if necessary. Spoon onto a serving plate and sprinkle with basil or coriander leaves.

CHICKEN WITH CHILLI JAM

CHILLI JAM, OR ROASTED CHILLI PASTE, IS USED AS A RELISH, CONDIMENT AND INGREDIENT IN VARIOUS THAI DISHES. HERE IT ADDS A MORE COMPLEX SWEET, CHILLI FLAVOUR THAN JUST USING CHILLIES. ADD THE SMALLER AMOUNT BEFORE TASTING, THEN ADD A LITTLE MORE IF YOU NEED TO.

2 teaspoons fish sauce
2 tablespoons oyster sauce
60 ml (¼ cup) coconut milk
    (page 279)
½ teaspoon sugar
2½ tablespoons vegetable oil
6 garlic cloves, finely chopped
1–1½ tablespoons chilli jam
    (page 283), to taste
500 g (1 lb 2 oz) skinless chicken
    breast fillets, finely sliced
a handful of holy basil leaves
1 long red or green chilli,
    seeded and finely sliced,
    for garnish

SERVES 4

MIX the fish sauce, oyster sauce, coconut milk and sugar in a small bowl.

HEAT the oil in a wok or frying pan and stir-fry half the garlic over a medium heat until light brown. Add half the chilli jam and stir-fry for another 2 minutes or until fragrant. Add half of the chicken and stir-fry over a high heat for 2 to 3 minutes. Remove from the wok. Repeat with the remaining garlic, chilli jam and chicken. Return all the chicken to the wok.

ADD the fish sauce mixture to the wok and stir-fry for a few more seconds or until the chicken is cooked. Taste, then adjust the seasoning if necessary. Stir in the basil leaves. Garnish with chilli slices.

Mixing the sauce ingredients together before you start cooking means you can just pour it in when you need to.

Salt harvested from the Gulf of Thailand.

The mushrooms and tofu are cut into similarly sized pieces so that they cook evenly in the wok.

Ringing the bells at Wat Phra That Doi Tung.

HET PHAT TAO-HUU

MUSHROOMS WITH TOFU

TOFU AND MUSHROOMS ARE COMMONLY USED TOGETHER IN CHINESE DISHES, JUST AS THEY ARE HERE IN THIS THAI DISH. THE BLANDNESS OF THE TOFU IS A CONTRAST TO BOTH THE TEXTURE AND FLAVOUR OF THE MUSHROOMS. FOR THE BEST FLAVOUR, USE THE TYPE OF MUSHROOMS SUGGESTED.

350 g (12 oz) firm tofu (bean curd)
1 teaspoon sesame oil
2 teaspoons light soy sauce
¼ teaspoon ground black pepper, plus some to sprinkle
1 tablespoon finely shredded ginger
5 tablespoons vegetable stock or water
2 tablespoons light soy sauce
2 teaspoons cornflour (cornstarch)
½ teaspoon sugar
1½ tablespoons vegetable oil
2 garlic cloves, finely chopped
200 g (7 oz) oyster mushrooms, hard stalks removed, cut in half if large
200 g (7 oz) shiitake mushrooms, hard stalks removed
2 spring onions (scallions), sliced diagonally, for garnish
1 long red chilli, seeded and finely sliced, for garnish

SERVES 2

DRAIN each block of tofu and cut into 2.5 cm (1 inch) pieces. Put them in a shallow dish and sprinkle with the sesame oil, light soy sauce, ground pepper and ginger. Leave to marinate for 30 minutes.

MIX the stock with the light soy sauce, cornflour and sugar in a small bowl until smooth.

HEAT the oil in a wok or frying pan and stir-fry the garlic over a medium heat until light brown. Add all the mushrooms and stir-fry for 3 to 4 minutes or until the mushrooms are cooked. Add the cornflour liquid, then carefully add the pieces of tofu and gently mix for 1 to 2 minutes. Taste, then adjust the seasoning if necessary.

SPOON onto a serving plate and sprinkle with spring onions, chilli slices and ground pepper.

PORK WITH GINGER

A HYBRID DISH, CHINESE IN STYLE WITH THE ADDITION OF FISH SAUCE FOR A THAI FLAVOUR, THIS

RECIPE IS BEST MADE WITH FIRM, YOUNG, TENDER GINGER WITH TRANSLUCENT SKIN. THE AROMA

OF THE WHOLE DISH SHOULD BE DISTINCTLY GINGERY AS IT ARRIVES AT THE TABLE.

15 g (½ oz) dried black fungus
  (about half a handful)
1 tablespoon fish sauce
1½ tablespoons oyster sauce
4 tablespoons vegetable or chicken
  stock, or water
½ teaspoon sugar
2 tablespoons vegetable oil
3–4 garlic cloves, finely chopped
500 g (1 lb 2 oz) lean pork,
  finely sliced
25 g (1 oz) ginger, julienned
1 small onion, cut into 8 wedges
2 spring onions (scallions),
  diagonally sliced
ground white pepper, for sprinkling
1 long red chilli, seeded and finely
  sliced, for garnish
a few coriander (cilantro) leaves,
  for garnish

SERVES 4

SOAK the black fungus in hot water for 2 to
3 minutes or until soft, then drain.

MIX the fish sauce, oyster sauce, stock and sugar
in a small bowl.

HEAT the oil in a wok or frying pan and stir-fry half
the garlic over a medium heat until light brown.
Add half the pork and stir-fry over a high heat for
2 to 3 minutes or until the pork is cooked. Remove
from the wok. Repeat with the remaining garlic
and pork. Return all the pork to the wok.

ADD the ginger, onion, black fungus and the
sauce mixture to the wok. Stir-fry for 1 to
2 minutes. Taste, then adjust the seasoning
if necessary. Stir in the spring onions.

SPOON onto a serving plate and sprinkle with
ground pepper, chilli slices and coriander leaves.

Selling vegetables in Chiang Mai.

STIR-FRIED GARLIC PRAWNS

TIGER PRAWNS ARE EXTENSIVELY FARMED IN THAILAND AND APPEAR IN MANY DISHES. YOU CAN, HOWEVER, USE DIFFERENT TYPES OF PRAWNS DEPENDING ON AVAILABILITY. THIS RECIPE HAS QUITE A LOT OF GARLIC SO CHOOSE NICE FRESH, SWEET BULBS TO MAKE THE BEST OF THE FLAVOUR.

500 g (1 lb 2 oz) large raw prawns
  (shrimp)
18–20 coriander (cilantro) roots,
  roughly chopped
4–5 garlic cloves, roughly chopped
10 black peppercorns
1 tablespoon light soy sauce
1½ tablespoons oyster sauce
½ teaspoon sugar
3 tablespoons vegetable oil
a few coriander (cilantro) leaves,
  for garnish
1 long red chilli, seeded and finely
  sliced, for garnish

SERVES 4

PEEL and devein the prawns and cut each prawn along the back so it opens like a butterfly (leave each prawn joined along the base and at the tail).

USING a pestle and mortar or a small blender, pound or grind the coriander roots and garlic into a rough paste. Add the peppercorns and continue to grind roughly.

MIX the light soy sauce, oyster sauce and sugar in a small bowl.

HEAT the oil in a wok or frying pan and stir-fry the coriander paste for 1 to 2 minutes or until the garlic starts to turn light brown and fragrant. Add the prawns and light soy sauce mixture and stir-fry for another 2 to 3 minutes or until the prawns open and turn pink. Taste, then adjust the seasoning if necessary. Sprinkle with coriander leaves and chilli slices.

MUU PHAT PRIAW WAAN
PORK WITH SWEET AND SOUR SAUCE

PORK IS THE MEAT PREFERRED IN MANY AREAS OF THAILAND. THIS RECIPE IS A THAI VERSION OF THE BETTER KNOWN CHINESE SWEET AND SOUR PORK. THE VEGETABLES CAN BE VARIED ACCORDING TO WHAT IS AVAILABLE, BUT CHOOSE ONES THAT WILL STILL BE CRUNCHY WHEN COOKED.

225 g (8 oz) tin pineapple slices in light syrup, each slice cut into 4 pieces (reserve the syrup)
1½ tablespoons plum sauce (page 284) or tomato ketchup
2½ teaspoons fish sauce
1 tablespoon sugar
2 tablespoons vegetable oil
250 g (9 oz) pork, sliced
4 garlic cloves, finely chopped
¼ carrot, sliced
1 medium onion, cut into 8 slices
½ red capsicum (pepper), cut into bite-sized pieces
1 small cucumber, unpeeled, halved lengthways and cut into thick slices
1 tomato, cut into 4 slices, or 4–5 baby tomatoes
a few coriander (cilantro) leaves, for garnish

SERVES 4

MIX all the pineapple syrup (about 6 tablespoons) with the plum sauce, fish sauce and sugar in a small bowl until smooth.

HEAT the oil in a wok or deep frying pan over a medium heat and fry the pork until nicely browned and cooked. Lift out with a slotted spoon and drain on paper towels.

ADD the garlic to the wok or pan and fry over a medium heat for 1 minute or until lightly browned. Add the carrot, onion and capsicum and stir-fry for 1 to 2 minutes. Add the cucumber, tomato, pineapple and pineapple syrup and stir together for another minute. Taste, then adjust the seasoning if necessary.

RETURN the pork to the pan and gently stir. Spoon onto a serving plate and garnish with coriander leaves.

Snake beans sometimes have a mottled dark colouring but this is perfectly normal.

THUA PHAT MUU

PORK WITH SNAKE BEANS

SNAKE BEANS ARE SOLD IN ASIAN FOOD SHOPS, EITHER COILED UP OR IN LONG BUNCHES. THEY TASTE SIMILAR TO EUROPEAN GREEN BEANS BUT HAVE A SLIGHTLY MORE LEATHERY SKIN. YOU CAN USE FRENCH OR ROUND GREEN BEANS IF YOU PREFER. THIS DISH GOES WITH ANY MEAL.

1 tablespoon oyster sauce
1 tablespoon light soy sauce
¼ teaspoon sugar
2 tablespoons vegetable oil
4 garlic cloves, finely chopped
350 g (12 oz) pork fillet, finely sliced
250 g (9 oz) snake beans, cut into
   5 cm (2 inch) pieces
½ long red chilli, seeded, shredded,
   for garnish (optional)

SERVES 4

MIX the oyster sauce, light soy sauce, sugar and 2 tablespoons water in a small bowl.

HEAT the oil in a wok or frying pan and stir-fry the garlic over a medium heat until light brown. Add the pork and stir-fry over a high heat for 3 to 5 minutes or until the pork is cooked. Add the beans and the sauce mixture and stir-fry for 4 minutes. Taste, then adjust the seasoning if necessary.

TRANSFER to a serving plate and garnish with chilli slices.

MUU PHAT KRA-TIAM PHRIK THAI

PORK WITH GARLIC AND PEPPER

A CLASSIC COMBINATION OF GARLIC AND PEPPER IS FOUND IN THIS CHINESE-STYLE DISH. THAI GARLIC IS LESS PUNGENT THAN MANY OTHER GARLICS. TRY TO BUY NEW SEASON GARLIC. CRUSH THE PEPPERCORNS JUST BEFORE YOU USE THEM. SERVE WITH A VEGETABLE DISH AND JASMINE RICE.

1½ teaspoons black peppercorns
1 whole bulb of garlic, cloves
    roughly chopped
8–10 coriander (cilantro) roots,
    roughly chopped
3 tablespoons vegetable oil
500 g (1 lb 2 oz) pork fillet, cut into
    5 cm (2 inch) squares
1 tablespoon fish sauce
1 tablespoon light soy sauce
½ teaspoon sugar
garlic and chilli sauce (page 283),
    to serve

SERVES 4

USING a pestle and mortar or a small blender, pound or blend the black peppercorns (just roughly) and spoon them into a small bowl.

POUND or blend the garlic and coriander roots into a paste and mix with peppercorns.

HEAT the oil in a wok or frying pan and stir-fry half the garlic and peppercorn paste over a medium heat for 1 to 2 minutes or until the garlic turns light brown and is fragrant. Add half the pork and stir-fry over a high heat for a minute, then reduce the heat and cook for 2 to 3 minutes, or until the meat is cooked. Remove from the heat. Repeat with the remaining paste and pork. Return all the pork to the wok.

ADD the fish sauce, light soy sauce and sugar to the wok. Stir-fry for 5 minutes or until the pork starts to turn brown. Serve with garlic and chilli sauce.

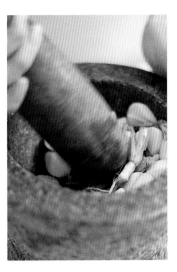

A granite pestle and mortar helps in many Thai recipes. A deep mortar is best when you have a lot of ingredients.

Chillies and garlic at a Bangkok market.

NOODLES & RICE

Stir the paste into the coconut cream before adding the chicken, soy sauce, sugar, stock and coconut milk.

KHAO SAWY

CHIANG MAI NOODLES

ONE OF CHIANG MAI'S WELL KNOWN DISHES, THIS IS FOUND ON RESTAURANT MENUS AND AT HAWKER STALLS, PARTICULARLY THOSE NEAR THE MOSQUE. SERVE WITH THE ACCOMPANIMENTS SUGGESTED AS THEY COMPLEMENT THE NOODLES PARTICULARLY WELL.

PASTE
3 dried long red chillies
4 Asian shallots, chopped
4 garlic cloves, crushed
2 cm (¾ inch) piece of turmeric, grated
5 cm (2 inch) piece of ginger, grated
4 tablespoons chopped coriander (cilantro) roots
1 teaspoon shrimp paste
1 teaspoon curry powder (page 287)

5 tablespoons coconut cream (page 279)
2 tablespoons palm sugar
2 tablespoons soy sauce
4 chicken drumsticks and 4 chicken thighs, with skin and bone
500 ml (2 cups) chicken stock or water
410 ml (1⅔ cups) coconut milk (page 279)
400 g (14 oz) fresh flat egg noodles
chopped or sliced spring onions (scallions), for garnish
a handful of coriander (cilantro) leaves, for garnish
lime wedges, to serve
pickled mustard greens or cucumber, to serve
roasted chilli sauce (page 283), to serve
Asian shallots, quartered, to serve

SERVES 4

TO MAKE the paste, soak the dried chillies in hot water for 10 minutes, then drain and chop the chillies into pieces, discarding the seeds. Put the chillies in a pestle and mortar with the shallots, garlic, turmeric, ginger, coriander roots and shrimp paste and pound to a fine paste. Add the curry powder and a pinch of salt and mix well.

PUT the coconut cream in a wok or saucepan and simmer over a medium heat for about 5 minutes, or until the cream separates and a layer of oil forms on the surface. Stir the cream if it starts to brown around the edges.

ADD the paste and stir until fragrant. Add the palm sugar, soy sauce and chicken and stir well, then add the stock and coconut milk and bring to the boil. Reduce the heat and simmer for 30 minutes or until the chicken is cooked and tender.

MEANWHILE, cook 100 g (3 oz) of the egg noodles by deep-frying them in very hot oil in a saucepan until they puff up. Drain on paper towels. Cook the remaining noodles in boiling water according to the packet instructions.

PUT the boiled noodles in a large bowl and spoon the chicken mixture over the top. Garnish with the crispy noodles, spring onions and coriander leaves. Serve the accompaniments alongside.

KIAW NAAM KUNG

WON TON SOUP WITH PRAWNS

WON TONS ARE A CHINESE-STYLE STUFFED NOODLE. USUALLY SERVED IN SOUPS, THEY ARE EASY TO PREPARE, AND WITH THIS LIGHT, FRESH PRAWN FILLING WON TONS MAKE A GOOD MEAL IN A BOWL AT ANY TIME OF DAY. CHICKEN OR FISH ARE ALSO SUITABLE FILLINGS.

225 g (8 oz) finely chopped prawns
  (shrimp)
6 garlic cloves, finely chopped
2 coriander (cilantro) roots,
  finely chopped
a sprinkle of ground white pepper
20 won ton sheets 7.5 cm
  (3 inches) square
1–2 tablespoons vegetable oil
935 ml (3¾ cups) chicken or
  vegetable stock
2 tablespoons light soy sauce
4 raw prawns (shrimp), peeled
  and deveined
100 g (4 oz) Chinese cabbage or
  spinach leaves, roughly chopped
100 g (1 cup) bean sprouts, tails
  removed
3 spring onions (scallions), slivered
ground white pepper, for sprinkling

SERVES 4

IN a bowl, combine the chopped prawns with 2 of the garlic cloves, the coriander roots, ground pepper and a pinch of salt. Spoon 1 teaspoon of the mixture into the middle of each won ton sheet. Gather up, squeezing the corners together to make a little purse.

HEAT the oil in a small wok or frying pan and stir-fry the remaining garlic until light golden. Remove from the heat and discard the garlic.

HEAT a saucepan of water to boiling point. Gently drop each won ton purse into the water and cook for 2 to 3 minutes. Lift each purse out with a slotted spoon and drop it into a bowl of warm water.

HEAT the stock in a saucepan to boiling point. Add the light soy sauce, prawns and Chinese cabbage and cook for a few minutes.

DRAIN the cooked won tons and transfer them to the stock saucepan.

DIVIDE the bean sprouts among individual bowls and divide the won tons and the soup mixture among the bowls. Garnish with spring onions, ground pepper and the garlic oil.

Spoon a small amount of mixture onto each won ton sheet, gather up and squeeze into a purse.

Score the insides of the squid tubes in a crisscross pattern.

EGG NOODLES WITH SEAFOOD

BA-MII ARE WHEAT FLOUR NOODLES, USUALLY MADE WITH EGG. STALLS SPECIALIZING IN BA-MII CAN BE FOUND ALL OVER THAILAND — NOODLE DISHES LIKE THIS ARE USUALLY EATEN AS A SNACK. SERVE WITH SLICED CHILLIES IN FISH SAUCE, DRIED CHILLI AND WHITE SUGAR FOR SEASONING.

8 raw prawns (shrimp)
2 squid tubes
250 g (9 oz) egg noodles
1 tablespoon vegetable oil
4 Asian shallots, smashed with the
    side of a cleaver
4 spring onions (scallions), cut into
    lengths and smashed with the
    side of a cleaver
2 cm (¾ inch) piece of ginger,
    finely shredded
2 garlic cloves, finely sliced
1 tablespoon preserved cabbage,
    rinsed and chopped (optional)
4 scallops, cut in half horizontally
1 tablespoon oyster sauce
2 teaspoons soy sauce
2 teaspoons fish sauce
½ bunch (1 cup) holy basil leaves

SERVES 4

PEEL and devein the prawns and cut each prawn along the back so it opens like a butterfly (leave each prawn joined along the base and at the tail, leaving the tail attached).

OPEN out the squid tubes and score the insides in a criss-cross pattern. Cut the squid tubes into squares.

COOK the egg noodles in boiling water, then drain and rinse.

HEAT the oil in a wok and add the shallots, spring onions, ginger, garlic and cabbage and stir-fry for 2 minutes. Add the prawns, squid and scallops one after the other, tossing after each addition, and cook for 3 minutes.

ADD the oyster and soy sauces and noodles and toss together. Add the fish sauce and holy basil and serve.

Preparing fish in Phetchaburi.

PHAT WUN SEN

HOT AND SOUR NOODLES WITH PRAWNS

200 g (7 oz) mung bean vermicelli
100 g (3 oz) minced (ground) pork
2 tablespoons oil
8 cooked prawns (shrimp), peeled
4 pickled garlic cloves, chopped
2 Asian shallots, finely sliced
4 bird's eye chillies, finely sliced
2 tablespoons fish sauce
1 tablespoon lime juice
2 tomatoes, seeded and cut into
   thin wedges
½ bunch (1 cup) Thai sweet basil
   leaves
½ bunch (1 cup) coriander (cilantro)
   leaves

SERVES 4

SOAK the noodles in hot water for 10 minutes or until soft. Drain the noodles and cut them into shorter lengths using a pair of scissors.

COOK the pork in boiling water for 2 minutes, breaking it up into small pieces, then drain.

HEAT the oil in a wok and add all the ingredients except the basil and coriander. Toss together for a minute or two. Add the herbs, toss briefly and serve.

Toss all the ingredients together before adding the herbs.

PHAT KHII MAO

STIR-FRIED NOODLES WITH HOLY BASIL

NOODLES ARE ONE OF THE MOST COMMON DISHES IN THAILAND, FOUND ON JUST ABOUT EVERY STREET CORNER. AS THEY ARE OF CHINESE ORIGIN THEY ARE USUALLY EATEN OUT OF A BOWL WITH CHOPSTICKS AND A SPOON. SERVE STRAIGHT OUT OF THE WOK.

450 g (1 lb) wide fresh flat rice
   noodles (sen yai)
2 teaspoons soy sauce
4 garlic cloves
4 bird's eye chillies, stems removed
4 tablespoons vegetable oil
200 g (7 oz) skinless chicken fillets,
   cut into thin strips
2 tablespoons fish sauce
2 teaspoons palm sugar
½ bunch (1 cup) holy basil leaves

SERVES 4

PUT the noodles in a bowl with the soy sauce and rub the sauce through the noodles, separating them out as you do so. Pound the garlic and chillies together with a pestle and mortar until you have a fine paste.

HEAT the oil in a wok and add the garlic and chilli paste and fry until fragrant. Add the chicken and toss until cooked. Add the fish sauce and palm sugar and cook until the sugar dissolves. Add the noodles and basil leaves, toss together and serve.

STIR-FRIED NOODLES WITH HOLY BASIL

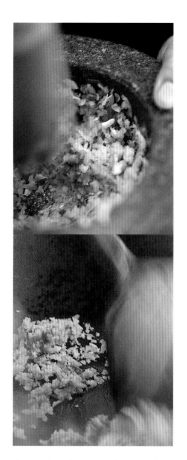

Pound the flavours into a paste.
Cook for a few minutes, then
add the rice and, when coated,
transfer to a clay pot.

Painting umbrellas at Bo Sang
village.

KUNG LAI SAI KRAWK NAI MAW DIN

PRAWNS AND SAUSAGE IN A CLAY POT

CLAY POT COOKING IS CHINESE IN STYLE. IF YOU HAVE FOUR SMALLER CLAY POTS YOU CAN MAKE
INDIVIDUAL DISHES TO SERVE INSTEAD OF ONE LARGE ONE. A HEAVY CASSEROLE WILL WORK JUST
AS WELL. THE INGREDIENTS IN THE DISH WILL FLAVOUR THE RICE AS IT COOKS.

12 raw small prawns (shrimp),
    peeled, deveined and roughly
    chopped
1 lemon grass stalk, white part only,
    finely chopped
2 large green chillies, chopped
1 teaspoon Thai whisky or rice wine
1 teaspoon fish sauce
1 teaspoon tapioca flour
2 garlic cloves, chopped
2 coriander (cilantro) roots, chopped
2 cm (¾ inch) piece of ginger,
    chopped
2 Asian shallots, chopped
200 g (1 cup) jasmine rice
2 tablespoons oil
2 Thai or Chinese sour sausages,
    finely sliced
2 tablespoons chopped coriander
    (cilantro), for garnish

SERVES 4

PUT the chopped prawns in a bowl with
1 tablespoon of lemon grass, the chillies, whisky,
fish sauce and tapioca flour. Stir to combine.

POUND the remaining lemon grass, garlic,
coriander roots, ginger and shallots in a pestle
and mortar or blend in a small food processor
to form a rough paste.

WASH the rice in cold water until the water runs
clear, then drain.

HEAT the oil in a wok, add the garlic paste and
cook for 3 to 4 minutes, stirring constantly. Add
the rice and cook for a minute to coat the rice
evenly in the mixture.

TRANSFER the rice into a large clay pot and add
water so there is 2 cm (¾ inch) of water above the
surface of the rice. Bring the water to a slow boil,
then place the sausage slices on top of the rice
and the prawn mixture on top of the sausages.
Cover the clay pot and cook over a low heat for
15 minutes or until the rice is cooked. Serve
sprinkled with the chopped coriander.

PHAT KUAYTIAW RAAT NAA MUU

STIR-FRIED WHITE NOODLES WITH PORK

NOODLES ARE ENJOYED WITH FERVOUR IN THAILAND. LARGE WHITE NOODLES ARE USED IN THIS DISH, WHICH IS ONE OF THE BEST-KNOWN NOODLE DISHES, SERVED AT ANY TIME OF THE DAY OR NIGHT. THE LIGHT, BITTER TASTE COMES FROM THE CHINESE KALE.

2 teaspoons oyster sauce
6 teaspoons light soy sauce
1 teaspoon sugar
2 teaspoons yellow bean sauce
1 tablespoon tapioca flour
450 g (1 lb) wide fresh flat rice
    noodles (sen yai)
4 tablespoons vegetable oil
4–5 garlic cloves, finely chopped
225 g (8 oz) pork or chicken fillet,
    finely sliced
175 g (6 oz) Chinese kale, cut into
    2.5 cm (1 inch) pieces, leaves
    separated
ground white pepper, for sprinkling

SEASONING
6 bird's eye chillies, sliced and
    mixed with 3 tablespoons
    white vinegar
3 tablespoons fish sauce
3 tablespoons roasted chilli powder
3 tablespoons white sugar

SERVES 4

MIX the oyster sauce, 4 teaspoons of the light soy sauce, sugar, yellow bean sauce and tapioca flour with 125 ml (½ cup) water in a bowl.

PUT the noodles in a bowl with 2 teaspoons of the soy sauce and rub the sauce through the noodles, separating them out as you do so.

HEAT 2 tablespoons oil in a wok or frying pan over a medium heat and stir-fry the noodles for 4 to 5 minutes or until the noodles are browning at the edges and beginning to stick. Keep them warm on a serving plate.

HEAT the remaining oil in a wok or frying pan and stir-fry the garlic over a medium heat until light brown. Add the pork and stir-fry for 2 to 3 minutes or until the meat is cooked. Add the stalks of Chinese kale and stir-fry for 1 to 2 minutes. Add the sauce mixture and the top leaves and stir together for another minute or so. Taste and adjust the seasoning if necessary.

SPOON the pork and Chinese kale on top of the noodles and sprinkle with white pepper. Serve the seasoning ingredients in small bowls on the side, for adjusting the flavour.

Stir-fry the noodles, then remove and stir-fry the garlic, pork and Chinese kale stalks. Add the sauce and kale leaves.

This melding of flavours with
noodles is popular in Thailand.

THAI FRIED NOODLES WITH PRAWNS

THIS IS ONE OF THE MOST FAMOUS DISHES IN THAILAND. EVERYONE WHO VISITS SHOULD TRY IT,
OTHERWISE THEY HAVE NOT REALLY BEEN THERE AT ALL. TO MAKE IT, YOU NEED TO USE SMALL
WHITE NOODLES OF THE DRIED SEN LEK VARIETY. YOU CAN SUBSTITUTE MEAT FOR PRAWNS.

150 g (5 oz) dried noodles *(sen lek)*
300 g (10 oz) raw large prawns
  (shrimp)
3 tablespoons tamarind purée
2½ tablespoons fish sauce
2 tablespoons palm sugar
3 tablespoons vegetable oil
3–4 garlic cloves, finely chopped
2 eggs
85 g (3 oz) Chinese chives
  (1 bunch)
¼ teaspoon chilli powder,
  depending on taste
2 tablespoons dried shrimp, ground
  or pounded
2 tablespoons preserved turnip,
  finely chopped
2½–3 tablespoons chopped
  roasted peanuts
180 g (2 cups) bean sprouts
3 spring onions (scallions), slivered
1 long red chilli, seeded and
  shredded, for garnish
a few coriander (cilantro) leaves,
  for garnish
lime wedges, to serve

SERVES 4

SOAK the noodles in hot water for 1 to 2 minutes
or until soft, then drain.

PEEL and devein the prawns and cut each prawn
along the back so it opens like a butterfly (leave
each prawn joined along the base and at the tail,
leaving the tail attached).

COMBINE the tamarind with the fish sauce and
palm sugar in a bowl.

HEAT 1½ tablespoons oil in a wok or frying pan
and stir-fry the garlic over a medium heat until light
brown. Add the prawns and cook for 2 minutes.

USING a spatula, move the prawns out from the
middle of the wok. Add another 1½ tablespoons oil
to the wok. Add the eggs and stir to scramble for
1 minute. Add the noodles and chives and stir-fry
for a few seconds. Add the fish sauce mixture,
chilli powder, dried shrimp, preserved turnip and
half of the peanuts. Add half of the bean sprouts
and spring onions. Test the noodles for tenderness
and adjust the seasoning if necessary.

SPOON onto the serving plate and sprinkle the
remaining peanuts over the top. Garnish with
shredded chillies and a few coriander leaves.
Place the lime wedges and remaining bean
sprouts and spring onions at the side of the dish.

MII KROB

CRISPY RICE NOODLES

THIS IS MADE BY DEEP-FRYING THE THINNEST RICE NOODLES INTO LIGHT AND CRISPY TANGLES. THESE ARE THEN TOSSED WITH SWEET AND SOUR SAUCE. THIS DISH SHOULD BE SERVED AS SOON AS IT IS COOKED OR THE NOODLES WILL LOSE THEIR CRISPINESS.

75 g (3 oz) rice vermicelli noodles
    (sen mii)
vegetable oil, for deep-frying
200 g (7 oz) firm tofu (bean curd),
    cut into matchsticks
75 g (3 oz) small Asian shallots or
    small red onions, finely sliced
150 g (5 oz) raw prawns (shrimp),
    peeled and deveined, tails intact
2 tablespoons fish sauce
2 tablespoons water or pickled
    garlic juice
1 tablespoon lime juice
2 tablespoons plum sauce
    (page 284) or tomato ketchup
1 tablespoon sweet chilli sauce
    (page 284)
4 tablespoons sugar
3 tablespoons palm sugar
3 small whole pickled garlic,
    finely sliced
110 g (1¼ cups) bean sprouts,
    tails removed, for garnish
3–4 spring onions (scallions),
    slivered, for garnish
1 long red chilli, seeded and
    cut into slivers, for garnish

SERVES 4

SOAK the noodles in cold water for 20 minutes, drain and dry very thoroughly on paper towels. Cut them into smaller lengths with a pair of scissors.

PUT the oil in the wok to a depth of about 8–10 cm (3–4 inches) and heat over a medium heat. Drop a piece of noodle into the wok. If it sinks and then immediately floats and puffs, the oil is ready. Drop a small handful of the noodles into the oil. Turn them once (it only takes seconds) and remove them as soon as they have swelled and turned a dark ivory colour. Remove the crispy noodles with a slotted spoon, hold over the wok briefly to drain, then transfer to a baking tray lined with paper towels to drain. Fry the remaining noodles in the same way. Break into smaller bits.

IN the same oil, deep-fry the tofu for 7 to 10 minutes or until golden and crisp. Remove and drain with a slotted spoon.

DEEP-FRY the shallots until crispy and golden brown. Remove with a slotted spoon and drain on paper towels.

DEEP-FRY the prawns for 1 to 2 minutes until they turn pink. Remove with a slotted spoon and drain on paper towels.

CAREFULLY pour off all the oil in the wok. Add the fish sauce, water, lime juice, plum sauce, sweet chilli sauce, sugar and palm sugar to the wok. Stir for 4 to 5 minutes over a low heat until slightly thick.

ADD half of the rice noodles and toss gently, mixing them into the sauce. Add the remaining noodles and tofu, prawns, pickled garlic and the shallots, tossing for 1 to 2 minutes until coated. Spoon onto a platter and garnish with bean sprouts, spring onions and chilli slivers.

Thai pickled garlic can be bought from Thai and Asian shops. Remove the crispy noodles and tofu with a slotted spoon.

STIR-FRIED EGG NOODLES WITH VEGETABLES

2 tablespoons oyster sauce
1 tablespoon light soy sauce
1 teaspoon sugar
2 tablespoons vegetable oil
4 garlic cloves, finely chopped
225 g (8 oz) mixed Chinese broccoli
    florets, baby sweet corn,
    snake beans cut into lengths,
    snow peas (mangetout) cut into
    bite-sized pieces
250 g (9 oz) fresh egg noodles
45 g (½ cup) bean sprouts
3 spring onions (scallions), finely
    chopped
½ long red or green chilli, seeded
    and finely sliced
a few coriander (cilantro) leaves,
    for garnish

SERVES 4

COMBINE the oyster sauce, light soy sauce and sugar in a small bowl.

HEAT the oil in a wok or frying pan and stir-fry the garlic over a medium heat until lightly brown. Add all the mixed vegetables and stir-fry over a high heat for 1 to 2 minutes.

ADD the egg noodles and oyster sauce mixture to the wok and stir-fry for 2 to 3 minutes. Add the bean sprouts and spring onions. Taste, then adjust the seasoning if necessary.

SPOON onto a serving plate and garnish with chilli and coriander leaves.

FRIED RICE WITH PRAWNS AND CHILLI JAM

225 g (8 oz) raw prawns (shrimp)
3 tablespoons vegetable oil
4 garlic cloves, finely chopped
1 small onion, sliced
3 teaspoons chilli jam (page 283)
450 g (1 lb) cooked jasmine rice,
    refrigerated overnight
1 tablespoon light soy sauce
½ teaspoon sugar
1 long red chilli, seeded and
    finely sliced
2 spring onions (scallions),
    finely sliced
ground white pepper, for sprinkling
a few coriander (cilantro) leaves,
    for garnish

SERVES 4

PEEL and devein the prawns and cut each prawn along the back so it opens like a butterfly (leave each prawn joined along the base and at the tail, leaving the tail attached).

HEAT the oil in a wok or frying pan and stir-fry the garlic and onion over a medium heat until light brown. Add the chilli jam and stir for a few seconds or until fragrant. Add the prawns and stir-fry over a high heat for 2 minutes or until the prawns open and turn pink.

ADD the cooked rice, light soy sauce and sugar and stir-fry for 3 to 4 minutes. Add the chilli and spring onions and mix well. Taste, then adjust the seasoning if necessary.

SPOON onto a serving place and sprinkle with the white pepper and coriander leaves.

FRIED RICE WITH PRAWNS
AND CHILLI JAM

KHAO PHAT SAPPAROT

FRIED RICE WITH PINEAPPLE

FRIED RICE ORIGINATED IN CHINA AND IS NOW A STAPLE SNACK IN THAILAND. IT IS NOT EATEN INSTEAD OF STEAMED RICE BUT ON ITS OWN. THIS IS A UNIQUE WAY OF PRESENTING FRIED RICE. IT IS A SPLENDID DISH TO SERVE WHEN PINEAPPLES ARE IN SEASON AND EASY TO FIND.

1 fresh pineapple, leaves attached
2 tablespoons vegetable oil
1 egg, beaten with a pinch of salt
2–3 garlic cloves, finely chopped
150 g (5 oz) raw prawns (shrimp), peeled and deveined
150 g (5 oz) ham, finely chopped
25 g (1 oz) sweet corn kernels
25 g (1 oz) peas
½ red capsicum (pepper), finely diced
1 tablespoon finely sliced ginger (optional)
280 g (1½ cups) cooked jasmine rice, refrigerated overnight
1 tablespoon light soy sauce
25 g (1 oz) ready-made roasted salted cashew nuts, roughly chopped
1 long red chilli, seeded and finely sliced, for garnish
a few coriander (cilantro) leaves, for garnish

SERVES 4

Carefully scoop out flesh of the pineapple leaving a shell for the fried rice filling.

PREHEAT the oven to 180°C/350°F/Gas 4. Cut the pineapple in half, lengthways. Scoop the flesh out of both halves using a tablespoon and a paring knife, to leave two shells with a 1 cm (½ inch) border of flesh attached. Cut the pineapple flesh into small cubes. Put half the cubes in a bowl and refrigerate the rest for eating later.

WRAP the pineapple leaves in foil to prevent them from burning. Place the shells on a baking tray and bake for 10 to 15 minutes. This will seal in the juice and prevent it leaking into the fried rice when it is placed in the shells.

HEAT 1 tablespoon oil in a wok or frying pan over a medium heat. Pour in the egg and swirl the pan so that the egg coats it, forming a thin omelette. Cook for 2 minutes, or until the egg is set and slightly brown on the underside, then flip over to brown the other side. Remove from the pan and allow to cool slightly. Roll up and cut into thin strips.

HEAT 1 tablespoon oil in the wok or frying pan and stir-fry the garlic over a medium heat until light brown. Add the prawns, ham, sweet corn, peas, capsicum and ginger. Stir-fry for 2 minutes or until the prawns open and turn pink. Add the cooked rice, light soy sauce and the bowl of fresh pineapple and toss together over a medium heat for 5 to 7 minutes. Taste, then adjust the seasoning if necessary.

SPOON as much of the fried rice as will fit into the pineapple shells and sprinkle with cashew nuts and omelette strips. Garnish with sliced chillies and coriander leaves.

Fresh and pickled fruit in Udon Thani.

HOT AND SOUR SOUP WITH NOODLES AND PRAWNS

THIS IS A TANGY SOUP VERSION OF A NOODLE SALAD. WUN SEN NOODLES ARE MADE FROM MUNG BEANS. THEY TURN CLEAR WHEN SOAKED AND ADD A SLIPPERY TEXTURE TO THIS SOUP. CUT THE NOODLES INTO SMALL PIECES TO MAKE THEM EASIER TO EAT.

150 g (5 oz) vermicelli or mung bean
   vermicelli (*wun sen*)
280 g (10 oz) raw medium prawns
   (shrimp)
920 ml (3⅔ cups) vegetable stock
2 lemon grass stalks, each cut into
   a tassel or bruised
2–2½ tablespoons fish sauce
1½–2 tablespoons chilli jam
   (page 283), depending on taste
   (optional)
1–2 small red and green chillies,
   slightly crushed
110 g (4 oz) mixed mushrooms
110 g (4 oz) baby tomatoes
   (about 10) or medium tomatoes,
   cut into 6 pieces
5 makrut (kaffir) lime leaves,
   torn in half
4 tablespoons lime juice
a few coriander (cilantro) leaves,
   for garnish

SERVES 4

SOAK the vermicelli in hot water for 1 to 2 minutes or until soft, then drain them well and cut into small pieces.

PEEL and devein the prawns and cut each prawn along the back so it opens like a butterfly (leave each prawn joined along the base and at the tail, leaving the tail attached).

HEAT the stock, lemon grass, fish sauce, chilli jam and crushed chillies to boiling point. Reduce the heat to medium, add the vermicelli, then cook for 1 to 2 minutes. Add the prawns and cook for another minute.

ADD the mushrooms, tomatoes, makrut lime leaves and lime juice. Cook for another 2 to 3 minutes, taking care not to let the tomatoes lose their shape. Taste, then adjust the seasoning if necessary. Discard the lemon grass. Spoon into a bowl and garnish with coriander leaves.

KHAO PHAT PUU

FRIED RICE WITH CRAB

FRIED RICE IS BEST MADE WITH DAY-OLD RICE, IN OTHER WORDS LEFTOVERS, THOUGH THE
LIKELIHOOD OF THERE BEING LEFTOVER RICE IN THAILAND IS REMOTE. USE A WOK FOR THE BEST
RESULTS. CRAB, PREFERABLY FRESH IF POSSIBLE, GOES PARTICULARLY WELL WITH THE RICE.

2 tablespoons vegetable oil
4 garlic cloves, finely chopped
2 eggs
450 g (2½ cups) cooked jasmine
   rice, refrigerated overnight
110 g (4 oz) crab meat
   (drained well if tinned)
½ small onion, sliced
175 g (6 oz) tin water chestnuts,
   drained and sliced
2 tablespoons finely julienned ginger
   (optional)
1 tablespoon light soy sauce
1 teaspoon sugar
4 cooked crab claws, for garnish
½ long red chilli, seeded and finely
   sliced, for garnish
2 spring onions (scallions), finely
   chopped, for garnish

SERVES 4

HEAT the oil in a wok or frying pan and stir-fry the
garlic over a medium heat until light brown. Using
a spatula, move the fried garlic to the outer edges
of the wok. Add the eggs and stir to scramble for
1 to 2 minutes. Add the cooked rice, crab meat
and onion, stirring for 1 to 2 minutes.

ADD the water chestnuts, ginger, light soy sauce
and sugar and stir together for 1 minute. Taste,
then adjust the seasoning if necessary.

SPOON onto a serving plate and garnish with
the crab claws. Sprinkle with sliced chilli and
spring onions.

Fresh water chestnuts.

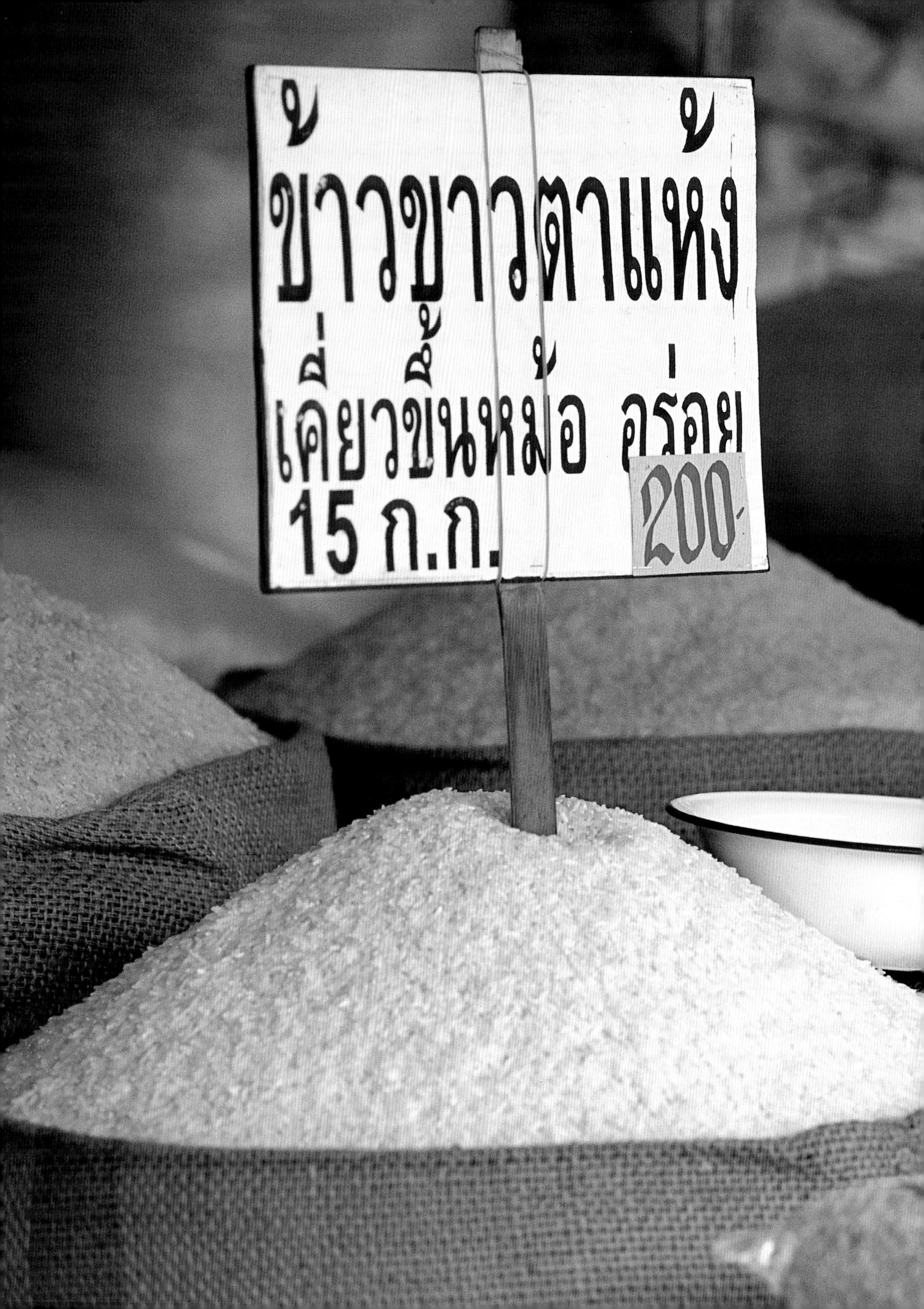
ข้าวขาวตาแห้ง
เคี่ยวขึ้นหม้อ อร่อย
15 ก.ก.
200-

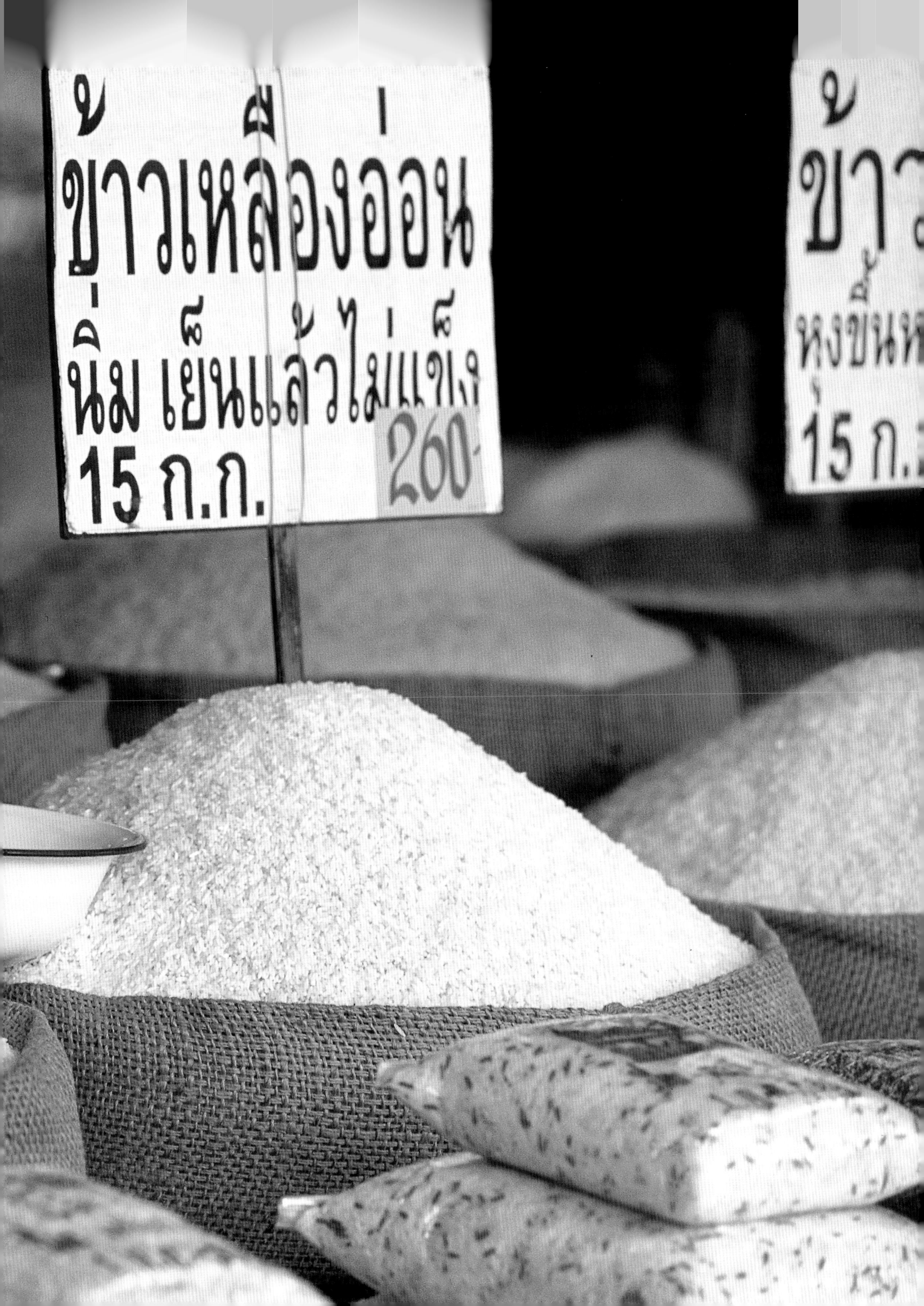
ข้าวเหลืองอ่อน
นิ่ม เย็นแล้วไม่แข็ง
15 ก.ก.
260-

COMMERCIAL RICE GROWING Rather than investing in large expanses of land on which to grow rice, many rice companies buy unhusked rice from farmers surrounding their mills. Once harvested, the rice is bagged up and taken to the mill to be tested: if it is good quality it is bought by the mill and processed. At the Chia Meng rice mill it is tested for ripeness and for the percentage of jasmine or fragrant rice in the

RICE

RICE (KHAO) IS NOT ONLY THE STAPLE FOOD OF THAILAND, IT IS A FUNDAMENTAL PART OF THAI LIFE, INTEGRAL TO ITS CULTURE AND TRADITIONS. THE GREETING KIN KHAO LAEW REU YANG MEANS 'HOW ARE YOU' BUT IS TRANSLATED AS 'HAVE YOU EATEN RICE YET?'. RICE IS NOT JUST PART OF A MEAL, IT IS THE MEAL. OTHER DISHES ARE ACCOMPANIMENTS.

The cultivation of rice may have started in Thailand. Wild rice originated somewhere in an area that now runs through Upper Assam, Burma, northern Thailand, South-West China and northern Vietnam, a fertile belt that is given over to rice cultivation today. The indigenous inhabitants of the area, were cultivating rice in what would eventually become part of the kingdom of Thailand at a time when most of China was still eating millet. The cultivation of rice led to settlements of people as paddy fields needed supervising.

Rice became important to the Thai economy as it became a staple elsewhere. Arab and Indian traders took rice to India and the Middle East and the Chinese absorbed rice into the cuisine until it became their staple as well. Rice also travelled throughout South-East Asia. Thailand is one of the world's major rice exporters and is self sufficient in this staple food.

TYPES OF RICE

Most of the rice eaten in Thailand comes from local paddy. Originally, sticky rice was predominant but gradually long-grain rice became popular. The North and North-East still

RICE NOODLES Rice is also used to make kuaytiaw or rice noodles. Rice flour is mixed with water, then this paste is spread out in trays and steamed before being cut into different widths. Wide noodles are sen yai or wide line, medium are sen lek or small line, and thin noodles are sen mii, line noodles. Rice noodles are sold fresh in markets or dried in packets and are used in soups or stir-fried and eaten with sauces.

mix. The rice is dried by spreading it out in the sun and is then cleaned of impurities, husked, polished and sorted into broken and whole grains. It is finally sieved to sort it into different sizes before being bagged. Broken and smaller grained rices are sold locally. New crop rice is often exported to Singapore, and older, harder rice to Hong Kong. Local companies may mix new and old rice to give a 'perfect' mix.

prefer sticky rice but elsewhere long-grain is more common. Sticky rice is also used for desserts in both its white and 'black' forms. Long-grain rice is served with every meal except snacks. A spoonful is usually eaten by itself before any other dish is added to it and it is never swamped with other food. Sticky rice is eaten by rolling some rice into a ball with one hand. It is then used to pick up food or to dip into a sauce. It is always eaten using your hand.

QUALITY

The quality of rice is of paramount importance to the Thais. Jasmine rice, which has a flowery fragrance, is considered to be the best variety of long-grain. Like wine connoisseurs, some Thais can tell how old rice is, and how and where it was grown. Rice is generally eaten within 12 to 18 months of harvesting. It is at its best after three months because when it is very new and still high in moisture, it is stickier. The drier rice becomes, the more water it needs to be cooked in.

STICKY RICE Sticky rice is often cooked in a container or wrapping. It is soaked in water overnight and then pushed into lengths of bamboo that are plugged at one end. Coconut milk mixed with salt and sugar is added and the bamboo then grilled over coals. Little parcels of sticky rice are also steamed in leaves. Banana, coconut and lotus leaves are all used as wrappings.

HILL TRIBE RICE Rice is cut and threshed by hand by the hill tribes of northern Thailand. The harvested rice is gathered up between two sticks and threshed against the sides of a giant woven bowl until the rice grains are shaken loose from the stalks. The grains are then tossed in the air and fanned, to blow away as much chaff as possible, before being transferred to a flat area where it is raked out and dried in the sun.

CULTIVATION

Rice is cultivated in several different ways depending on the area in which it is grown. An average crop of rice takes between 100 and 200 days to mature depending on variety and growing climate. Quick-maturing crops give some areas two rice harvests a year and in other regions quick and slow growing crops are planted together to string out the harvest and make it more manageable.

Rice can be grown in paddy fields — that is, in water — or in fields that are dry except for rainfall. Rice that relies on rainfall is mainly grown by hill tribes in northern Thailand. These farmers rotate their fields as the land becomes exhausted, cutting down new areas of jungle as they need them.

Technology is relatively primitive in these areas and there are few labour-saving devices. Families within each tribal group help each other. Planting takes place in the monsoon season, July to October, and sometimes in November.

Paddy rice is either grown by sowing seed where it is to grow, a less labour intensive but less regular way of planting, or by initially growing the rice in small nursery fields, where it can be nurtured, and then transplanting it to larger fields. Paddy fields, which are sunken, with raised dams around them, are irrigated with water channels. The channels are filled by rainfall supplied by Thailand's monsoonal climate. Rice is harvested, dried and husked by the farmer or village collective, or taken to a rice mill to be sold as raw rice.

Paddy fields are a common sight in Thailand where farmers help each other with planting and harvesting by growing crops in rotation.

VEGETABLES

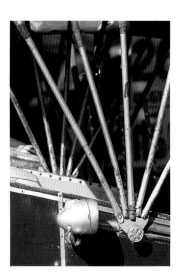

BABY EGGPLANT AND CHERRY TOMATO STIR-FRY

ALTHOUGH A MIXTURE OF THAI EGGPLANTS OF DIFFERENT COLOURS WILL MAKE THIS DISH MORE VISUALLY APPEALING, JUST ONE TYPE WILL DO FINE. THE EGGPLANTS MAY DISCOLOUR WHEN YOU COOK THEM BUT DON'T WORRY AS THE FLAVOUR WON'T BE AFFECTED.

12 small round Thai eggplants
    (aubergines), green, yellow
    or purple
1 teaspoon fish sauce,
    plus 1 tablespoon
1 tablespoon vegetable oil
1 small red chilli, chopped
1 tablespoon finely sliced ginger
2 Asian shallots, finely chopped
1 garlic clove, chopped
150 g (5 oz) cherry tomatoes
2 tablespoons black vinegar
2 tablespoons palm sugar
12–18 Thai sweet basil leaves

SERVES 4

CUT each eggplant in half and toss them in a bowl with 1 teaspoon fish sauce. Put about 8 cm (3 inches) of water in a wok and bring to the boil. Place the eggplants in a bamboo steamer, place the steamer over the boiling water and steam the eggplants for 15 minutes.

HEAT the oil in a wok, add the chilli, ginger, shallots and garlic and cook for 15 seconds. Add the eggplants and tomatoes and toss well. Add the black vinegar, sugar and remaining fish sauce and cook for 2 to 3 minutes, until the sauce thickens. Stir in the basil leaves and serve.

STIR-FRIED BROCCOLI WITH
OYSTER SAUCE

STIR-FRIED BROCCOLI WITH OYSTER SAUCE

350 g (12 oz) Chinese broccoli,
    cut into pieces
1 tablespoon vegetable oil
2 garlic cloves, finely chopped
1 tablespoon oyster sauce
1 tablespoon light soy sauce

SERVES 4

BLANCH the Chinese broccoli in boiling salted water for 2 to 3 minutes, then drain thoroughly.

HEAT the oil in a wok or frying pan and stir-fry the garlic over a medium heat until light brown. Add the Chinese broccoli and half of the oyster sauce and the light soy sauce. Stir-fry over a high heat for 1 to 2 minutes until the stems are just tender. Drizzle with the remaining oyster sauce.

WING BEAN SALAD

THIS IS A FRESH, CRUNCHY SALAD THAT LOOKS GOOD ON THE TABLE. WING BEANS HAVE FOUR

FRILLY EDGES TO THEM AND AN INTERESTING CROSS SECTION WHEN CUT.

oil, for frying
75 g (3 oz) Asian shallots,
   finely sliced
175 g (6 oz) wing beans
55 g (2 oz) cooked chicken, shredded
1 lemon grass stalk, white part only,
   finely sliced
2 tablespoons dried shrimp, ground
1½ tablespoons fish sauce
3–4 tablespoons lime juice
½ long red chilli or 1 small red chilli,
   finely chopped
55 g (2 oz) whole salted roasted
   peanuts
125 ml (½ cup) coconut milk
   (page 279), for garnish

SERVES 4

HEAT 2.5 cm (1 inch) oil in a wok or deep frying pan over a medium heat. Deep-fry the shallots for 3 to 4 minutes until they are light brown (without burning them). Lift out with a slotted spoon and drain on paper towels.

SLICE the wing beans diagonally into thin pieces. Blanch the wing beans in boiling water for 30 seconds, then drain and put them in cold water for 1 to 2 minutes. Drain and transfer to a bowl. Add the cooked chicken, lemon grass, dried shrimp, fish sauce, lime juice, chilli and half the peanuts. Mix with a spoon. Taste, then adjust the seasoning if necessary.

PUT the wing bean salad in a serving bowl, drizzle with coconut milk and sprinkle with the crispy shallots and the rest of the peanuts.

STIR-FRIED WATER SPINACH

THE VEGETABLE THAT THE CHINESE CALL 'ONG CHOY' IS POPULAR IN THAILAND WHERE IT'S CALLED

'PHAK BUNG'. IT HAS LONG THIN STALKS AND LEAFY TOPS, ALL OF WHICH ARE GOOD TO EAT. BUY IT

FROM ASIAN SUPERMARKETS WHERE IT IS SOMETIMES CALLED MORNING GLORY.

1½ tablespoons oyster sauce
1 teaspoon fish sauce
1 tablespoon yellow bean sauce
¼ teaspoon sugar
1½ tablespoons vegetable oil
2–3 garlic cloves, finely chopped
350 g (12 oz) water spinach, cut
   into 5 cm (2 inch) lengths
1 red bird's eye chilli, slightly
   crushed (optional)

SERVES 4

MIX the oyster sauce, fish sauce, yellow bean sauce and sugar in a small bowl.

HEAT the oil in a wok or a frying pan and stir-fry the garlic over a medium heat until light brown. Increase the heat to very high, add the stalks of the water spinach and stir-fry for 1 to 2 minutes. Add the leaves of the water spinach, the sauce mixture and the crushed chilli and stir-fry for another minute.

STIR-FRIED WATER SPINACH

PHAT THUA FAK YAO

STIR-FRIED SNAKE BEANS

SNAKE BEANS ARE VERY LONG GREEN BEANS AND ARE USUALLY SOLD IN COILS. YOU CAN LEAVE OUT THE CHICKEN IF YOU PREFER, BUT REMEMBER THAT THIS STILL WON'T BE A VEGETARIAN DISH AS IT CONTAINS RED CURRY PASTE, WHICH HAS FISH SAUCE AND SHRIMP PASTE IN IT.

2 tablespoons vegetable oil
2 teaspoons red curry paste
  (page 276) or bought paste
350 g (12 oz) skinless chicken
  breast fillet, finely sliced
350 g (12 oz) snake beans,
  cut diagonally into 2.5 cm
  (1 inch) pieces
1 tablespoon fish sauce
25 g (1 oz) sugar
4 makrut (kaffir) lime leaves,
  very finely shredded

SERVES 4

HEAT the oil in a wok or frying pan and stir-fry the red curry paste over a medium heat for 2 minutes or until fragrant. Add the chicken and stir for 4 to 5 minutes or until the chicken is cooked. Add the beans, fish sauce and sugar. Stir-fry for another 4 to 5 minutes.

TRANSFER to a serving plate and sprinkle with the makrut lime leaves.

PUMPKIN WITH CHILLI AND BASIL

PHAT FAK THAWNG KUB PHRIK

PUMPKIN WITH CHILLI AND BASIL

3 tablespoons dried shrimp
½ teaspoon shrimp paste
2 coriander (cilantro) roots
10–12 white peppercorns
2 garlic cloves, chopped
2 Asian shallots, chopped
125 ml (½ cup) coconut cream
  (page 279)
300 g (10 oz) butternut pumpkin
  (squash), cut into 4 cm (1½ inch)
  cubes
2 large red chillies, cut lengthways
125 ml (½ cup) coconut milk
  (page 279)
1 tablespoon fish sauce
1 tablespoon palm sugar
2 teaspoons lime juice
12 Thai sweet basil leaves

SERVES 4

SOAK 2 tablespoons of the dried shrimp in a small bowl of water for 20 minutes, then drain.

PUT the remaining dried shrimp, shrimp paste, coriander roots, peppercorns, garlic and shallots in a pestle and mortar or food processor and pound or blend to a paste.

BRING the coconut cream to a boil in a saucepan and simmer for 5 minutes. Add the paste and stir to combine. Cook for another 2 to 3 minutes, then add the pumpkin, chillies, rehydrated shrimp and coconut milk. Stir to combine all the ingredients and simmer for 10 to 15 minutes, until the pumpkin is just tender. Don't let the pumpkin turn to mush.

ADD the fish sauce, palm sugar and lime juice to the pan and cook for another 2 to 3 minutes. Stir in the basil leaves before serving.

STIR-FRIED MIXED VEGETABLES

CARROTS, SNOW PEAS AND ASPARAGUS ARE NOT TYPICALLY THAI BUT THEY ARE NOW WIDELY GROWN AND EATEN. THE NORTH-WEST OF THAILAND HAS THE RIGHT CLIMATE FOR GROWING COLDER WEATHER VEGETABLES, PARTICULARLY PLACES LIKE THE KING'S PROJECT NORTH OF CHIANG MAI.

4 thin asparagus spears
4 baby sweet corn
50 g (2 oz) snake beans
110 g (4 oz) mixed red and yellow
  capsicums (peppers)
½ small carrot
50 g (2 oz) Chinese broccoli or
  broccoli florets
25 g (1 oz) snow peas (mangetout),
  topped and tailed
2 cm (¾ inch) piece of ginger,
  finely sliced
1 tablespoon fish sauce
1½ tablespoons oyster sauce
2 tablespoons vegetable stock
  or water
½ teaspoon sugar
1½ tablespoons vegetable oil
3–4 garlic cloves, finely chopped
2 spring onions (scallions), sliced

SERVES 4

CUT off the tips of the asparagus and slice each spear into 5 cm (2 inch) lengths. Cut the sweet corn in halves lengthways and the beans into 2.5 cm (1 inch) lengths. Cut both on an angle. Halve the capsicums and remove the seeds, then cut into bite-sized pieces. Peel the carrot and cut into batons.

BLANCH the asparagus stalks, sweet corn, beans and broccoli florets in boiling salted water for 30 seconds. Remove and place in a bowl of iced water to ensure a crispy texture. Drain and place in a bowl with the capsicum, carrot, snow peas, asparagus tips and ginger.

MIX the fish sauce, oyster sauce, stock and sugar in a small bowl.

HEAT the oil in a wok or frying pan and stir-fry the garlic over a medium heat until light brown. Add the mixed vegetables and the sauce mixture, then stir-fry over a high heat for 2 to 3 minutes. Taste, then adjust the seasoning if necessary. Add the spring onions and toss.

Vegetables for stir-fries should be cut into a uniform size.

SPICY TOMATO DIPPING SAUCE

THIS FAMOUS DIPPING SAUCE FROM CHIANG MAI SHOULD BE SERVED AS A MAIN COURSE WITH BLANCHED VEGETABLES SUCH AS WEDGES OF EGGPLANT OR CABBAGE, PIECES OF SNAKE BEAN OR PUMPKIN, AND ASPARAGUS SPEARS. PIECES OF DEEP-FRIED PORK SKIN ARE ALSO SUITABLE.

1 dried long red chilli
1 lemon grass stalk, white part only, finely sliced
4 Asian shallots, finely chopped
2–3 garlic cloves, roughly chopped
½ teaspoon shrimp paste
1½ tablespoons vegetable oil
175 g (6 oz) minced (ground) fatty pork
450 g (1 lb) tomatoes, finely chopped
2 tablespoons fish sauce
1 tablespoon sugar
3 tablespoons tamarind purée
mixed vegetables, such as wedges of eggplant (aubergine), pieces of snake bean, wedges of cabbage, asparagus spears, baby corn, pieces of pumpkin, to serve
a few coriander (cilantro) leaves, for garnish
pieces of pork skin, deep-fried, to serve

SERVES 4

SLIT the chilli lengthways with a sharp knife and discard all the seeds. Soak the chilli in hot water for 1 to 2 minutes or until soft, then drain and chop roughly. Using a pestle and mortar, pound the chilli, lemon grass, shallots and garlic into a paste. Add the shrimp paste and mix well. Alternatively, use a small processor or blender to grind or blend the chilli, lemon grass, shallots, garlic and shrimp paste into a smooth paste.

HEAT the oil in a saucepan or wok and stir-fry the paste over a medium heat for 2 minutes or until fragrant. Add the minced pork and stir for 2 to 3 minutes. Add the tomatoes, fish sauce, sugar and tamarind. Reduce the heat and gently simmer for 25 to 30 minutes or until the mixture is thick.

BLANCH briefly any tough vegetables such as eggplant, snake beans, asparagus and pumpkin. Drain well.

TASTE the sauce, then adjust with more tamarind, sugar or chilli if necessary. This dish should have three flavours: sweet, sour and lightly salted. Spoon into a serving bowl and garnish with coriander leaves. Serve with a mixture of blanched vegetables and deep-fried pork skin.

NAAM PHRIK KA-PI

SHRIMP PASTE DIPPING SAUCE

THAI HOT DIPPING SAUCE IS USED TO ACCOMPANY GRILLED OR DEEP-FRIED FISH, PIECES OF OMELETTE, AND FRESH VEGETABLES AND FRUIT SUCH AS EGGPLANT, CUCUMBER, WING BEANS AND SNAKE BEANS. YOU CAN VARY THE NUMBER OF CHILLIES, DEPENDING ON HOW HOT YOU LIKE IT.

3–4 garlic cloves
2 teaspoons shrimp paste
2–3 small red and green chillies
3–4 Thai eggplants (aubergines)
  (optional)
1 teaspoon sugar
1 tablespoon fish sauce
2 tablespoons lime juice
mixed raw vegetables and fruit
  such as pieces of Thai eggplant
  (aubergine), cucumber batons,
  wing beans, pieces of snake
  bean, spring onions (scallions),
  pomelo segments, pieces of rose
  apple, to serve

SERVES 4

USING a pestle and mortar, pound the garlic into a rough paste. Add the shrimp paste and grind together. Add the chillies and lightly bruise to release the hot taste. (Do this gently so the liquid won't splash.) Add the eggplants and lightly pound. Add the sugar, fish sauce and lime juice and lightly mix in. Taste the sauce, then adjust the seasoning if necessary.

TO MAKE without a pestle and mortar, put the finely chopped garlic in a bowl and, using the back of a spoon, scrape the garlic into a paste. Add the shrimp paste and mix well. Add the chillies and break them up with a fork. Add the eggplant and squash it gently against the side of the bowl. Add the sugar, fish sauce and lime juice and lightly mix.

SPOON into a small serving bowl and serve with the mixed vegetables.

When you have pounded the ingredients together, stir in the sugar, fish sauce and lime juice.

SHRIMP PASTE DIPPING SAUCE

DESSERTS

STICKY RICE WITH MANGO

IN THAILAND THE MANGO SEASON IS IN APRIL. SOME MANGOES TASTE BETTER WHEN GREEN, CRISP AND CRUNCHY, OTHERS WHEN THEY ARE RIPE. EITHER WAY, THERE IS A LOT OF VARIETY AND MANY DIFFERENT FLAVOURS. THIS STICKY RICE WITH MANGO IS ARGUABLY THE BEST THAI DESSERT.

4 large ripe mangoes
1 quantity of steamed sticky rice
  with coconut milk (page 280)
170 ml (⅔ cup) coconut cream
  (page 279) mixed with ¼ teaspoon
  salt, for garnish
2 tablespoons dry-fried mung beans
  (optional)

SERVES 4

PEEL the mangoes and slice off the two outside cheeks of each, removing as much flesh as you can in large pieces. Avoid cutting very close to the stone where the flesh is fibrous. Discard the stone. Slice each cheek lengthways into four or five pieces.

ARRANGE the mango pieces on a serving plate. Spoon a portion of steamed sticky rice with coconut milk near the mango slices. Spoon the coconut cream garnish on top and sprinkle with mung beans. Serve at room temperature.

BANANA IN COCONUT CREAM

BANANA IN COCONUT CREAM

THERE ARE MORE THAN 20 VARIETIES OF BANANA IN THAILAND, ALL OF WHICH ARE USED IN COOKING. USE NICE SWEET BANANAS FOR THIS RECIPE AND AVOID PARTICULARLY LARGE ONES.

400 ml (1⅔ cups) coconut milk
  (page 279)
4 tablespoons sugar
5 just-ripe bananas
½ teaspoon salt

SERVES 4

PUT the coconut milk, sugar and 125 ml (½ cup) water in a saucepan and bring to a boil. Reduce the heat and simmer until the sugar dissolves.

PEEL the bananas and cut them into 5 cm (2 inch) lengths. If you are using very small bananas, leave them whole.

WHEN the sugar in the coconut milk has dissolved, add the bananas and salt. Cook gently over a low to medium heat for 5 minutes or until the bananas are soft.

DIVIDE the bananas and coconut cream among four bowls. Serve warm or at room temperature.

TAPIOCA PUDDING WITH YOUNG COCONUT

Stir the tapioca and pandanus leaves occasionally.

170 ml (⅔ cup) coconut milk
   (page 279)
¾ teaspoon salt
110 g (4 oz) tapioca or sago
6 pandanus leaves
60 g (¼ cup) caster (superfine) sugar
150 g (5 oz) young coconut meat in
   syrup (from a tin), drained

SERVES 4

IN a small saucepan, stir the coconut milk with ½ teaspoon salt until combined.

BRING 1 litre (4 cups) water to a rolling boil in a medium saucepan. Add the tapioca and pandanus leaves and stir occasionally with a wooden spoon for 15 to 20 minutes while simmering over a medium heat. Stir until all the grains are swollen, clear and shiny. Reduce the heat if necessary. Add the sugar and ¼ teaspoon salt to the saucepan and stir until the sugar has dissolved. The tapioca should now be almost cooked. Add the coconut meat and gently mix. Remove the pandanus leaves. Leave to thicken for 5 minutes before dividing among individual bowls. Drizzle coconut milk on top. Serve warm.

DEEP-FRIED BANANAS

YEARS AGO MOST THAI PEOPLE WERE BROUGHT UP ON THIS DELICIOUS SNACK BUT IT IS NOT AS EASY TODAY TO FIND IT ON THE STREET. HOWEVER, YOU CAN EASILY MAKE IT AT HOME, JUST AS MANY THAI PEOPLE DO. ANOTHER VERSION USES SWEET POTATOES WITH THE BANANAS.

DEEP-FRIED BANANAS

BATTER
125 g (1 cup) self-raising flour
½ teaspoon baking powder
2 teaspoons sugar
¼ teaspoon salt
25 g (1 oz) grated coconut
   (page 279) or desiccated coconut
2 tablespoons sesame seeds
350 ml (1⅓ cups) water, at room
   temperature

vegetable oil, for deep-frying
4 ripe bananas

SERVES 4

PUT the flour, baking powder, sugar, salt, coconut and sesame seeds in a bowl. Add the water and lightly mix with a spoon or fork until smooth.

HEAT 7.5 cm (3 inches) oil in a wok or deep-frying pan over a medium heat. When the oil seems hot, drop a little batter into the oil. If it sizzles immediately, the oil is ready. It is important not to have the oil too hot or the batter will burn.

HALVE the bananas lengthways, then cut them into 5 cm (2 inch) chunks. Preheat the oven to 150°C/300°F/Gas 2. Dip the banana chunks one at a time into the batter, then lower into the hot oil. Deep-fry about 5 pieces at a time for 3 to 4 minutes or until golden, then lift out with a slotted spoon or a pair of chopsticks. Drain on paper towels and keep warm in the oven. Transfer to a serving plate and serve warm.

When you have coloured and floured the water chestnuts, cook them in two batches. When they float, lift them out.

Detail from a Wat in Ratchaburi.

CRISP RUBIES

CRISP RUBIES RESEMBLE JEWEL-LIKE PIECES OF POMEGRANATE. THE COMBINATION OF INGREDIENTS MAY SOUND SOMEWHAT ODD, BUT CRISP RUBIES ARE VERY POPULAR AND ARE ACTUALLY QUITE DELICIOUS, ESPECIALLY WHEN SERVED WITH ICE AND COCONUT CREAM.

8–10 drops of pink or red food colouring
2 x 225 g (8 oz) tins water chestnuts, drained and each chestnut cut into 10–12 pieces
150 g (5 oz) tapioca flour
250 g (1 cup) sugar
185 ml (¾ cup) coconut milk (page 279)
¼ teaspoon salt
crushed ice, to serve

SERVES 6

ADD the food colouring to 60 ml (¼ cup) water in a bowl. Add the water chestnuts and mix with a spoon. Leave for 10 minutes until the pieces turn pink, then drain and leave to dry.

PUT the tapioca flour in a plastic bag. Add the pink water chestnuts and shake the bag to coat them well. Dust off any excess flour. Bring a saucepan of water to boiling point. Add half of the water chestnuts and cook for 1 to 2 minutes or until they float to the surface. Lift out with a slotted spoon and put them in a bowl of cold water. Repeat with the remaining water chestnuts. Drain all the pieces.

IN a small saucepan, heat 250 ml (1 cup) water and the sugar until the mixture boils, stirring constantly. Lower the heat to medium and simmer for 5 to 10 minutes until the liquid reduces to a thick syrup.

MIX the coconut milk and salt in a small saucepan and cook over a medium heat for 1 to 2 minutes until slightly creamy.

DIVIDE the water chestnuts among individual bowls and top with a few spoonfuls each of sugar syrup and creamy coconut milk. Sprinkle with ice and serve cold.

KHAO NIAW DAM
BLACK STICKY RICE WITH TARO

VEGETABLES LIKE TARO ARE OFTEN USED IN THAI DESSERTS. BLACK STICKY RICE IS SIMPLY WHITE RICE WITH THE BRAN LEFT ON AND IS ACTUALLY MORE PURPLE THAN BLACK. YOU MUST COOK THE RICE BEFORE ADDING ANY SUGAR OR IT WILL TOUGHEN AND NEVER BECOME TENDER.

175 g (6 oz) black sticky rice
  (black glutinous)
280 g (10 oz) taro, cut into 1 cm
  (½ inch) squares and soaked in
  cold water
150 g (5 oz) palm sugar
1 teaspoon salt
185 ml (¾ cup) coconut milk
  (page 279)

SERVES 6

PUT the rice in a bowl and pour in cold water to come 5 cm (2 inches) above the rice. Soak for at least 3 hours, or overnight if possible.

DRAIN the rice and add clean water. Scoop the rice through your fingers four or five times to clean it, then drain. Repeat two or three times with clean water to remove the unwanted starch. (The water will never be completely clear when using black rice, even when all the unwanted starch has gone.) Put the rice in a saucepan and add 625 ml (2½ cups) cold water.

BRING to the boil, stirring the rice frequently as it reaches boiling point. Reduce the heat to medium. Stir and simmer for 30 to 35 minutes or until nearly all the liquid has been absorbed. The rice should be very moist, but with hardly any water remaining in the bottom of the saucepan. (Taste a few grains to check whether the rice is cooked.)

MEANWHILE, drain the taro, spread it on a plate and transfer it to a bamboo steamer or other steamer. Taking care not to burn your hands, set the basket over a pan of boiling water over a high heat. Cover and steam for 8 to 10 minutes or until the taro is cooked and tender.

WHEN the rice is cooked, add the sugar and gently stir until the sugar has dissolved. Add the taro and gently mix.

MIX the salt into the coconut milk. Divide the pudding among individual bowls and drizzle coconut milk on top. Serve warm.

Black sticky rice is commonly used for desserts and, when cooked, is actually a dark purplish-red.

Akah bracelets for sale.

Cut off the tops of the pumpkins and scrape out the seeds. Sieve the custard, discard the leaves, then pour into the pumpkins.

PUMPKIN WITH CUSTARD

THIS TRADITIONAL THAI DESSERT, MADE WITH COCONUT MILK AND PALM OR COCONUT SUGAR, IS SWEET AND RICH IN TASTE. CHOOSE HONEY-COLOURED PUMPKINS, EITHER ONE SMALL TO MEDIUM, OR FOUR VERY SMALL ONES. WHEN COOKED AND COOLED, CUT THEM INTO WEDGES FOR SERVING.

2 tablespoons coconut milk
    (page 279)
2 eggs
150 g (5 oz) palm sugar, cut or
    shaved into very small pieces
2–3 pandanus leaves, dried
    and cut into small pieces,
    and bruised, or 1 teaspoon
    vanilla essence
1 small to medium or 4 very small
    pumpkins

SERVES 4

TO make a custard, stir the coconut milk, eggs, palm sugar, pandanus leaves and a pinch of salt in a bowl, using a spoon, for 10 minutes or until the sugar has dissolved.

POUR the custard through a sieve into a jug to discard the pandanus leaves. Pour the custard into the pumpkin/s, filling to within 2.5 cm (1 inch) from the top.

CAREFULLY cut off the top of the pumpkin/s. Try not to pierce the pumpkin at any other point with the knife as it is more likely to crack or leak around such punctures. Using a spoon, scrape out and discard all the seeds and fibres.

FILL a wok or a steamer pan with water, cover and bring to a rolling boil over a high heat. Place the pumpkin/s on a plate. Use a plate that will fit on the rack of a traditional bamboo steamer basket or on a steamer rack inside the wok. Taking care not to burn your hands, place the plate on the rack or steamer inside the wok. Cover, reduce the heat to low and cook for 30 to 45 minutes or until the pumpkin is cooked and the custard puffed up. Check and replenish the water every 10 minutes or so.

TURN off the heat and remove the cover. Carefully remove the pumpkin and set aside to cool. If you prefer, you can leave the pumpkin in the steamer to cool to room temperature.

CUT the pumpkin into thick wedges for serving. Serve at room temperature or chilled.

AS an alternative, you can steam the mixture in a shallow tin, such as a pie tin or cake pan, and serve it in small spoonfuls on top of mounds of steamed sticky rice with coconut milk (page 280).

SANGKAYA

CUSTARDS

THE CLASSIC CUSTARD COOKED IN A PUMPKIN IS JUST ONE OF MANY POPULAR CUSTARDS IN THAILAND. AS HERE, COCONUT, SWEET POTATO, JACKFRUIT AND TARO ARE ALSO USED AS FLAVOURINGS. SERVE IN BANANA CUPS, AS SHOWN, OR POUR THE MIXTURE INTO BABY PUMPKINS.

banana leaves
80 ml (⅓ cup) coconut milk
   (page 279)
7 eggs
275 g (10 oz) palm sugar, cut into
   very small pieces
¼ teaspoon salt
5–6 fresh pandanus leaves, dried
   and cut into small pieces, bruised,
   or 3 teaspoons vanilla essence
100 g (3 oz) young coconut meat,
   cut into small pieces, or orange
   sweet potato, jackfruit or taro,
   cut into matchsticks

MAKES 6

TO SOFTEN the banana leaves and prevent them from splitting, put them in a hot oven for about 10 seconds, or blanch them briefly. Cut the banana leaves into 12 circles about 13 cm (5 inches) in diameter with the fibre running lengthways. Place one piece with the fibre running lengthways and another on top of it with the fibre running across. Make a 1 cm (½ inches) tuck 4 cm (1½ inch) long (4 cm in from the edge and no further) and pin securely with a small sharp toothpick. Repeat this at the opposite point and at the two side points, making four tucks altogether. Flatten the base as best you can. Repeat to make 6 square-shaped cups. Alternatively, use a small shallow rectangular tin such as a brownie tin.

COMBINE the coconut milk, eggs, sugar, salt and pandanus leaves in a bowl, using a spoon, for 10 minutes or until the sugar has dissolved. Pour the custard through the sieve into a bowl to discard the pandanus leaves.

ADD the coconut, orange sweet potato, taro or jackfruit to the custard and lightly mix. Spoon the mixture into each banana cup, filling to within 1 cm (½ inch) from the top.

HALF FILL a wok or a steamer pan with water, cover and bring to a rolling boil over a high heat. Place the banana cups on a plate. Use a plate that will fit on the rack of a traditional bamboo steamer basket or on a steamer rack inside the wok or pan. Taking care not to burn your hands, place the plate on the bamboo steamer or steamer rack inside the wok or pan. Cover, reduce the heat to low and cook for 10 to 15 minutes. Check and replenish the water after 10 minutes. Serve at room temperature or chilled. The custards can be covered and refrigerated for up to 3 to 4 days.

Make and balance the cups carefully so none of the liquid spills out.

Preparing durian for sale.

ICE CREAM KRA TI

COCONUT ICE CREAM

400 ml (1⅔ cups) coconut milk
(page 279)
250 ml (1 cup) thick (double/heavy)
cream
2 eggs
4 egg yolks
160 g (⅔ cup) caster (superfine)
sugar
¼ teaspoon salt

SERVES 10

POUR the coconut milk and cream into a medium saucepan. Stir over a gentle heat without boiling for 2 to 3 minutes. Remove from the heat, cover and keep warm over a bowl of boiling water.

PUT the eggs, egg yolks, sugar and salt in a large heatproof bowl. Beat the mixture with electric beaters for 3 minutes or until frothy and thickened.

PLACE the bowl over a pan of simmering water. Continue to beat the egg mixture, slowly adding all the coconut mixture until the custard thickens lightly. This process will take 8 to 10 minutes. The mixture should be a thin cream and easily coat the back of a spoon. Do not boil it or it will curdle. Set aside until cool. Stir the mixture occasionally while it is cooling. Pour into a freezer box or churn in an ice cream machine. If you are using a freezer box, take the mixture out of the freezer and beat it with electric beaters at least twice during the freezing. You want it to get plenty of air whipped into it. Cover and freeze completely. To serve, remove from the freezer for 10 to 15 minutes until slightly softened. Serve in scoops with slices of coconut.

ICE CREAM MAMUANG

MANGO SORBET

3 ripe mangoes
150 g (5½ oz) palm sugar
zest and juice from 1 lime

SERVES 4

PEEL the mangoes and cut the flesh off the stones. Chop into small pieces. Put the sugar and 185 ml (¾ cup) water in a saucepan and bring to the boil. Reduce the heat and simmer until the liquid reduces by half. Put the sugar syrup, mango and lime zest and juice in a food processor or blender and whiz until smooth.

POUR into a freezer box or churn in an ice cream machine. If you are using a freezer box, take the mixture out of the freezer and beat it with electric beaters at least twice during the freezing time. You want it to have plenty of air whipped into it or it will be too icy and hard. Cover and freeze completely.

MANGO SORBET

PALMS Phetchaburi province is famous for its sweets. It is also the land of the palm tree. Both coconut and sugar palms supply the sweet-makers with raw ingredients to ply their trade. Coconut is used both fresh and dried. When fresh, the flesh is soft and jelly-like with lots of liquid inside and these coconuts are sold for drinking (left). Older, drier coconut flesh, however, is shredded (bottom centre) and used as a garnish

SWEETS

PEOPLE IN THAILAND USE THE TERM KHWANG WAAN, LITERALLY MEANING SWEET STUFF, TO REFER TO ANYTHING THAT IS SWEET, INCLUDING DESSERTS, SWEET SNACKS OR SWEETS THEMSELVES. MOST KHWANG WAAN ARE EATEN AS SNACKS RATHER THAN AS DESSERTS BUT NEVERTHELESS MEALS CAN BE FINISHED ON A SWEET NOTE.

In Thailand sweet things have always been part of the cuisine, originally made with crushed beans, coconut, rice, sugar and fruit. These were supplemented with the use of eggs and pastry, ideas that arrived with the Portuguese. Even more recently, ice cream has become popular.

TEXTURES, COLOURS AND FLAVOURS

Thai sweets differ from European ones in both texture and flavour. Though egg custards and pastries may be reminiscent of European desserts, they are often much sweeter. Unlike in Europe, salt is used as a flavour in coconut desserts and sweets, to offset sweetness. Flower and leaf perfumes such as jasmine and pandanus are used in sugar syrups. Favourite textures include jellies, custards and sticky,

Coconut is used to flavour sticky rice, which is steamed in leaves (opposite page bottom right and this page bottom left). Palm sugar comes in different grades, the best being from Phetchaburi province. It is usually sold in discs or log shapes (bottom centre) though softer types can come in tubs. Palm sugar is used to sweeten Thai style waffles (top) and used in perfumed syrups for 'wet' sweets and layered sweets (right).

chewy ingredients like rice. Often combinations of textures are eaten together, particularly in desserts like 'green strings' where 'strings' made of green dough are served with crushed ice, sugar syrup and coconut juice. Colours come from pandanus (green), egg yolks (yellow), and coconut ash and sesame (black). Crunch is often added by adding lotus seeds, beans, sweet corn kernels and water chestnuts. Fruit is eaten fresh and is also candied and preserved.

FESTIVALS
Some sweets are associated with ceremonies and in many cases are thought to sweeten the gods. Other sweets are eaten at particular times of the year, ash pudding at Thai New Year, and sticky rice with banana at the end of Thai Lent.

CUSTARDS

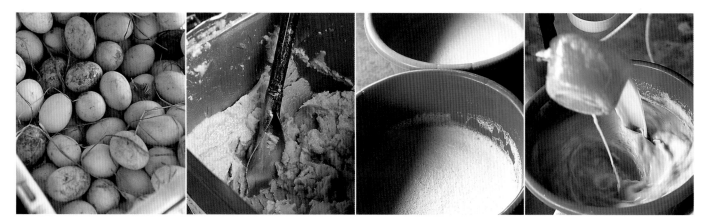

COCONUT CUSTARDS *(sangkaya)* These popular baked coconut custards are made with duck eggs, palm sugar and coconut milk at the Mei Kim Lui sweet factory. Hundreds of custards are made every morning and sent out to the shops owned by the factory. The ingredients are all local to Phetchaburi, a province famous for its palm sugar. The cook mixes the custard in large quantities and pours it into small tin

containers set out on baking sheets. The custards are baked in an oven for about an hour before being cooled. They are then sold in their containers. Some custards have different toppings: sliced garlic, shallots or peanuts are particularly popular. The use of egg to make custard-type sweets is probably based on Portuguese desserts introduced in the 14th and 15th centuries.

PALM SUGAR

PALM SUGAR Palm sugar is made by boiling the sap of sugar palms *(ton taan)*. The sap is collected twice a day, in the early morning and early evening. It is then boiled until it reaches the desired thickness. Pandanus leaves are used to flavour some syrups, others are left plain. The thinnest syrup is sold in bottles to be sold as juice, which is drunk poured over ice. The thickest crystallizes to a solid sugar.

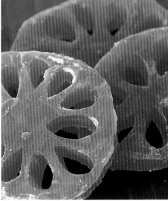

CANDIED LOTUS ROOT
Candied fruit and vegetables are popular sweets. Slices of lotus root are simmered in a sugar syrup until they candy.

GOLDEN FLOWERS These are made by piping duck egg yolks into simmering sugar syrup to form golden flowers. Here they are piled into little pastry cups.

PALM FRUIT IN SUGAR SYRUP Palm fruit in sugar syrup is sold by the scoop in small plastic bags. Coconut milk is added as a garnish.

BEAN PASTE SWEETS Thick sweetened mung bean paste is moulded into a variety of different attractive fruit shapes. Here they resemble mangosteens.

COCONUT PUDDINGS These puddings have a transparent sweet jelly with chestnut or lotus seeds on the bottom and a salty coconut jelly on top.

COCONUT CUSTARDS *(sangkaya fak thawang)* These are a common sweet snack. Coconut custard is steamed in small hollowed out pumpkins.

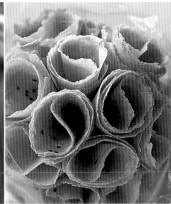

COCONUT WAFERS These thin, crisp coconut wafers are made with coconut, rice flour and palm sugar. Rolled into cones and packed in cellophane.

CHINESE CAKES These Chinese-style pastry cakes are filled with green mung beans or red beans. Often given as gifts at weddings and birthdays.

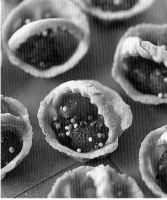

PASTRY CUPS This is a modern Thai sweet made by filling a pastry cup with a dark sweet palm sugar mixture. Hundreds and thousands add colour.

DIPPED FRUITS *(luuk chup)* These are the most intricate Thai sweets. Made from soy bean paste and dipped into a clear jelly that dries to a waxy glaze.

JELLIES These jellies are made with durian (brown), pandanus leaves (green) and sesame (black). Each jelly is wrapped in a piece of cellophane.

BLACK STICKY RICE This is a popular dessert made with a sticky rice that is purple rather than black. Sold in little bags with some salted coconut cream.

BASICS &
ACCOMPANIMENTS

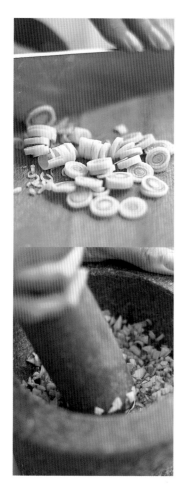

Pound the chopped ingredients until a smooth paste is formed.

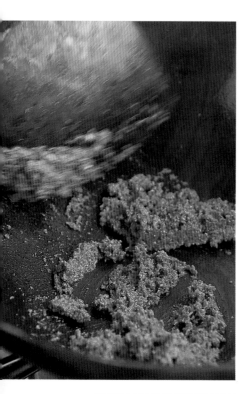

CHIANG MAI CURRY PASTE

KHREUANG KAENG PHANAENG

DRY CURRY PASTE

2 dried long red chillies, about
   13 cm (5 inches) long
2 lemon grass stalks, white part
   only, finely sliced
2.5 cm (1 inch) piece of galangal,
   finely chopped
4–5 garlic cloves, finely chopped
3–4 Asian shallots, finely chopped
5–6 coriander (cilantro) roots,
   finely chopped
1 teaspoon shrimp paste
1 teaspoon ground cumin,
   dry-roasted
3 tablespoons unsalted peanuts,
   chopped

MAKES 80 G (⅓ CUP)

REMOVE the stems from the chillies and slit the chillies lengthways with a sharp knife. Discard the seeds and soak the chillies in hot water for 1 to 2 minutes or until soft. Drain and roughly chop.

USING a pestle and mortar, pound the chillies, lemon grass and galangal into a paste. Add the remaining ingredients one at a time and pound until the mixture forms a very smooth paste.

ALTERNATIVELY, you can use a food processor or blender to blend all the ingredients together into as smooth a paste as possible. Add cooking oil, as needed, to assist the blending.

USE as required or keep in an airtight jar. The paste will keep for at least two weeks in the refrigerator and for two months in a freezer.

KHREUANG KAENG HANGLEH

CHIANG MAI CURRY PASTE

1 tablespoon coriander seeds
2 teaspoons cumin seeds
2 dried long red chillies, about
   13 cm (5 inches) long
½ teaspoon salt
5 cm (2 inch) piece of galangal,
   grated
1 lemon grass stalk, white part only,
   finely chopped
2 Asian shallots, chopped
2 garlic cloves, chopped
1 teaspoon grated turmeric or
   a pinch of ground turmeric
1 teaspoon shrimp paste
½ teaspoon ground cassia
   or cinnamon

MAKES 185 G (¾ CUP)

DRY-ROAST the coriander seeds in a small frying pan for 1 minute until fragrant, then remove from the pan. Repeat with the cumin seeds. Grind them both to a powder with a pestle and mortar.

REMOVE the stems from the chillies and slit the chillies lengthways with a sharp knife. Discard the seeds. Soak the chillies in hot water for 1 to 2 minutes or until soft. Drain and roughly chop.

USING a pestle and mortar, pound the chillies, salt, galangal, lemon grass, shallots, garlic and turmeric to as smooth a paste as possible. Add the shrimp paste, ground coriander, cumin and cassia and mix until the mixture forms a smooth paste.

ALTERNATIVELY, use a small processor or blender to blend all the ingredients into a very smooth paste. Add a little cooking oil, as needed, to ease the grinding.

GREEN CURRY PASTE

1 teaspoon ground coriander
1 teaspoon ground cumin
8–10 small green chillies, seeded
2 lemon grass stalks, white part
  only, finely sliced
2.5 cm (1 inch) piece of galangal,
  finely chopped
1 teaspoon very finely chopped
  makrut (kaffir) lime skin or makrut
  lime leaves (about half the skin
  from a makrut lime or 4–5 leaves)
4–5 garlic cloves, finely chopped
3–4 Asian shallots, chopped
5–6 coriander (cilantro) roots,
  finely chopped
a handful of holy basil leaves, finely
  chopped
2 teaspoons shrimp paste

MAKES 125 G (½ CUP)

DRY-ROAST the coriander in a small frying pan for 1 minute until fragrant, then remove from the pan. Repeat with the cumin.

USING a pestle and mortar, pound the chillies, lemon grass, galangal and makrut lime skin or leaves into a paste. Add the garlic, shallots and coriander roots and pound together. Add the remaining ingredients and dry-roasted spices one at a time and pound until the mixture forms a smooth paste.

ALTERNATIVELY, you can use a food processor or blender to blend all the ingredients into as smooth a paste as possible. Add cooking oil as needed to assist the blending.

USE as required or keep in an airtight jar. The paste will keep for at least two weeks in the refrigerator and for two months in a freezer.

Whether using makrut lime skin or leaves, chop them very finely. Dry-roasting the ground spices helps to bring out the flavour.

YELLOW CURRY PASTE

3 teaspoons coriander seeds,
  dry-roasted
1 teaspoon cumin seeds,
  dry-roasted
2–3 dried long red chillies
2 lemon grass stalks, white part
  only, finely sliced
3 Asian shallots, finely chopped
2 garlic cloves, finely chopped
2 tablespoons grated turmeric or
  1 teaspoon ground turmeric
1 teaspoon shrimp paste

MAKES 250 G (1 CUP)

GRIND the coriander seeds to a powder with a pestle and mortar. Grind the cumin seeds.

REMOVE the stems from the chillies and slit the chillies lengthways with a sharp knife. Discard the seeds and soak the chillies in hot water for 1 to 2 minutes or until soft. Drain and roughly chop.

USING a pestle and mortar, pound the chillies, lemon grass, shallots, garlic and turmeric to as smooth a paste as possible. Add the shrimp paste, ground coriander and ground cumin and pound until the mixture forms a smooth paste. Alternatively, use a small processor or blender, blend all the ingredients into a very smooth paste. Add cooking oil as needed to ease the grinding. Use as required or keep in an airtight jar. The paste will keep for at least two weeks in the refrigerator and for two months in a freezer.

YELLOW CURRY PASTE

Before soaking the dried chillies in hot water, slit them lengthways and remove all the seeds.

RED CURRY PASTE

3–4 dried long red chillies, about 13 cm (5 inches) long

8–10 dried small red chillies, about 5 cm (2 inches) long, or 10 fresh small red chillies, seeded

2 lemon grass stalks, white part only, finely sliced

2.5 cm (1 inch) piece of galangal, finely sliced

1 teaspoon very finely chopped makrut (kaffir) lime skin or makrut lime leaves (about half the skin from a makrut lime or 4–5 leaves)

4–5 garlic cloves, finely chopped

3–4 Asian shallots, finely chopped

5–6 coriander (cilantro) roots, finely chopped

2 teaspoons shrimp paste

1 teaspoon ground coriander, dry-roasted

MAKES 125 G (½ CUP)

REMOVE the stems from the dried chillies and slit the chillies lengthways with a sharp knife. Discard the seeds and soak the chillies in hot water for 1 to 2 minutes or until soft. Drain and roughly chop.

USING a pestle and mortar, pound the chillies, lemon grass, galangal and makrut lime skin or leaves into a paste. Add the remaining ingredients and pound together until the mixture forms a smooth paste.

ALTERNATIVELY, you can use a food processor or blender to blend all the ingredients into as smooth a paste as possible. Add cooking oil, as needed, to assist the blending.

USE as required or keep in an airtight jar. The paste will keep for at least two weeks in the refrigerator and for two months in a freezer.

MASSAMAN CURRY PASTE

MASSAMAN CURRY PASTE

2 dried long red chillies, about 13 cm (5 inches) long

1 lemon grass stalk, white part only, finely sliced

2.5 cm (1 inch) piece of galangal, finely chopped

5 cloves

10 cm (4 inch) piece of cinnamon stick, crushed

10 cardamom seeds

½ teaspoon freshly grated nutmeg

6 garlic cloves, finely chopped

4 Asian shallots, finely chopped

4–5 coriander (cilantro) roots, finely chopped

1 teaspoon shrimp paste

MAKES 250 G (1 CUP)

REMOVE the stems from the chillies and slit the chillies lengthways with a sharp knife. Discard the seeds and soak the chillies in hot water for 1 to 2 minutes or until soft. Drain and roughly chop.

USING a pestle and mortar, pound the chillies, lemon grass, galangal, cloves, cinnamon, cardamom seeds and nutmeg into a paste. Add the garlic, shallots and coriander roots. Pound and mix together. Add the shrimp paste and pound until the mixture is a smooth paste.

ALTERNATIVELY, use a food processor or blender to grind or blend all the ingredients into as smooth a paste as possible. Add cooking oil, as needed, to assist the blending. Use as required or keep in an airtight jar. The paste will keep for two weeks in the refrigerator and for two months in a freezer.

KA-THI

COCONUT MILK AND CREAM

GRATED COCONUT IS BEST WHEN IT IS FRESH. DRIED OR DESICCATED COCONUT CAN ALSO BE USED TO MAKE COCONUT MILK BUT IT NEEDS TO BE SOAKED, THEN CHOPPED MORE FINELY OR GROUND TO A PASTE, OTHERWISE IT WILL BE FIBROUS. IF YOU CAN, BUY A PROPER COCONUT GRATER.

1 coconut
  (yields about 300 g/10 oz flesh)

MAKES 125 ML (½ CUP) COCONUT CREAM AND 250 ML (1 CUP) COCONUT MILK

DRAIN the coconut by punching a hole in two of the dark, coloured eyes. Drain out the liquid and use it as a refreshing drink. Holding the coconut in one hand, tap around the circumference firmly with a hammer or pestle. This should cause the coconut to split open evenly. (If the coconut doesn't crack easily, put it in a 150°C/300°F/ Gas 2 oven for 15 minutes. This may cause it to crack as it cools. If it doesn't, it will crack easily when hit with a hammer.)

IF YOU would like to use a coconut grater, the easiest ones to use are the ones that you sit on at one end, then scrape out the coconut from each half on the serrated edge, catching the grated coconut meat in a large bowl. If you don't have a coconut grater, prise the flesh out of the shell, trim off the hard, brown, outer skin and grate either by hand on a box grater or chop in a food processor. Grated coconut can be frozen in small portions until it is needed.

MIX the grated coconut with 125 ml (½ cup) hot water and leave to steep for 5 minutes. Pour the mixture into a container through a sieve lined with muslin, then gather the muslin into a ball to squeeze out any remaining liquid. This will make a thick coconut milk, which is usually called coconut cream.

REPEAT the process with another 250 ml (1 cup) water to make thinner coconut milk.

Tap the coconut until it splits open. Pull it apart, scrape out the coconut and soak it in hot water before draining in a sieve.

STICKY RICE

STEAMED STICKY RICE WITH
COCONUT MILK

STEAMED RICE

400 g (2 cups) jasmine rice

SERVES 4

RINSE the rice until the water runs clear. Put the rice in a saucepan and add enough water to come an index-finger joint above the rice. Bring to the boil, cover and cook at a slow simmer for 10 to 15 minutes. Remove from the heat and leave it to rest for 10 minutes.

STICKY RICE

400 g (2 cups) sticky rice

SERVES 4

PUT the rice in a bowl and pour in cold water to come 5 cm (2 inches) above the rice. Soak for at least 3 hours, or overnight. Drain and transfer to a bamboo basket specially made for steaming sticky rice, or to a steamer lined with a double thickness of muslin. Spread the rice in the steamer. Bring the water in the bottom of the steamer to a rolling boil. Taking care, set the rice over the water. Lower the heat, cover and steam for 20 to 25 minutes or until the rice swells and is glistening and tender. The cooking time will vary depending on the soaking time. Check and replenish the water every 10 minutes or so.

WHEN the rice is cooked, tip it onto a large tray and spread it out to help it cool quickly. If it cools slowly it will be soggy rather than sticky. Serve warm or cold.

STEAMED STICKY RICE WITH COCONUT MILK

200 g (1 cup) sticky rice
170 ml (⅔ cup) coconut milk
  (page 279), well stirred
1 tablespoon palm sugar
  (not too brown)
½ teaspoon salt

SERVES 4

COOK the sticky rice according to the instructions in the recipe above.

WHILE the rice is cooking, stir the coconut milk, sugar and salt in a small saucepan over low heat until the sugar has dissolved. As soon as the rice is cooked, use a wooden spoon to gently mix it with the coconut milk. Set aside for 15 minutes.

NAAM JIM PHRIK
CHILLI JAM

80 ml (⅓ cup) oil
2 Asian shallots, finely chopped
2 garlic cloves, finely chopped
40 g (1½ oz) dried chilli flakes
¼ teaspoon palm sugar

MAKES 185 G (¾ CUP)

HEAT the oil in a small saucepan and fry the shallots and garlic until brown. Add the chilli flakes and palm sugar and stir well. Season with a pinch of salt. Use as a dipping sauce or accompaniment. The sauce can be stored in a jar in the refrigerator for several weeks.

NAAM PHRIK PHAO
ROASTED CHILLI SAUCE

oil, for frying
20 Asian shallots, sliced
10 garlic cloves, sliced
3 tablespoons dried shrimp
7 dried long red chillies, chopped
3 tablespoons tamarind purée or
  3 tablespoons lime juice
6 tablespoons palm sugar
1 teaspoon shrimp paste

MAKES 250 G (1 CUP)

HEAT the oil in a wok or saucepan. Fry the shallots and garlic together until golden, then transfer from the wok to a blender or food processor.

FRY the dried shrimp and chillies for 1 to 2 minutes, then add these to the blender along with the remaining ingredients. Add as much of the frying oil as necessary to make a paste that you can pour. Put the paste back in the clean saucepan and bring to a boil. Reduce the heat and simmer until thick. Be careful because if you overcook this you will end up with a caramelized lump. Season the sauce with salt or fish sauce. Chilli jam is used as base for recipes, especially stir-fries, as well as a seasoning or accompaniment. It will keep for several months in an airtight jar in the refrigerator.

ROASTED CHILLI SAUCE

NAAM JIM AAHAAN THALEH
GARLIC AND CHILLI SAUCE

4 garlic cloves, finely chopped
3 bird's eye chillies, mixed red and
  green, stems removed, lightly
  crushed
2 tablespoons lime juice
1 tablespoon fish sauce
1 teaspoon sugar

MAKES 125 ML (½ CUP)

MIX all the ingredients together in a small bowl. The sauce can be stored in a jar in the refrigerator for several weeks.

GARLIC AND CHILLI SAUCE

SWEET CHILLI SAUCE

7 long red chillies, seeded and
  roughly chopped
185 ml (¾ cup) white vinegar
8 tablespoons sugar
½ teaspoon salt

MAKES 60 ML (¼ CUP)

USING a pestle and mortar or a small blender,
pound or blend the chillies into a rough paste.

IN a small saucepan, boil the vinegar, sugar and
salt over a high heat to boiling point, stirring
constantly. Reduce the heat to medium and
simmer for 15 to 20 minutes until the mixture
forms a thick syrup. Spoon the paste into the
syrup, cook for 1 to 2 minutes, then pour into
a bowl ready to serve.

PLUM SAUCE

PLUM SAUCE

185 ml (¾ cup) white vinegar
8 tablespoons sugar
1 preserved plum (available in jars)
  without liquid

MAKES 60 ML (¼ CUP)

IN a small saucepan, heat the vinegar and sugar
quickly, stirring constantly, until it reaches boiling
point. Lower the heat to medium and simmer for
15 to 20 minutes until it forms a thick syrup.

ADD the preserved plum and mash it with a spoon
or fork. Cook for 1 to 2 minutes to form a smooth
paste, then pour into a bowl ready to serve.

PEANUT SAUCE

2 garlic cloves, crushed
4 Asian shallots, finely chopped
1 lemon grass stalk, white part only,
  finely chopped
2 teaspoons Thai curry powder
  (page 287) or bought powder
1 tablespoon tamarind purée
1 tablespoon chilli paste
160 g (1 cup) unsalted roasted
  peanuts, roughly chopped
375 ml (1½ cups) coconut milk
  (page 279)
2 teaspoons palm sugar

MAKES 375 G (1½ CUPS)

HEAT 1 tablespoon vegetable oil in a saucepan
and fry the garlic, Asian shallots and lemon grass
for a minute. Add the Thai curry powder and stir
until fragrant.

ADD the remaining ingredients and bring slowly
to the boil. Add enough boiling water to make
a spoonable sauce and simmer for 2 minutes.
Season with salt to taste.

PEANUT SAUCE

KHAI KEM
SALTED EGGS

10 fresh duck eggs (if available),
    or large chicken eggs, cleaned
175 g (6 oz) salt
a preserving jar, big enough to
    hold all the eggs

MAKES 10

IN a saucepan, heat 625 ml (2½ cups) water and
the salt until the salt has dissolved. Allow to cool.

BEING very careful not to crack the shells, place
the eggs into a large jar. Pour in the cool salt
water. Seal the jar and leave for only three weeks.
If you leave them any longer they will get too salty.
Salted eggs will last for up to two months in their
jar. Drain and use as required: boil the eggs, then
scoop out the yolks and discard the whites.

CURRY POWDER

PHONG KARII
CURRY POWDER

1 tablespoon black peppercorns
2 teaspoons white peppercorns
1 tablespoon cloves
3 tablespoons coriander seeds
3 tablespoons cumin seeds
1 tablespoon fennel seeds
seeds from 8 cardamom pods
3 tablespoons dried chilli flakes
2 tablespoons ground ginger
3 tablespoons ground turmeric

MAKES 125 G (½ CUP)

DRY-ROAST the peppercorns, cloves, coriander,
cumin and fennel seeds, doing one ingredient at a
time, in a frying pan over a low heat until fragrant.

TRANSFER to a spice grinder or pestle and mortar
and grind to a powder. Add the remaining
ingredients and grind together. Store in an
airtight container.

CUCUMBER RELISH

AJAT
CUCUMBER RELISH

4 tablespoons rice vinegar
125 g (½ cup) sugar
1 small red chilli, seeded and
    chopped
1 teaspoon fish sauce
80 g (½ cup) peanuts, lightly roasted
    and roughly chopped
1 Lebanese cucumber, unpeeled,
    seeded, finely diced

MAKES 185 G (¾ CUP)

PUT the vinegar and sugar in a small saucepan
with 125 ml (½ cup) of water. Bring to the boil, then
reduce the heat and simmer for 5 minutes.

ALLOW to cool before stirring in the chilli, fish
sauce, peanuts and cucumber.

GLOSSARY OF THAI FOOD AND COOKING

Asian shallots *(hawn)* Small reddish-purple shallots used in South-East Asia. French shallots can be used instead.

bamboo shoots *(naw mai)* The edible shoots of bamboo. Available fresh when in season, otherwise preserved in jars or canned. Fresh shoots should be blanched (possibly more than once) if they are bitter.

banana flower *(hua plii)* **or blossom** This is the purple, teardrop-shaped flower of the banana plant. The purple leaves and pale yellow buds that grow between them are discarded. Only the inner pale core is eaten and this needs to be blanched in boiling water to remove any bitterness. It is advisable to wear rubber gloves to prepare banana flower as it has a gummy substance that can stain your fingers. Shredded banana flowers appear in salads and sometimes in curries.

banana leaves *(bai tawng)* Large green leaves, which can be used as a wrapping (dip briefly in boiling water or put in a hot oven for 10 seconds to soften them before use) for foods, or to line plates. Young leaves are preferable. Available from Asian food shops.

bananas *(kluay)* There are more than 20 different types of banana available in Thailand, all of which are used in cooking and are very popular. Varieties differ in flavour, with the small sugar bananas being the sweetest.

basil There are three types of basil used in Thai cuisine.

Thai sweet basil (bai horapha) is the most common. This has purplish stems, green leaves and an aniseed aroma and flavour. It is aromatic and is used in curries, soups and stir-fries, as well as sometimes being served as an accompaniment to *naam phrik*.

Holy basil (bai ka-phrao) is either red or green with slightly pointed, variegated leaves. Holy basil is used in stir-fries and fish dishes.

Lemon basil (bai maeng-lak) is also called mint basil. It is less common and is used in curries and stir-fries and as a condiment with rice noodles.

bean curd *see* tofu.

betel leaves *(bai cha-phluu)* Known also as piper leaves or wild tea leaves, these are not true betel but are a close relative. They are used to wrap some snacks. Use baby spinach leaves if you can't get betel leaves.

black fungus A funghi that is available fresh and dried, this has a cartilaginous texture and very little flavour. Dried fungus is soaked before use. It is used in Chinese-style soups and stir-fries.

cardamom *(luuk kra-waan)* A round white variety of cardamom is used in Indian- or Muslim-influenced curries such as massaman. Common green cardamom can be used instead.

Ready-ground cardamom quickly loses flavour. Use the pods whole or crushed.

cha om A bitter green vegetable resembling a fern. *Cha om* is used in omelette-style dishes and in stir-fries.

chilli jam *(naam jim phrik)* A thick, sweet chilli relish that can also be used as a sauce. Make it yourself (see page 283) or buy it ready-made.

chilli sauce The common name for siracha chilli sauce *(naam phrik sii raachaa)*, this is used more than any of the many other types of chilli sauce. Usually served alongside grilled fish, this thick orange sauce is named after the seaside town famous for its production. Chilli sauce goes with anything.

chillies *(phrik)* Red and green chillies are widely used in Thai cuisine. Recipes usually give a variety, rather than a colour. Generally, with Thai chillies, the smaller they are the hotter they are.

Bird's eye or mouse dropping chillies *(phrik khii nuu)* are the smallest and hottest. Most commonly green, but red can be used in most recipes.

Dragon's eye chillies *(phrik khii nuu suan)* are slightly larger and less hot.

Sky-pointing or long chillies *(phrik chii faa)* are about 5 cm (2 inches) in length and milder than the smaller ones. Used in stir-fries, salads and curry pastes.

Orange chillies *(phrik leuang)* are hot but not as hot as bird's eye chillies.

Banana chillies *(phrik yuak)* are large fat yellow/green (almost fluorescent) chillies with a mild flavour. They are used in stir-fries as well as in salads.

Dried chillies *(phrik haeng)* Dried red chillies are either long chillies or bird's eye. They are sometimes soaked in hot water to soften them. Remove the seeds if you prefer less heat.

Chinese kale *(phak kaa-naa)* Known as gai laan in Chinese food shops.

Chinese keys *(kra-chai)* A rhizome with skinny fingers that hang down like a bunch of keys. Has a peppery flavour. Available tinned, or preserved in jars, from Asian food shops.

cloves *(kahn pluu)* The dried, unopened flower buds of the clove tree. Brown and nail-shaped, they have a pungent flavour and so should be used in moderation. Use cloves whole or ground.

coconut *(maphrao)* The fruit of a coconut palm. The inner nut is encased in a husk which has to be removed. The hard shell can then be drained of juice before being cracked open to extract the white meat. Coconut meat is jellyish in younger nuts and harder in older ones. Medium-hard coconuts, which are perfect for desserts, are sold as grating coconuts in Thailand. The method for cracking and grating coconuts is shown on page 279.

coconut cream *(hua ka-thi)* This is made by soaking freshly grated coconut in boiling water and then squeezing out a thick, sweet coconut-flavoured liquid. It is available tinned but if you want to make your own, see page 279. Coconut cream is sometimes 'cracked' in order to fry curry pastes. This means it is boiled until the water evaporates out and it separates into oil and solids.

coconut milk *(haang ka-thi)* A thinner version of coconut cream, made as above but with more water or from a

second pressing. Available tinned, but to make your own, see page 279.

coconut sugar *(naamtaan maphrao)* This sugar is made from the sap from coconut trees. Dark brown in colour, it is mainly used in sweet dishes. Palm sugar or unrefined soft brown sugar can be used instead.

coriander *(phak chii)* Fresh coriander leaves are used both as an ingredient and as a colourful garnish. The roots *(raak phak chii)* are chopped or ground and used in curry pastes and sauces. Buy bunches that have healthy green leaves and avoid any that are yellowing.

coriander seeds *(met phak chii)* The round seeds of the coriander plant have a spicy aroma and are used in some curry pastes, especially those that are Indian in style. To intensify the flavour, dry-roast the seeds until aromatic, before crushing them. Best freshly ground for each dish. They are available whole or ground.

corn *(khao phoht)* Now commonly grown in northern Thailand, corn is eaten freshly grilled as a healthy snack. Baby corn *(khao phoht awn)* is often used in stir-fries and curries.

cumin seeds *(met yiiraa)* The elongated ridged seeds of a plant of the parsley family, these have a peppery, slightly bitter flavour and are used in some curry pastes. To intensify the flavour, dry-roast the seeds before crushing them. Best freshly ground for each dish. Available whole or ground.

curry pastes *(khreuang kaeng)* Most often homemade in Thailand, though they can be bought freshly made in markets, and packaged in supermarkets. All curry pastes are ground and pounded together in a pestle and mortar until they are very smooth. The most common ones are red or hot *(kaeng phet)*, green *(kaeng khiaw-waan)*, panaeng or dry

(kaeng phanaeng), matsaman or massaman *(kaeng matsaman)*, sour orange *(kaeng som)*, yellow *(kaeng leuang)*, Chiang Mai or hangleh *(kaeng hangleh)* and jungle or forest *(kaeng paa)*.

curry powder *(phong karii)* Usually bought ready-made in Thailand as it is not widely used except in a few stir-fries, marinades, sauces and in curry puffs.

dried fish *(plaa haeng)* Used extensively in Thai cuisine and a common roadside sight near the coast, dried fish is usually fried and crumbled and used in dips, salads and pastes.

dried shrimp *(kung haeng)* These are either ground until they form a fine fluff or rehydrated and used whole. Look for dark pink ones.

durian *(thurian)* The most infamous of fruit with a notoriously noxious aroma and sweet, creamy flavour and texture. It is banned from airlines and hotels.

eggplant *(makheua)* There are lots of varieties of eggplant (aubergine) used in Thai cuisine and, unlike in the West, bitterness is a prized quality. Common eggplants include Thai eggplant *(ma-kheua phraw)* which are pale green, orange, purple, yellow or white and golf-ball sized. Long eggplant *(ma-kheua yao)* are long, skinny and green. Pea eggplant *(ma-kheau phuang)* are tiny, bitter and look like large peas. Cut eggplant using a stainless steel knife and store in salted water to prevent them from turning black.

fish sauce *(naam plaa)* Made from salted anchovy-like fish that are left to break down naturally in the heat, fish sauce is literally the liquid that is drained off. It is the main source of salt flavouring in Thai cooking and is also used as a condiment. It varies in quality. Look for Tiparos or Golden Boy brands. A fermented version *(naam plaa raa)* is used in the North and North-East.

galangal or galingale *(khaa)* A rhizome, similar to ginger, used extensively in Thai cooking, usually in place of ginger. It is most famously used in *tom khaa kai.*

garlic *(kra-tiam)* Thai garlic has tiny cloves and is usually smashed with the side of a cleaver rather than being crushed before use. Deep-fried garlic is used as a garnish as is garlic oil. Deep-fried garlic can be bought in jars.

ginger *(khing)* The rhizome of a tropical plant which is sold in 'hands'. Fresh young ginger should have a smooth, pinkish beige skin and be firm and juicy. As it ages, the skin toughens and the flesh becomes more fibrous. Avoid old ginger which is wrinkled as it will be tough. Ginger is often measured in centimetre (inch) pieces and this means pieces with an average-sized width.

jackfruit *(kha-nun)* A large spiky fruit with segmented flesh enclosing large stones. It tastes like fruit salad and is used unripe in curries.

ketchap manis A thick, sweet soy sauce used as a flavouring.

lemon grass *(ta-khrai)* This ingredient is used in many Thai dishes. The fibrous stalk of a citrus perfumed grass, it is finely chopped or sliced or cut into chunks. Discard the outer layers until you reach a softer purple layer.

limes *(ma-nao)* Limes and lime juice are used extensively in Thai cuisine. Lime juice is a souring agent though Thai limes are sweeter than their Western counterparts. Lemon juice is not a particularly good substitute but can be used. Limes are often cut into cheeks rather than wedges.

lychees *(linchii)* Small round fruit with a red leathery skin and translucent white flesh surrounding a brown stone. Very perfumed and often available peeled and seeded in a syrup as a dessert.

makrut (kaffir) limes *(luk makrut)* These knobbly skinned fruit are used for their zest rather than their bitter juice. Leaves *(bai makrut)* are double leaves with a fragrant citrus oil. They are used very finely shredded or torn into large pieces. Frozen leaves are available but less fragrant than fresh ones.

mangoes *(ma-muang)* Green unripe mangoes are used in relishes, curries, soups and salads, or preserved in brine. Ripe mangoes are eaten out of the hand or alongside sticky rice as a dessert.

mint *(sa-ra-nae)* Mint is used in salads such as *laap* as well as being served alongside salads and rice-noodle soups.

mung bean sprouts *(thua ngawk)* These are used in stir-fries, soups and salads. Keep them in a bowl of cold water in the fridge to prolong their life.

mung beans *(thua leuang)* Whole beans are puréed or ground and used in desserts. Also used to make a type of noodle.

mushrooms *(het)* Straw mushrooms *(het faang)* are usually found tinned except in Asia. Replace them with oyster mushrooms if you need to. Shiitake *(het hawm)* are used both fresh and dried. Dried ones need to be soaked in boiling water before they are used.

noodles Rice noodles *(kuaytiaw)* are made of rice flour and water and steamed in sheets before being cut into widths. Wide line or *sen yai* noodles are about 2.5 cm (1 inch) wide, small line *(sen lek)* are 5 mm (¼ inch) in width and line noodles *(sen mii)* are 1–2 mm. Rice noodles are sold fresh and dried. The widths can be used interchangeably. Wheat noodles *(ba-mii)* are usually made with egg. Mung bean starch noodles *(wun sen)* are very thin white translucent noodles that go clear when soaked. They are much tougher than rice noodles. Both *wun sen* and *sen mii* are referred to as vermicelli.

oyster sauce Use the Thai version of the Chinese sauce if you can. It has a stronger oyster flavour.

palm sugar *(naamtaan piip)* Palm sugar is made by boiling sugar palm sap until it turns into a granular paste. Sold in hard cakes of varying sizes or as a slightly softer version in tubs. Malaysian and Indonesian brands of palm sugar are darker in colour and stronger in flavour. Unrefined, soft light brown sugar can be used instead.

pandanus leaves *(bai toey)* These long green leaves are shaped like blades and are used as a flavouring in desserts and sweets, as well as a wrapping for small parcels of food. Pandanus are also called screwpine. Essence can be bought in small bottles from speciality Asian food shops. Pandanus leaves are often sold frozen.

peanuts *(thua lisong)* Peanuts are used raw in some curries, deep-fried as a garnish, or in dipping sauces. Buy raw peanuts and fry them yourself for the best results.

peppercorns *(phrik thai)* Green peppercorns are used fresh in curries. Dried white peppercorns are used as a seasoning in dishes and as a garnish but black pepper is seldom used.

pickled garlic *(kra-tiam dong)* Eaten as an accompaniment, pickled garlic has a sweet/sour flavour. Preserved as whole heads that can be used as they are. Available at Chinese food shops.

pickled ginger *(khing dong)* Eaten as an accompaniment to curries and snacks. Buy ready-made from Asian food shops.

preserved cabbage *(phak gaund dong)* Salted and preserved cabbage is usually sold shredded. It sometimes comes in eathenware pots and is labelled Tianjin preserved vegetables. Available at Asian food shops.

preserved plums Salty, sour, preserved plums are used in sweet/sour dishes, to make plum sauce, and with steamed fish. Can be bought at Asian food shops.

preserved radish *(tang chai)* Salted and preserved radish is sold shredded or as strips. It is also referred to by the Japanese name, daikon, or the Indian, mooli. Comes salty and sweet/salty. Buy from Asian food shops.

rambutan *(ngaw)* A small round fruit with a red skin covered in soft, fine red spikes. Buy rambutan when they are vibrant in colour.

rice *(khao)* Jasmine (long-grain) and sticky rice are the two main varieties eaten in Thailand. Sticky rice comes in white and black, which is quite purple in reality. Much of the rice that is eaten is grown locally and it is nearly always white and polished. Jasmine rice is steamed, boiled or, more traditionally, cooked in a clay pot. Sticky rice is soaked and then steamed, either in a steamer or packed into lengths of bamboo.

rice flour *(paeng khao)* Made from white and black rice, this is also known as ground rice and is used in desserts.

roasted chilli powder *(phrik bon)* Both bird's eye and sky-pointing chilies are used to make chilli powder. Buy from Asian food shops or make your own by roasting and grinding whole chillies.

roasted chilli sauce *(naam phrik phao)* This sauce is made from dried red chillies roasted in oil, hence the name. It usually includes shrimp paste and palm sugar. Roasted chilli sauce comes in mild, medium and hot and is sold in jars and plastic pouches. To make your own, see page 283. Use as a flavouring and as a relish.

rose apple (chom-phuu) A crisp, watery fruit with no overwhelming taste, except for sweetness. Eaten on its own as a fruit and sometimes as an accompaniment to dips such as *naam phrik*.

sago *(saku)* Small dried balls of sago palm sap, which are used for milky desserts and savoury dishes. Cooked sago is transparent and soft with a silky texture.

shrimp paste *(ka-pi)* A strong smelling dark brownish-pink paste sold in small tubs that are usually sealed with wax. It is made from salted, fermented and dried shrimp. Buy a Thai version as those from other Asian countries vary. Used as it is or roasted first and refrigerated. This is very strong smelling and is a main ingredient in dips such as *naam phrik.*

snake beans *(thua fak yao)* Also called long beans or yard-long beans, these are sold in coils or tied together in bunches. Eaten fresh and cooked. Green beans can be used instead.

sour sausage Thai sausages can be bought ready-made or you can make them yourself (see page 42). They sometimes come wrapped in cellophane or banana leaves, or are strung together. Chinese sausages can be used instead.

soy sauce *(sii-yu)* Both light soy sauce *(sii-yu khao)* and dark soy *(sii-yu dam)* are used in Thai cooking. The dark one is sweeter than Chinese-style soy sauce.

spring roll sheets Wheat and egg dough wrappers that can be bought from Asian food shops and some good supermarkets. Look in the refrigerator or freezer sections. Squares of filo can also be used.

tamarind *(ma-khaam)* A fruit whose flesh is used as a souring agent. Usually bought as a dried cake or prepared as a purée, tamarind is actually a pod filled with seeds and a fibrous flesh. If you buy tamarind cake, then it must be soaked in hot water and then rubbed and squeezed to dissolve the pulp around the fibres. The fibres are then sieved out.

Pulp is sold as purée or concentrate but is sometimes referred to as tamarind water in recipes. Freshly made tamarind water has a fresher, stronger flavour.

tapioca flour Made from ground, dried cassava root, this flour is used in desserts, dumpling wrappers and as a thickener. It is sold in small plastic bags in Asian food shops.

tofu *(tao-huu)* Also called bean curd, this can be firm or silken (soft).

turmeric *(kha-min)* A rhizome like ginger and galangal. In Thailand turmeric comes in white and yellow varieties. The yellow type is often referred to as red and is used fresh in curry pastes. Dried, it adds a yellow colour to curries, particularly Northern *khao sawy.* The white type is often eaten raw as a vegetable accompaniment to *naam phrik.*

vinegar *(naam som)* White coconut vinegar is the most common. Any mild white vinegar or better still, rice vinegar, can be used as a substitute.

water spinach *(phak bung)* Also called kang kong, morning glory, ong choy and water convolvulus, this is a leafy green vegetable that has hollow stems. Used as an ingredient as well as an accompaniment.

wing beans *(thua phuu)* Also called angle beans, these have four frilly edges. Used cut into cross sections in salads and stir-fries. Buy as fresh as you can.

won ton sheets These sheets or wrappers are available from the refrigerator or freezer cabinets of Asian food shops. Some are yellow and include egg in the pastry and others are white. Gow gee and gyoza wrappers can also be used.

yellow bean sauce *(tao jiaw)* This paste made of yellow soy beans adds a salty flavour to dishes.

INDEX

BIBLIOGRAPHY

Bhumichitr, Vatcharin, *The Taste of Thailand*, Pavilion Books, 1988.

Cummings, Joe, *World Food Thailand*, Lonely Planet, 2000.

Davidson, Alan, *Oxford Companion to Food*, Oxford University Press, 1999.

Hargreave, Oliver, *Exploring Chiang Mai, City, Valley and Mountains*, Within Books, 1997.

Loha-Unchit, Kasma, *It Rains Fishes, Legends, Traditions and the Joys of Thai Cooking*, Pomegranate Art Books, 1995.

Solomon, Charmaine, *Encyclopedia of Asian Food*, Hamlyn, 1996.

Thompson, David, *Classic Thai Cuisine*, Ten Speed Press, 1993.

Thompson, David, *Thai Food*, Chrysalis Books, 2002.

Yu, Su-Mei, *Cracking the Coconut, Classic Thai Home Cooking*, William Morrow, 2000.

THE FOOD OF THAILAND

Published in 2003 by Murdoch Books®, a division of Murdoch Magazines Pty Ltd.

Murdoch Books® Australia
GPO Box 1203, Sydney, NSW 2001
Phone: (612) 4352 7000   Fax: (612) 4352 7026

Murdoch Books® UK Limited
Ferry House, 51–57 Lacy Road, London SW15 1PR
Phone: (020) 8355 1480   Fax: (020) 8355 1499

Food Editor: Lulu Grimes
Recipes: Oi Cheepchaiissara   www.modernthaifood.com
Additional Recipes: Ross Dobson
Design Concept: Marylouise Brammer
Designer: Susanne Geppert
Production: Fiona Byrne
Editorial Director: Diana Hill
Editor: Wendy Stephen
Photographer (location and recipes): Alan Benson
Additional Photography (recipes): Ian Hofstetter
Stylist: Mary Harris
Additional Styling: Katy Holder
Stylist's Assistant: Wendy Quisumbing
Map: Berit Kruger-Johnsen

Publisher: Kay Scarlett
Chief Executive: Juliet Rogers

National Library of Australia Cataloguing-in-Publication Data
Oi Cheepchaiissara. The Food of Thailand. Includes index.
ISBN 1 74045 223 2.
1. Cookery, Thai. I. Title. 641.59593

PRINTED IN CHINA by Leefung-Asco Printers Ltd. First published 2003.

© Text, design, photography and illustrations Murdoch Books® 2003

ACKNOWLEDGMENTS

The Publisher wishes to thank the following for all their help in making this book possible:

The Dusit Group: Werachej Lelanuja, Jakkris Supeerajit, Holger Jakobs, Andrew Swatdipakdi, Saravuth Manuthasna,
Victor Sukseree, Chanok Chaisiri, Ingo Räuber, Peter Held; Randall Marketing: Angela Blair; World Travel Services:
Jack Painchokdee, Praphan Jandeng; Thailand Tourist Board Australia: Leanne Ward; Valcom: Ms. Huai Hui Lee,
Ms. Chritravee Suwanag, Mr. Vitsnu Pongsmai; Tang Sang Hah Co. Ltd.: Worachet Pongpairoj, Jarin Pongpairoj,
Patiphan Pongpairoj, Kobkiat Pongpairoj, Marosak, V. (QC), Ekaphol Chueroongrueng; Chiang Mai Thai Cookery School:
Sompon and Elizabeth Nabnian, Pom and all the staff; Chia Meng Co. Ltd.: Mr. Tavol Manathanya, Mrs. Prapit Manathanya,
Mrs. Mayura Manathanya, Mr. Somsak Kamjornkitbaworn, Ms. Walaiporn Phuhiran; Mei Kim Lui factory, Phetchaburi;
Oriental Merchant: Hannah Yiu.